SHIFTY'S WAR

SHIFTY'S WAR

The authorized biography of
Sgt. Darrell "Shifty" Powers, the
legendary sharpshooter from
the Band of Brothers

Marcus Brotherton

BERKLEY CALIBER, NEW YORK

THE BERKLEY PUBLISHING GROUP
Published by the Penguin Group
Penguin Group (USA) Inc.
375 Hudson Street, New York, New York 10014, USA
Penguin Group (Canada), 90 Eglinton Avenue East, Suite 700, Toronto, Ontario M4P 2Y3, Canada
(a division of Pearson Penguin Canada Inc.)
Penguin Books Ltd., 80 Strand, London WC2R 0RL, England
Penguin Group Ireland, 25 St. Stephen's Green, Dublin 2, Ireland (a division of Penguin Books Ltd.)
Penguin Group (Australia), 250 Camberwell Road, Camberwell, Victoria 3124, Australia
(a division of Pearson Australia Group Pty. Ltd.)
Penguin Books India Pvt. Ltd., 11 Community Centre, Panchsheel Park, New Delhi—110 017, India
Penguin Group (NZ), 67 Apollo Drive, Rosedale, Auckland 0632, New Zealand
(a division of Pearson New Zealand Ltd.)
Penguin Books (South Africa) (Pty.) Ltd., 24 Sturdee Avenue, Rosebank, Johannesburg 2196,
South Africa

Penguin Books Ltd., Registered Offices: 80 Strand, London WC2R 0RL, England

The publisher does not have any control over and does not assume any responsibility for author or
third-party websites or their content.

This book is an original publication of the Berkley Publishing Group.

*This work is a posthumous memoir that reflects the recollections of Shifty Powers's experiences and
the author's retelling of those experiences in Shifty's voice.*

FIRST EDITION: May 2011

Library of Congress Cataloging-in-Publication Data

Brotherton, Marcus.
Shifty's war : the authorized biography of Sergeant Darrell "Shifty" Powers, the legendary
sharpshooter from the Band of Brothers / Marcus Brotherton.—1st ed.
    p. cm.
  Includes bibliographical references.
  ISBN 978-0-425-24097-7
  1. Powers, Shifty, 1923–2009.   2. United States. Army. Parachute Infantry Regiment, 506th.
Company E.   3. Soldiers United States—Biography.   4. Shooters of firearms—United States—
Biography.   5. World War, 1939–1945—Biography.   6. World War, 1939–1945—Campaigns—
Western Front.   7. World War, 1939–1945—Regimental histories—United States.   8. United
States. Army—Parachute troops—History—20th century.   I. Title.
  D769.348506th .B757 2011
  940.54'8173—dc22
  [B]

                                                                            2010047531

PRINTED IN THE UNITED STATES OF AMERICA

10   9   8   7   6   5   4   3   2   1

DEDICATED TO THE 98 YOUNG MEN
FROM DICKENSON COUNTY, VIRGINIA,
WHO FOUGHT IN WORLD WAR II AND
NEVER CAME HOME.

CONTENTS

CONTENTS

INTRODUCTION

Shifty Powers was a soft-spoken machinist who never aspired to greatness. He was born, grew up, got married, raised his family, worked, retired, and died in Clinchco, a remote mining town in southwest Virginia. Aside from a few years he spent working in California and his years in the war, he seldom traveled outside his tiny hometown. Shifty was a self-described mountain man, a hillbilly. He enjoyed fishing, hunting, working in his vegetable garden, and shooting rifles at targets from his front porch. He began the war as a lowly private and ended the war as a squad leader, never leading a group larger than twelve men. After the war, he was never the boss of anything. He never held public office. He never made much money. He never chased any of the contemporary definitions of success—popularity, power, or position. Yet, despite this humble life, the world knows his name today.

Why?

Certainly much of Shifty's notoriety has to do with his association with the Band of Brothers. Shifty Powers was a soldier with the now-legendary Easy Company, 506th Parachute Infantry Regiment, 101st Division, an elite group of World War II fighters.

The Band of Brothers formed and trained at Camp Toccoa, Georgia, under the tough and controversial Captain Herbert Sobel. After training stateside, the men rode the troop ship *Samaria* to Aldbourne, England, for further battle preparation. They parachuted into Normandy on D-day and later into Holland for Operation Market-Garden. They fought their way through Belgium, France, and Germany, faced overwhelming odds, liberated concentration camps, and drank a toast to victory in April 1945 at Hitler's hideout in the Alps. Along the way they encountered horrors and victories, welded themselves into a family of soldiers, and helped swing the tide of World War II and, ultimately, the course of history.

The company was first chronicled in 1992 by historian Stephen Ambrose in his book *Band of Brothers*. In 2001, Tom Hanks and Steven Spielberg turned Ambrose's book into a ten-part HBO miniseries by the same name. The series won six Emmys and numerous other awards, and still runs frequently on various networks around the world.

Shifty Powers fit well into this group of elite soldiers. His paratrooper unit didn't have snipers by name, but if a man was particularly handy with a rifle, he could qualify as an "expert marksman." Shifty Powers was one of only two men in a company of 140 soldiers who initially achieved this designation. When it came to shooting rifles—and hitting what needed to be hit—he was the best of the best.

Fellow soldier Earl "One Lung" McClung described Shifty this way:

He was an excellent shot, as well as an excellent friend. On patrols, he knew exactly what he was doing—that's why he was one of the very few old-timers in the company who was never wounded. He had the best ears of any man in the company. He could hear anything, including enemy sentries, better than most men, so he would often lead our patrols. Shifty Powers was a great man, one of the kindest people I've ever known. I've never heard him say anything bad about anyone.

Despite his fame today, Shifty wasn't portrayed prominently in the book or the series. He wasn't a main character, such as Major Dick Winters. Shifty didn't have a single episode in the miniseries that focused on him, such as Doc Roe did. You never heard Shifty's interior monologue throughout an episode, such as you did with Carwood Lipton's. So why has Shifty Powers become so well-known today? I believe for three reasons.

First, Shifty Powers, played by actor Peter Youngblood Hills, was one of just a handful of men to be portrayed in all ten episodes of the HBO series. He's seldom seen in a main role, but he's solidly (and perhaps strategically) placed in the background of many scenes. He was the rifle expert in Bastogne whom men asked to verify what kind of weapon was being fired at them. He could do it just by the sound. He was the sharpshooter in Carentan whom men called upon when they needed a particularly difficult shot taken. Shifty Powers was the type of quiet go-to man that others could always depend on. That's admirable.

Second, Shifty Powers (in real life, in addition to the series) was a gentleman. He was the good friend to everyone. For instance, when Private Walter Gordon is shown being ordered by Captain Sobel to run Mount Currahee alone as punishment for committing some minor infraction, Shifty is one of three men who voluntarily join Gordon on the run. Friends who knew him well say that he was exactly this sort of man in real life, one with a deeply altruistic and kind spirit. His granddaughter-in-law, Dawnyale Johnson, described him this way:

> You just fell in love with him. He had this warmth about him. He didn't care what you looked like or if you had a PhD. He was very honest—what you saw was what you got. He'd be the same person to Tom Hanks as he'd be to the person working at Food City.

And third, Shifty is well known today because his death on June 17, 2009, came at an arguably hero-starved time in American history. Reporter Mary Katherine Ham, praising the plethora of tribute websites for Shifty that sprang up almost overnight after Shifty died, noted that "sometimes, in between uploading videos of stupid cat tricks, sustaining the careers of such blights . . . as Lindsay Lohan, and obsessively critiquing Jennifer Love Hewitt's bikini bod, the Internet community can up and do something admirable."* (See the epilogue for more of the story of how Shifty's life continued to influence people for good even after his death.)

Shifty is widely admired because his example helps us sort out what's truly valuable in life. He was an ordinary man who trained to become the best and ultimately did extraordinary things. He did a difficult job well and didn't call attention to himself. He came

---

* Mary Katherine Ham, "Remember Darrell Shifty Powers Today," *Weekly Standard*, July 20, 2009, http://www.weeklystandard.com/weblogs/TWSFP/2009/07/remember_darrell_shifty_powers.asp, accessed May 24, 2010.

home from the war with his life intact and chose to live it in service to his family and community. Shifty's life story is inspiring because it sounds so simple. It's inspiring because it's so rare.

Shifty's Story in Shifty's Words

Although I spoke with Shifty Powers several times over the phone, I never had the privilege of meeting him face-to-face. The information for this book came from several sources: face-to-face interviews with Shifty's immediate family, friends, and hometown acquaintances; interviews with the men from Easy Company who fought alongside him; research from articles and what's been written about him in other books; the phone interviews I did with Shifty before he died, for another book I wrote, titled *We Who Are Alive and Remain*; and recorded stories in archived audio and visual material in which Shifty told about his own life.

These recorded interviews really opened up this book's feel and tone for me. I had the rare opportunity to access about ten interviews, and spent weeks transcribing the recordings—literally allowing Shifty's specific phrasings and word choices to pass through my ears and flow through my brain to my hands. That opportunity prompted me to write this book in an unusual, even controversial format.

You'll notice the book is written in first person (the "I" voice), as opposed to third person (the "he" voice) in which most posthumous memoirs are written. I need to state and perhaps overstate a clear caveat up front: Shifty Powers did not write this book. Rather, I am presenting Shifty's voice as accurately as I can. This book is thoroughly based on fact, yes. It's also an imagined memoir, yes. I chose this format because I wanted you to be able to picture Shifty sitting down in a room with you, telling his stories in his own voice. Your invitation is to bypass me as author and meet Shifty Powers directly. You can see his life through his eyes and hear things with his ears. I want you to be able to get to know him in the closest way possible through the pages of a book.

The Powers family is in agreement with this choice. It was their love and admiration of their father, husband, and brother that led to this book's creation in the first place. Shifty's widow, Dorothy; his children, Wayne Powers and Margo Johnson; and his last surviving sibling, Gaynell Sykes, have all read and approved advance copies of this book.

I used first person for another, more basic reason. Shifty talked like only Shifty could talk. He told stories like only he could tell stories. He spoke in a colloquial, Southern manner, and I wanted to capture that feeling and tone throughout the book.

For instance, Shifty said the words "you know" after almost every sentence. He frequently described scenes using parallel sentence construction—he'd deliver a compound sentence, then he'd repeat the first part of the sentence but with a different ending. He often used past and present progressive tense with his verbs (a lot of "I am going . . . he was saying . . . I was shooting . . ."). He used colloquial phrases, such as "I'm studying this" to mean he was thinking about something. He was "aggravated" rather than angry. Often he interspersed his sentences with filler words such as "see" and "well." Wherever possible in this book, I've used Shifty's exact phrasing and speech patterns from transcriptions of his recorded words. I wanted you to hear and feel the words of Shifty firsthand.

Peter Youngblood Hills described Shifty's mannerisms as reflective of the man's character. Shifty was a great man leading a quiet life, and he spoke from the overflow of a good heart. Peter said this about Shifty:

His speech—it was like a song, how he talked. His speech patterns contained a depth of character—his voice was comforting to listen to—but it also contained a softness and lightness. He would often talk very slowly, often ending his phrases by letting his voice go high. But it wasn't like the highness of a woman's voice. The highness contained a quality of bringing you close. He'd say things like, "Well . . . now . . . I declare," and end up very high on the last words. You almost need to say it out loud for yourself to know what I mean. He spoke as one sure of himself, but who didn't want to speak without being heard.

Shifty could be humble to the point of being self-deprecating. He called himself "an old hillbilly in the holler," and he would understate almost everything he said—whether his own accomplishments or how horror-filled the war had been. For instance, he described the war to me by saying simply, "It wasn't a good time." Certainly Shifty sensed the gravity of what he had done and where he had been. But he understated things because he never wanted to be a person to blow his own horn. Although he was an ordinary man living through an extraordinary time, he never lost the sense of who he was at heart.

Even in his old age, when I met him, Shifty walked with a spring in his step, as if well connected to the earth. He had Cherokee blood running through his ancestry, and his skin was smooth and contained a pale reddish tint. He asked questions of other people and spoke as if he was listening to you as much as talking. He was always listening to his surroundings, yes, whether what was happening up on the hill or out in the field.

But he also talked as if listening to what you had to say. Shifty Powers wanted to bring you along in whatever amazing journey was happening.

I like that last phrase a lot: Shifty Powers wanted to bring you along in his amazing journey.

What follows is the story of Sergeant Darrell C. "Shifty" Powers, the legendary sharpshooter featured in the Band of Brothers. In the pages ahead, I invite you to meet this man, get to know him, and come to respect him deeply.

—Marcus Brotherton
August 2010

"Dig your foxhole deep.
Keep your head down.
And make damn sure your rifle doesn't jam."

—SHIFTY POWERS, AT AGE 81,
WORDS TO A YOUNG SOLDIER

1

GENERAL TAYLOR'S LOTTERY

Austria, 1945

B y my twenty-second birthday, you know, I had killed eight men. Eight that I was certain of, eight that I could plainly count. That information was stuffed deep within my gut, and if anyone ever asked if I killed someone during the war, particularly if a child ever asked, I vowed I'd shake my head no, that information was never coming out.

Less than a month after my birthday, the war was declared over. Everybody drank a lot of champagne, then this weariness set in. Everybody just wanted to go home. I think it was weariness we were feeling, anyway. It was hard to rightly put the feeling into words. Frustration, maybe. Like everybody else, home is where I longed to be, but I wasn't heading stateside soon. A man needed 85 points to be discharged from the army, and though I had trained at Toccoa as one of the original men in the company and served every day on the front as rifleman, scout, and sharpshooter in every campaign from Normandy forward, I didn't have enough points. I was missing one piece of important battle experience when it came to Army thinking. Maybe it was a special angel looking over my shoulder, don't rightly know, but I had dodged all bullets aimed my direction. Unlike most men in Easy Company, I had no Purple Hearts. In a company that suffered 150 percent casualties, I was an acute rarity. You see, I'd never been wounded.

Wasn't complaining, mind you, wasn't talking to anybody about the trouble I felt. Come war's end we was pulling occupation duty in Zell am See, a middling-sized town in Austria near the foot of the Alps. Fine country to be soldiering in. No one was doing much work no more, some running maybe, some drilling to keep us sharp. Was a beautiful place, truly, with that glassy lake in the center of town. Why shoot—compared to the aggravation we'd just fought through, the place we now stayed made a fellow feel almost lighthearted in spite of his weariness, as if he was relaxing on his front porch after a hard day's work.

Not even the Krauts felt like stirring things much up. Most days you'd see enemy soldiers hike out of the Alps and surrender to allied troops. They came down by the hundreds all hungry and beat down, such a far sight from the killing and fussing we'd just been through with them. A lot of those soldiers—well, I've thought about this often—that man and I might have been good friends. We might've had a lot in common. He might have liked to fish. He might have liked to hunt. Course, they was doing what they was supposed to do, and I was trying to do what I was supposed to do. But under different circumstances we might have been good friends. When they surrendered, we'd set a couple guards on them, feed 'em, and that was how it was for us come the end of the war.

It's funny how passing through a heap of combat draws your

outfit tight as brothers. I guess some of the fellows in the company got to grumbling among themselves on my behalf. The high points men only had about three weeks before they'd go home, but me, well, it might be another six months or year or maybe more. Rumors floated around about us joining the fight in the Pacific, and I was never one to shirk duty if it came to that. But if it was just the same as not, and hopefully that war in Japan soon would be finished, too, then I'd surely rather go home now and not later. I'd seen enough gore to last me forever.

Those same fellows must have been fussing loud enough for someone important to hear, because one sunny afternoon Captain Speirs led us in a troop formation near the town square, and I noticed one or two old-timers with unmistakable twinkles in their eyes. Wasn't no doubt something was up, but I couldn't rightly say what. Such a fine day it was that same afternoon, early June 1945, when all 140 of us in Easy Company assembled in the square. Most fellows you didn't even recognize anymore. Replacements, they came in when one of us got wounded or killed. You'd try your best to pair up a replacement with one of the older men, a fellow who'd seen combat already and made it to the other side. If you made that pairing, well, you might get the replacement used to what was going on, he might get settled in, he might even make it. Was easier said than done, though. I know a few old-timers got so they didn't care to learn a replacement's name. As soon's you did, why, you'd turn around and the boy's guts would be bleeding, he'd be screaming for his mama, and after it happened more than once like that, well, you needed a certain wariness of who became your friend.

Three platoons formed a half circle around Captain Speirs. He barked out the usual "Company, platoons, 'tenshun!" and the stamp of our boots and clack of our rifles echoed off the cobblestones.

Bordering the square was a manor and a steepled church, and when Captain Speirs growled "At ease!" the echo wasn't as noticeable then, and we stepped apart and shook our shoulders a bit.

"General Taylor is aware," Captain Speirs called out, "that many veterans—including Normandy veterans—still do not have the eighty-five points required to be discharged. On this, the anniversary of D-day, the general has authorized a lottery to send one man home in each company. Effective immediately."

Several men gave low whistles at the good news. A fellow to my side swallowed loudly, his throat dry from possibility. Lieutenant Harry Welsh, a gutsy scrapper and our unit's staff officer, fished his fingers around in an outstretched helmet filled with slips of paper that each bore a man's name. Lieutenant Welsh paused, leveled his eyebrows at the helmet for a moment, smirked, I guess, then handed his chosen slip of paper to our commander. Captain Speirs unfolded it and read the name silently to himself, then straightened his shoulders, his expression unchanged. We all leaned in and listened for the lucky name. I noticed a calm breeze stirring the early summer leaves of a beech tree to my right. Somewhere up on the forested hillside behind the manor came the high-pitched *ti-ti-ti-ti-ti* call of a grouse. "C'mon, c'mon, c'mon," a man behind me muttered.

"For Easy Company . . . ," Captain Speirs drew his words out for emphasis," . . . the winner is . . . serial number one, three, zero, six, six, two, six, six . . . Sergeant Darrell C. Powers." His voice rose like a radio announcer as he said the last part of my name. The captain, known mostly for his fearless and killing ways, musta had a softer spot to him after all.

Cheers erupted from the men. Lieutenant Welsh's smirk had turned into an indisputable laugh. "That's how it's done, Shifty!"

someone hollered. I think it was George Luz, the fellow everybody got along with and who could do a dead-on mimic of anyone. Bull Randleman, a bear of a man and a fine soldier, grinned from several rows over and looked like he wanted to slap my back. "Congratulations, Shifty!" Randleman bawled. "It couldn't have happened to a better man!"

I shook my head in disbelief. I had won General Taylor's lottery. *Home*—I needed to let that sink in for a minute. A slight smile spread its way across my lips. Me, Shifty Powers, I was going home at last.

As soon as the formation was dismissed, two replacements ran up to me and grabbed my arm. "I'll give you a thousand dollars for that trip home," said one, all breathless. The other looked like he'd do the same. Wasn't no doubt they was serious. A few men won heaps of money gambling and such, and well, it was true: a thousand dollars would've meant a hill of money to a fellow like me. But I didn't need to roll that decision over in my mind before I shook my head and said, "No, I think I'll just go home." So that was that.

One of the old-timers, Sergeant Paul Rogers, strolled up just as the replacements were leaving. Everyone called him Hayseed. He smiled as big as a sunrise and shook my hand. He was one of my best friends in the company still alive, and I was mighty glad he made it to war's end. I didn't know what to say to him except "Shoot, Paul, I've never won anything in my life."

Hayseed smiled even wider and shook my hand harder. "We all wanted this for you, Shifty." His eyes bore that same twinkle I had seen earlier in some of the men. He handed me an empty duffel bag like he had been preparing for this and added, "C'mon, I've got something to show you."

Hayseed was our platoon sergeant, a man tasked with caring for the soldiers nearest him. I didn't have much gear to gather up, not many souvenirs from combat. Back when we went through Berchtesgaden I swiped one of those big red banners of Hitler's with its black swastika. Didn't know what I'd ever do with that big ole ugly banner, but I figured a find like that was something a down-home fellow like me didn't come across every day. That's about all I had.

We started walking. I guessed Hayseed was just leading me back to the barracks to help gather my gear, but soon we turned and headed toward a supply building a few streets away where I had spotted comings and goings. A single guard nodded to us when we reached the door. He rattled the lock and let us in. The building was windowless, pitch-dark inside. Hayseed switched on the overhead light. I gasped.

"Now, Shifty," he said, "you go pick out whatever you want."

Dadgum, if there wasn't a whole room full of 'em. Confiscated from the Krauts. Stacked in boxes and lying on shelves and filling the floor. Guns. Heaps of guns, mounds of guns. Rifles and pistols and carbines and shotguns and submachine guns. A grin spread wide across my face.

"Figured it would make a fitting going-away present for the best shot in Easy Company," Hayseed said, and handed me the duffel bag.

"Aw nah," I said, and stepped forward. "You're forgetting Buck Taylor. He's a much better shot than I ever was. And Earl McClung, that's for sure, best in the company by far. Now, back home in Virginia, you know, my daddy . . . now, there was a man who could shoot. Daddy was an excellent shot, yes he was. Why, that man could shoot the wings off a fly . . ."

"Just fill your sack, Shifty," Hayseed said. But he wasn't aggravated, not really.

I chose pistols, easiest to carry I reckoned. I'd already be taking my M1 home and didn't need the extra nine pounds of another rifle, so it was just pistols then. Ten, maybe twelve went into the duffel bag, fine pistols. As best find of the collection I spotted two .25 automatics, matched sets, pearl-handled, mighty fine pistols. Next to them lay two shoulder holsters for the pistols, one for the left, one for the right. I strapped those pearl-handled pistols directly on under my uniform jacket and beamed like I was getting ready to eat one of my mama's homemade chocolate pies, my favorite dessert.

"Truck's leaving soon," Hayseed said. "Better shake a leg." He shook my hand again for good measure. I nodded. Wasn't no time for saying proper good-byes. I think we both knew the limitations of a man's words at a time like that, for he swatted me on the shoulder, grinned wide again, and I nodded again. That was how we said good-bye.

Hayseed walked back to join the company. One more thing was needed before leaving, though—needed to ask a question. I knew what it was, but didn't know how to coax that dang question out of me so it made sense when I asked it. It sprung from a particular feeling that'd been gnawing on my insides ever since the war was declared over. Really, I'd been feeling it longer than that, but the war's end made me realize I was gonna need to get it out of me someday, maybe sooner, maybe later. It was rammed in my craw like a stuck piece of cornbread. That's where I held it tight. So, I reckoned if any man would know the answer to that question, it'd be Major Dick Winters.

The major was quartered some streets away in officers' housing. Upstairs and through the drawing room, the guard said when I knocked on the door, and the wood floors made nary a creak as I padded up. The major sat outside on the drawing room's balcony. He was framed with sunlight, in contrast to the dark drawing room through which I glimpsed him at first. As I walked toward him, I noticed he worked at a small desk he had carried out there for his paperwork. A glass of drinking water rested on his desk. Far behind him, an afternoon mist lay hazy and warm on the hills overlooking the lake.

Major Dick Winters was with us in the beginning. Back at Camp Toccoa when we started training three long years earlier, he was a regular officer, a lieutenant and platoon leader in Easy Company, maybe forty, fifty men in his charge. He fought shoulder to shoulder with us and led us all through Normandy, where he became company commander. He was there in the rain and wind of Holland, the snow and blood of Bastogne, the shelling and muck of Haguenau. The higher brass all saw what an admirable leader he was, and all the time he rose through the ranks swift as a hawk taking off from its perch. By the time we were in Austria he had replaced Colonel Robert Strayer as commander of our battalion. Major Winters was now responsible for leading some seven hundred men.

"Don't mean to interrupt you sir. Just wanted to say good-bye."

The major concentrated on the chart in front of him. He finished what he was reading, stood, and nodded at me.

"You know, sir . . . you was . . ." I searched for words, and tried again. "You was . . ." I stopped, listened. Somewhere to my left water burbled from a creek. I decided to try again. "Well . . . it's been a long time . . ." Wasn't nearly the point I wanted to get across.

The major set down his pen on the table. "Got everything you need, Sergeant Powers?" His voice was unruffled, steady as it ever was.

"Yes, sir. I gathered up my loot. Pistols mainly. Paperwork will be done soon. I'll get my back pay when I get down to headquarters."

The major's head gave a slight tilt to one side, inviting me to say what was truly on my mind. I shifted my dress cap from my right hand to my left.

"Well, back home in Virginia . . ." I began, then wobbled at the knees. A thought flew through my mind. It unfolded all at once, over and done with quicker than a hair trigger's pulled, but I'll try to lay it all out for you here so you see how my mind was churning just so.

Was that image of the water glass resting on the major's desk that jumbled everything. That water—so clean—just sitting there anytime a fellow felt like a sip. It sparked a recollection of a time Easy Company was holding the line at Bastogne. We was completely surrounded by the Krauts, all freezing in the snow. Hungry, cold, dirty, smelly. Scared. Near our foxholes lay a frozen creek and we'd chop it for water. You seldom had a chance to light fires for ice melting, surely never when the Krauts'd see you. So our throats were dry most way through Bastogne.

This particular day the thirst's got the company real bad, you know, and ole Wild Bill Guarnere and Babe Heffron are talking. They're two of the toughest men in Easy Company and Bill says, "Babe, pick up that jerry can over there. We need to get some water for the men." One of the guys from another company had been out to the creek the day before with his bayonet, hacking away at the ice. His helmet was lying there now with a hole dead center from a .50-caliber. Some other fellow saw what happened. "Oh yeah," the other fellow says. "A P-47 came down and was strafing and hit him—he was a kid from I Company—killed him instantly." Babe says, "Geez, one of our own planes—friendly fire."

In spite of the danger, we got to have water, you know, so Babe decides to go. The creek's maybe two hundred yards away. All the time he's in the open, he's glancing into the woods and we're listening up into the sky, nervous at what we all know is out there but can't be seen as yet. He's near where that helmet is because it's the only place to go, and fills the jerry can quick and shuffles through the snow lickity split back to us in the woods. Bill hollers in a whisper, "Come on up, guys, one at a time, fill your canteens." That's the strategy. You couldn't line up in a bunch. If a shell came in, it'd wipe out the whole group.

So the fellas go up one by one and get their water, and I'm near the end and I come up holding my canteen. They turn over the jerry can into the container and Babe says, "Goddam, Bill, look at this," and Bill says, "Aw Jesus," and he's looking at the last little bit of water in the can. They can only now see the state of affairs for what it is, now that the jerry can's nearly empty. It's got pieces of the kid's brains floating in the water, the kid killed by the P-47. Babe says to Bill, "What do you want me to do?" All our canteens are full of the stuff, and Bill's like, "You gonna drink yours?" And Babe turns behind to the guys and hisses, "Throw your goddam water purification pills in your canteens." So that's what we drank.

"You see, sir . . ." It was back to the sunlight on the balcony, and I tried forming my question again in front of Major Winters, although my voice had a clear-cut crack in it now. "I . . . I just don't rightly know how I'm gonna explain all this back home. . . . The things I've done. The things I've seen." I swallowed hard again.

The major's eyes glanced down at the table, then focused on me again. "You're a hell of a fine soldier, Shifty. There's nothing you need to explain."

I got to studying his words a moment and my chin became more resolute. It was truly time for me to go. "Thank you sir," I said, and saluted.

The major returned the salute, then, to my surprise, held out his hand like a man might to a friend. We shook. As I turned to go, I noticed the glass still resting on his desk. The water still looked cool and clear, though tiny beads of condensation had slipped from its sides and made the table the slightest bit wet. Just like maybe the major's eyes were. Maybe not.

The truck's motor idled with a growl. The driver slapped his hand against the side of the door. "You the guy from Easy Company? Get in. Gotta get a move on." Three other men lounged in the bed of the truck, the other lucky lottery winners, from Dog, Fox, and Headquarters companies. I didn't recognize them further than that. The kid from F Company offered me a hand climbing up and the truck began to roll. Zell am See, Easy Company, K-rations, sleeping on the ground, the war—it was all behind me now. I regretted not getting a chance to say good-bye to my good buddy Earl McClung. He thought he had died and gone to heaven in Austria and was seldom around. His job was to hunt stag and chamois, those little goats with the hooked horns, so we had something to feed ourselves and the prisoners. Mostly he stayed up in the hills around town and camped out. We saw McClung maybe once or twice a week. I'd write him a long letter once I got stateside.

"Where ya heading, Jack?" the kid from D Company asked me. He had sandy hair and long legs that stretched in front of him. I wondered if he played basketball before the war, just like me.

"Clinchco, Virginia. Little coal mining town in the southwest corner of the state. You?"

"Other side of the country. Got a girl there. Gonna get married soon. It's all home now."

We grinned. The truck picked up speed and the wind whistled past our ears. The truck was taking us to headquarters so we could clear up our paperwork. From there it was a straight shot to the coast and a boat ride home. An American GI car pulled in tight behind us and looked like it might pass on the curvy road. It honked and the blare echoed off the mountain rock. I craned my neck up. Over the top of our truck I glimpsed another GI truck heading toward us as it rounded a curve. The driver must have been searching for something because he was inching across the center line. Maybe he was drunk.

"Get any good souvenirs?" asked the kid from D Company. "Me, I got some—"

Don't remember no fuss. Don't remember no sound of metal against metal. Just remember flying ragdoll-style over the top of our truck with this car horn going off behind us. Echoing. Echoing. Bouncing off those rock walls. My wrist hit the middle of the road first and broke like someone snaps a twig while walking through the forest. My pelvis hit the blacktop next and something inside me rattled and busted, like a rock hitting a windowpane. My head hit the pavement last and I skidded along, still with the mindset to wish the car behind wouldn't run me over. All was black and blue for a moment and I fought to come back. My mind returned, and rubber tires were squealing and gravel was flying, striking my arms and chest like we was under fire. I saw the mashed-up cab of our truck from my periphery. That other truck was crunched into us, head-on. Steam and smoke gushed up and the motors were rammed into each other's cab. I propped myself up, trying to scramble out of the way, but my arm buckled and my insides jumbled and I scrunched my eyes and tried not to holler at the pain.

A woman bent over me. She wore a long gray coat-dress, and her hat bore a tiny crimson cross. Don't know how much time passed. The side of the road looked closer now, and she was flicking the seal of a morphine syrette, getting ready to stick my leg. The kid from D Company lay a few feet away, the kid going home to his girl. His sandy hair was matted red now, his long legs motionless, his complexion colorless when a medic pulled a blanket overtop his face.

The drug hit and everything got swirly and I thought about heading in for my mother's homemade chocolate pie. So creamy and good, and I was there sitting in our kitchen again. Mama wore her Sunday dress with her best apron tied behind her and she was telling me to stay at the table and have seconds on dessert. Don't worry about me, Mama, I said. My name's Sergeant Darrell C. Powers, and I won General Taylor's lottery. I'm coming home soon, Mama, I'm really coming home soon.

2

NO ORDINARY COUNTRY

Maybe a young man needs to travel to another country before he fully appreciates his home. He needs to abandon everything familiar, you know, travel a road that heads another direction. Then it dawns on him how good he had it at first. He remembers all over again being a boy and the rasp of his daddy's chin against his cheek, keeping within him that warmth of knowing his daddy would be home again after work. Or maybe he remembers the thick, salty smell of bacon sizzling in his mama's pan, so different from the cold bean soup the chow cook just sloshed in his mess kit. A home filled with bacon smells and a father coming home each night is how it is for some boys growing up, some boys who have it real lucky. That's how it was for me.

I was eight years old, nine maybe, and Daddy was walking softly off my left when he stopped fast in the bottom of a holler and held his hand up for me to do the same. He shaded his eyes then started walking again. We were hunting squirrels deep up on Frying Pan, the name given to the mountain Daddy's folks had owned longer than anybody could remember. Two cabins squatted up on Frying Pan. Daddy's family stayed up top in the smaller cabin in summers, then come winters they moved down to the bigger cabin on the river bottom where they was closer to town. I never lived in either of Frying Pan's cabins myself; we lived in a rented house in town by the time I was born, but the mountain was still as much our land as our skin was our skin, and on that mountain of bounty was where we hunted our food.

I must explain that folks in southwest Virginia throw round the word holler a lot, but it don't always mean yelling. A holler is a depression between two hills, like a valley, but not as deep. Frying Pan was filled with hollers, stacked on each other, and Daddy and I was climbing through these hollers to get to the top. I'd been to the summit plenty of times already in my young life and knew once we got there we were in for a treat. We'd look out and see more of the same thing, ridge after ridge, the sky coming down and brushing those mountaintops, coloring them blue. That's why you hear of the Blue Ridge Mountains running through this state and others. Those mountains are blue for real. The sun rose as Daddy and me walked, our breathing hung smoky in the early air, and we inhaled the crisp, cool smell of soil and bark. Lots of trees cover Frying Pan. "Deciduous" was the big word Daddy used. It was early fall and those leaves flamed in their colors—yellows, oranges, rubies, and golds.

"Listen," Daddy said. He held his hand up again. With the other, he carried his rifle. "What do you hear?"

"Nothing." I shrugged. We were the only folks around for miles.

"It's not what you think." Daddy hushed his words, not being harsh with me, but offering me again that question to wrestle with.

My heart pumped hard in my chest, I heard that—the blood flowing back of my eardrum—was that what Daddy was asking? We'd been hiking for some time already and I was glad to stop and rest. Daddy knew everything about hunting and shooting and he was schooling me in his ways. His name was Barnum Powers and he'd been a private in the 363rd Infantry during the First World War. He fired rifles through the Battle of St. Mihiel and came home alive to love Mama. She was a Scotch-Irish beauty named Audrey, and flowing somewhere deep in her bloodline was American Indian. I knew these things because Daddy told me, but that's all I knew, particularly about his shooting ways, so I wrinkled my nose and said, "I don't hear nothing, Daddy, nothing at all."

Daddy hiked over to me, his movements whisperlike on the forest floor, and laid his hand thick but gentle over the top of my face. He spread his fingers once for me to see his eyes were shut, too, then gathered his fingers so all was dark. "You're thinking about only what you know is true, son, but a good hunter uses more than his eyes, you know. Let me ask you again: What do you hear?"

I tried to hush the pounding in my ears. I tried to see all around me by listening to what I heard. Finally I said, "Dripping, Daddy. I hear dripping from water off leaves."

"Good, son. What else?"

"Wind."

"What kind of wind?"

"A little breeze, I guess. Comes in puffs."

"What direction?"

"From the holler over yonder. North, maybe."

"What else?"

"A sort of a rustling. Mushy. Leaves are moving someplace."

"Where from?"

"Up in that big ole Maple to our right."

"Good. And why might those leaves be rustling, son?

"I dunno. I guess—"

Bang! Daddy's hand was off my eyes. He was bringing his rifle down from his shoulder. Smoke drifted out of the end. A bushytailed squirrel lay on the ground, some twenty-five yards to our right.

"You'll get the next one, you know," Daddy said. His eyes were still closed. I don't know if they were closed while he shot, or if he only closed them again afterward, like a man might do at a sacred place. He had heard that squirrel rustling through the leaves in the tree, same as I had, but he was more certain of what he heard. I didn't ask more because Daddy was already walking to where the squirrel lay. He crouched over it and unsheathed his knife and I followed his motions. Squirrel is dark meat, flavorful and tender if young. Old squirrels are fit for stewing only, but Mama would brush butter on this in her roasting pan, and it'd make fine eating.

Daddy removed all four paws at the wrist joint. He used small, careful cuts to open the belly skin without nicking into the muscle wall. He cut down the insides through all four legs and around the rectum at the base of the tail. He handed me the knife and I stripped the skin away from the meat and cut the tail off at the bone. There were seven of us in our family and I knew that Daddy made a hundred dollars a month. In a boy's figuring, I didn't know if that was a heap or a little, but Mama said we ate on a dollar a day, and she stretched it hard to go that far, so these squirrels kept us fed. We ate 'em all the time, as well as Mama's garden in season, chickens that we raised ourselves, and a hog or two we kept up on the hillside.

Daddy wiped his knife. "Promise me this, son—"

"Yes, Daddy?"

"People think hunting's just being out walking in the woods, but it's lots more than that. You see things. You hear things. You learn to know everything that moves around you. Might be squirrel, deer, turkey, grouse, might be another man, you know. So you aim well, and aim for the eyes. It means a smaller target, but you have to promise me this—quick, clean kills only. Understand?"

I nodded without knowing the total of what I was agreeing to, whether Daddy was referring to squirrel hunting only, or to something he learned during the war, or if he knew enough about the troubling ways of the world to fear that his son would someday need to fight similar battles as he had. Soon enough we had that squirrel dressed and were hiking the sides of the hollers again, Daddy and me, this time with me listening for more than I could see.

Daddy took me hunting a few more times, but mostly I was with my brothers, friends, or on my own. I'd head out before the sun rose, just like Daddy taught me, and start by looking fifty feet ahead, then scan left to right. Then I'd hike out further and scan right to left and so on, just like that. I practiced my blank stare, where you're not looking at anything solid, but you become aware of everything in front of you all the way back to your shoulders. Daddy's words about movement being the biggest giveaway became second nature to me, and I always had an ear inclined to what might be in the trees. I heard wind. I heard snow crunch. I heard raindrops. If a leaf fell behind me, I knew. Might have been a year after Daddy first took me hunting that I came into the house with two squirrels tucked under my arm. Daddy looked them over and said, "Well that's pretty good shooting, son, you shot 'em both through the eyes, you know." It was the best compliment he'd ever given me, and I never felt prouder.

Daddy soon told me I needed to buy my own ammunition, so that meant I needed to earn money. I didn't know what a boy like me could do around our hometown of Clinchco. All the jobs were for men. Ever heard of Clinchco? Probably not. Picture a bunch of mountains all grouped together with narrow, winding roads lacing through them. Clinchco's a little speck by the side of one of those roads, far in the southwest tip of the triangle of Virginia. If you climb high enough on any ridge round Clinchco and spit hard enough, you'll cross one of three state lines and land it on Kentucky, Tennessee, or North Carolina. If you look on a map, you'll see that Virginia's midway up the country, but everybody still considers us part of the South. Not Deep South like Alabama, we don't talk with as much drawl, but we ain't Yankees, that's for sure. If you travel about an hour away from Clinchco to the big town of Bristol, you'll see tan-bricked houses with wide white Greek columns out front, built Southern style, and folks will be real neighborly and ask you your business or make it their business to find out. They'll be belted solid in the Bible, maybe Methodist, or Baptist like our family, and they'll believe in God and Jesus Christ and go to church more Sundays than not. Most of 'em vote Democrat on account of the labor unions, and they'll expect you to work hard if you live among them. They'll help you if you're down on your luck, and smoke cigarettes on your porch, and they'll feed you the best ham and baked beans you've ever eaten if you come to visit a spell.

Oh, I knocked on plenty doors around Clinchco looking for work, but it wasn't no use. A fella needed to work for the company, and that was that. I'm talking the Clinchfield Coal Mine Company, which was much the only reason our little town ever existed. A few pioneers settled the area mid 1880s and built a grist mill; then come 1913, a railway pushed its way from Spartanburg, South Carolina, to Elkhorn City, Kentucky, and eighteen houses sprung up overnight. One of the railway contractors was a hefty fella named Moss, so that's what our town was first named. Four years later a post office was built and folks wanted things renamed in honor of the mining company, which began operations that same year. So Moss was no more, and Clinchco now was, and the railroad brought in workers, and that's the way our town began.

They came for jobs in all four of the original Clinchfield mines, hardscrabble folks from all over the globe—Greeks, Hungarians, Italians, blacks—mostly by route of Ellis Island; I grew up with a real smattering of ethnic kids. The company needed services for its workers, so it built a school and barber's office, a church and store. That big ole store had everything in it, groceries, meat, clothes, furniture, and that's the only place you shopped if you lived in Clinchco. The store had a post office in one end and a drug store on the other, and every year come first of December they'd stock a heap of toys in the front window for our delight. Clinchco, oh, it was a booming place in those years. Maybe two thousand people in its heyday, maybe three thousand, though if you travel there today, the boom is long over and about four or five hundred folks call it home now.

The company owned our house. The company paid you what they reckoned to pay. At first, Daddy received script. Then the company changed the system, and in the latter 1930s and early 1940s, Daddy was paid cash money, silver dollars. Come payday you'd see this armored truck drive up and two guards climb out with their guns drawn. Later in the 1940s, the company switched to credit cards. Daddy got his card, and how much it said was how much he spent.

Tennessee Ernie Ford wrote that song about a company store owning a man's soul, but it didn't feel that way for our family. Few folks in Clinchco ever complained out loud. Most was into hard work and good behavior. Wasn't actually a police force in town, but we had a security guard. He'd make sure all the doors were locked and check the office buildings, things like that. One time some boys broke into the drugstore and were caught. Their families had to move away. So that's what it was. Kids were taught to behave themselves. If you didn't, your daddy lost his job.

Never even felt like we were poor, to me. It was the Great Depression, but most all the fathers I knew kept their jobs. Maybe a man worked at the Number 7 Coal Tipple, or he processed at Number 9. Plenty of folks round America had it worse than we did, but it wasn't all smooth in Clinchco. Coal business goes by jumps, you know. It'll go along with a lot of demand, then tables turn sudden-like. A lot of business depends on what they call lake orders—when lakes thaw up north, they haul coal across to sell it, but when lakes are frozen too long, then everything slows, and times get hard for a coal town. Daddy kept his job all through the Depression, thankfully, and he never worked down in the actual mines, thankfully. His job was superintendent of supplies, so he bought, stocked, and issued out the various parts the company needed to fix machinery, that's what he did.

It took me a week or two of knocking on doors and coming up empty on jobs, but finally I figured I'd need to create my own work. So I found a cloth and turned over a wooden box and shined shoes outside the commissary. Grown-ups like it when a young boy's polite, and pretty soon I earned enough to buy a real shoeshine kit. From then on I had it made. Every Saturday I coated and buffed those boots and shoes till they shined brown and black. Every dime I earned from my business went into bullets for shooting practice. Well, that's not true; I kept a few coins for myself. Had heard of an experiment I wanted to try, you know, but was probably twelve years old before I had enough jingle in my pocket to give it a real go.

Me and a kid named Frank Powers went into the woods one day to test the experiment. Frank had the same last name as me but was no relation. He was my best buddy in all Clinchco and the kids at school called him Pete, but I couldn't tell you why. An alley ran between the back of our house and the back of Pete's house, so whenever Pete headed out his door for school he ran through our house on his way down the street. Nobody in my family seemed to mind. Mama often spooned up a second helping of banana pudding on Pete's plate if he stopped long enough at our kitchen table.

"Ain't no way," Pete said. "Not a chance in hell."

"Just stand back," I said, real quiet, and loaded a bullet in my rifle. I fished around in my pocket and took out a silver dollar. Now, it took a quarter just to buy a box of .22 rifle shorts, so the sacrifice of a whole silver dollar meant I was making a real investment on glory. I flicked the coin high in the air, maybe eight, ten feet, grabbed my rifle hard with both hands, and fired.

Pete shook his head. "Never woudda believed it," he said. "Never ever, if I hadn't seen it with my own eyes."

That big ole silver dollar was sent sailing. Never did see where it landed. A .22 wouldn't be powerful enough to blow a hole through the center of it, but we both knew I had shot the silver dollar.

"You're here to witness, right?"

Pete nodded. He was no slouch when it came to shooting,

neither, but this was my experiment. I fished around in my pocket again, took out a smaller half dollar this time, flipped it high in the air, and pulled the trigger. Pete's mouth plumb dropped out of his jaw. "Wild Bill Hickok ain't got nothing on you," he whispered.

"Ain't done yet," I said. This experiment had cost me a buck-fifty already, but nothing was stopping me now. I pulled a quarter out of my pocket, smaller still, gave 'er a flip, and blasted it clean into the trees.

"Nickel next?" Pete asked.

"Nickel." My voice was still confident. See, I had been planning this experiment for months in advance, practicing by myself with all my spare change. Already I had shot a nickel and knew I could do it. I just hadn't told Pete about it, so it would look fresh to him. I flipped the nickel and blasted it good.

"Nice," Pete said.

Was the dime I was worried about. Try as I might, I never could hit a dime when I practiced before. None of the kids at school would care about a penny. But they'd ask about the dime. Shoot—I wasn't even doing this to impress the kids, you know, I was doing it to challenge myself and become good at aiming. So maybe Pete would think the nickel was all that's needed. Or maybe I had jumped ahead of time and called him to witness the experiment before I was truly ready. There wasn't any man or boy I knew who could hit a dime with a rifle. I decided to call it quits with the nickel, so I said, "Well, I guess we'll call it a day then."

"Well, hold on," Pete said. "You're forgetting something."

I toed the dirt with my shoe and sighed. I pulled a dime out of my pocket, flipped it in the air, and pulled the trigger. The dime landed straight down in front of my nose. "Pete," my shoulders slumped, "that nickel might be all that gets it today."

Pete was solemn. "Give it another go," he said.

I flipped the dime again. Again no luck. A box of .22 shorts held a hundred rounds. I flipped and fired and flipped and fired and flipped and fired. Finally, my box was empty, my dime still rested in front of me in the dirt.

"Shit," Pete said.

"Shit's right," I said. I wasn't smiling.

He looked at the dime on the ground and slugged me in the shoulder, a small grin on his face. Not a hard slug. Just friendly. "A nickel it is, then."

I nodded. "A nickel it is."

High school hit, and Pete and me stayed friends. Always on each other's side, that's the way we were. Math was my favorite subject in school, came real natural to me, and Pete was good at it, too. Pete and me competed to see who'd get the best grades in math. It was always only a point or two difference, and we never fussed either way. For one year our family moved eleven miles away to a town called Clintwood, then moved back to Clinchco. All our friends still felt real close despite our leaving and coming home again. Us kids did more than hunt and shoot for fun, you know. True, we was always outdoors growing up. But we had baseball, softball, football, and basketball, no television then, but a few good radio stations to tune in to. We listened to *Amos and Andy*, and had cookouts, picnics, and there was always swimming, fishing, things like that.

Our family was always close knit. All seven of us looked after each other. They called my older brother Barnum Junior then just Junior for a while, then just Barney later on. He was older than me by three years. Then I had another brother, James, younger by three years, we called him Jimmy. My pretty sister Gaynell was four years younger than me. Then Franklin came along, the baby of the family, and we called him Frankie. Don't ever remember fighting with my sister—sure, I'd tease her sometimes, but I always kept a good lookout for her. Us brothers sometimes argued about who brought in the coal and kindling wood, but other than that we never fought or carried on like some families do. Never did see my dad drunk. He had maybe two drinks a night, vodka and Wild Turkey were his favorites. Mother wasn't necessarily stricter than he was, it's just that Daddy left her in charge of making us behave, because he was off at work. So she assumed the role of disciplinarian. If we needed it, Mama dealt it out.

We always wanted to please Daddy. Mama, too, but we were with her all the time so it was different. Once my little brother Frankie was late coming in. Supper was ready and he wasn't home. Daddy said, "Just wait till that boy gets here. Just wait." I don't know if he was gonna spank him or what. Finally Frankie came in, he'd been down at the river fishing. Before Daddy could say anything, Frankie held up his mud bucket and said, "Look what I got." Daddy's tone changed real quick, "What'd you get, son?" Frankie's bucket was fat with trout, and he told him where in the river he was, and Daddy said, "Well, get us some minnows, and we'll go back next morning real early and get us some more." That's the kind of daddy he was. Our parents raised us with a lot of love and fun, and that's what they passed along to us.

When we lived in Clintwood, it came Easter and we had a terrible snow, so much that we weren't able to go on our usual picnic Easter egg hunt. It wasn't much trouble to me, but I could tell my little sister was getting choked up. She was in fifth grade and it was important to her. So I told her we'd hunt the eggs in our living room this year. Sis was so impatient, as was the littlest, Frankie.

I wanted to give them a real good hunt, so I hid those eggs all over the room, then called them in, daring them to find them all. They squealed and laughed and ran about, and when the hunt was over, three eggs couldn't be found for nothing. About a day or two later, I let them in on the secret. One egg I taped under the bottom of the table. The second, I hid in the back of our radio. I took off the cover, took out the tubes, hid the egg, then replaced the tubes. Third egg I ate, then opened the window, put the shells outside, and waited for the snow to cover them up. That's why Sis and Frankie needed to wait outside the room so long, for those shells to be covered in snow. That's the type of family we were. We made our own fun.

I played a lot of basketball for the high school, and that's where I got my nickname. They thought I was kinda shifty on my feet, you know—quick-like, so they named me Shifty and it stuck. All the kids on the team had nicknames. There was Slick and Red and Pete and Flirty. It got so you didn't remember what a boy's real name was, but that was part of the fun.

When we moved to Clintwood, I played basketball there, and that year the Clintwood team won the county championship. I was also elected best dressed boy in school, but I don't know if that's something you'd care about. It's not that I had better clothes than anybody, I was just careful, clean, everything had to be pressed neat. I had been tubby as a kid. Shoot—I weighed ten pounds as a newborn baby. But by the time I got to high school I had a long, lean build. Girls seemed to think I was a fine-looking fella, and I liked that real fine. Girls, I mean. I liked a lot of girls. Went with several. Nothing serious. Don't even remember a steady girlfriend in high school, but we always went to dances and movies and for walks holding hands under the trees.

None of the kids I knew wanted to leave Dickenson County.

Didn't think of things in other places we might want to see. Maybe a few of us did, but we had it real fine in our hometown, so we just figured, why go anywhere else? Wasn't any money for us to travel, besides. Wasn't many vehicles in those days, you know. Maybe we'd go see a movie in Clintwood and we'd put a quarter's worth of gas in the car. Or we'd gather a carload and drive over to Norton, about thirty miles. They had a big swimming pool in Norton. It was a real treat to swim there. That's as far away from home as any of us ever went.

Mostly, I just kept hunting. I'd go to school, and shine shoes on Saturdays, and help around the yard, and hang out with friends, and play basketball, and every other spare moment I had I was out in the woods, squinting down the end of a rifle barrel. People ask me if I grew up something of a mountain man, and I say more or less. When I got into the army, I thought everybody knew how to do the things I did growing up—you know, scout the land, shoot with a rifle. I never took food or water with me when I hunted. I just went out, usually all day. We did a lot of that in the Army, and I got hungry same as any man, but it might not have bothered me as much as it did the other fellas. Maybe because I had been out there and looked at the forest and the sky and learned the types of trees and which ones have fruit or nuts that you can eat. Never hurt me at all, in fact it came in handy later.

Time has a way of changing what you've always known. The further I got in high school, the more I knew I'd need to find a trade for my life. Times seemed to be changing for a lot of folks. The radio was on each night, and we weren't much listening to *Amos and Andy* anymore. There was a war on in Europe. Crazy things were afoot. The chancellor of Germany seemed intent on gobbling up one country after another. President Roosevelt declared a draft in September 1940, the month I started eleventh grade, but the war in Europe was on the other side of the world, the draft only for twenty-one-year-olds at first, and that age still seemed a long way off. I was still dreaming of doing something beyond shining shoes, so I got a job picking slate for the company. You ever picked slate?

Don't.

Wasn't the hard work I hated. Was the dust. The coal car comes up out of the mine and dumps its load, see, and you pick out the junk rock from the coal by hand. This big black dust cloud rises up and there are times when you can't see the other fella on the other side of the car. You'd have to wait till the air moved before you could see again. I worked Saturdays and was paid fifty-eight cents an hour. The first day I worked ten hours and made five dollars and eighty cents. At the end of the day the company made me go buy some hard-toe shoes and a hard hat. When I came out of the commissary with my new gear, I owed the company eight dollars. So I picked slate most of that year and the next, but I knew it wasn't my future. I needed an occupation, even if I wanted to live in Clinchco the rest of my life, which I did. I needed to learn how to do something more than pick slate.

That meant I needed to leave home.

3

THE FUN AND THE FEAR

I t's a road you don't want to meet another car on. No way can two vehicles fit. The road's paved, you know, but spotty with potholes, and they sneak up without warning and bounce hell out of your shocks and springs. We was heading down the road, Pete and me, on our way toward a town called Haysi. You drive up one mountain, then shoot off the side of another, then coil around the roads a bit, and that's how you get where you're going. A trout stream beckoned us, one we heard was stocked flush, but to get there meant we needed to drive through Low Gap, and that's what had us worried. Well, at least Pete, for he was behind the wheel.

Everybody in Dickenson County knows the legend of Low Gap. If you dare to drive through Low Gap at night and it's foggy, they say your car will stall and roll to the bottom, then start up again, real sudden without you ever touching the ignition. One of our buddies told us how it happened to his cousin. Seems the cousin was heading that direction one murky night with the radio playing full blast. He was enjoying his drive, just meandering down that old road, but when nearing Low Gap everything shut off— ghost hushed—and he floated through the gap like a shadow over water. While coming through he heard voices, laughing and cackling, shivering things best left untold. By the time he rolled beyond a certain hollowed-out oak tree, his car came to life again and the radio roared up and he kept on driving. Only this time with his accelerator floored.

"You afraid? I ain't afraid," Pete said, but his knuckles showed white where his hands gripped the wheel.

"Tall tales always got a cousin in 'em," I said, and lit a cigarette. "Why can't things ever happen to the guy actually telling the story? A fella can make up anything if he says it happened to his cousin."

Low Gap lay directly in front of us now. A pothole grabbed the right front tire and the Pontiac pitched and swayed. It was early morning, clear, misty, but no fog.

"Goddam road," Pete said.

"Want me to turn the radio up?" I asked. "That way we'll know for sure when it cuts out."

"Just shut your yap."

I was teasing Pete, aggravating him like I always did. Wasn't no real fear in our lives, you know, nothing that actually pressed our luck. Sure, legends ran the course of the county, and everybody's cousin was always into trouble whenever you told tall tales. Just like the legend of Low Gap, an abandoned schoolhouse sits up in the hills that everybody claims is haunted. We called it Dave's Ridge, though there's another name, can't remember what. Sometimes we'd go up there just for fun and act like the place was haunted. We'd camp out overnight with some school buddies, maybe shinny out of our sleeping bags around midnight and bang on walls. Supposedly you could hear an old widow woman's voice yelling "Get out!" but I've got real good ears and never heard nothing. Those were our only fears around Dickenson County.

"Radio seems fine to me, Pete," I said. In the side mirror I could make out Low Gap behind us now. Pete relaxed his grip on the wheel. Our car hadn't shut off, and we were still heading for the stream and a day of fishing.

"How much time you got left, anyway?" Pete asked.

"Eight days."

"Well, we'll catch our limit this morning for sure." He paused and shifted into third, then added, "You think you'll ever come back to live in Clinchco?"

"That's my hope. Just as soon as I can."

Pete smacked the wheel. "It'll be good to have you back," he said.

Sure enough, we caught our limit, beautiful fat brown trout, and scaled them on the bank and packed them in a bucket to take back for Mama to fry for supper. Eight days later I said my good-byes all around and set out for Norfolk. It was clear on the other side of the state and the farthest I'd ever been from home. Norfolk was a big city, couple hundred thousand people, I guessed, and the September sun felt warm on my face as I walked through Town Point Park on the Elizabeth River. The river led to the deep-water channels of the nearby Chesapeake Bay where fresh and salt water merged together, the only bay in the United States where that happens, and seagulls from the Atlantic Ocean squawked over my head and swooped. Norfolk felt like nowhere I'd ever been.

I'd enrolled for a machinist course at a vocational school in Norfolk. Figured I could learn that skill, then come home and work for the company at a better job than picking slate. It was fall

1941 when I started the course. I was eighteen years old and had just graduated from high school the spring before, and only a tiny twinge of regret gnawed at me that I wasn't heading off to college instead. Math was my best subject, you know, and maybe if I ever went to college I could learn to be one of those engineers. Build roads, bridges, buildings maybe. But, well, nobody I knew ever went to college, and I wasn't sure what I'd ever do in Clinchco with a college education. And, well, maybe I'd still do that college thing later on after the machinist training. Life still held out plenty of time for me, I reckoned.

Come my first day of vocational school I shook hands with a wildcat named Robert E. Wynn, Jr. He had a cheerful, broad face and was from South Hill, Virginia, over in Mecklenburg County. Everybody called him Popeye. He suggested we go find ourselves a beer before classes started in earnest, and I grinned and reckoned me and Popeye were going to get along real fine.

It was good to make a friend right away. Right off, Popeye and me start picking on each other in a good-natured way, just little aggravations, funny things. About a week after we met he says, "Shifty, I'm gonna take you bowling." Well, I had never bowled in my life, never even seen a bowling ball, and I told him that, but he gave me good odds on a five-dollar bet just to make things interesting, so we went over to the lanes. He stood up to bowl, and I watched real close on how he did things, see. His ball bee-lined down the lane, and I was a fair athlete, too, so I copied all his moves, how he held his leg back and so on, and my ball hit a good number of pins. He said, "You've bowled before, Shifty. The bet's off." And I said, "No, I haven't. The bet's on." Well, we kept bowling and he won that game anyway and kept his five dollars and three of mine, but at least I didn't look like a fool.

Norfolk was a government training program, and the administration paid us ten dollars a month for essentials while at school, but September rolled on, and then October, and it seemed like both months we'd come near to the end and I was out of cigarettes. Popeye kept a pouch of tobacco and a rolling machine and he asked me if I felt like a smoke. I said sure and he said he'd roll one for me, then roll one for himself. I stood at the door of the room and he rolled one for me and I handed it to a guy as he passed down the hallway. "Need another," I said. Popeye shrugged, rolled a second cigarette, handed it to me, and I handed that one to a different guy as he walked on by. "Better roll one more," I said. Popeye kept rolling them and handing them to me, and as fast as he'd roll them, I kept giving them away. Oh, Popeye got good and mad about that, and it set me to laughing real hard. Then Popeye started laughing hard, too, and that was that. Popeye was fast becoming somebody I knew really well, almost as well as if he'd come from back home, and I felt fine about having a friend as good as Popeye.

Meeting new people in the outside world didn't intimidate me. Good thing, too, because all manner of young men signed up for that course. They bunked us on campus and we got to know the fellas around us, and plenty of them were tough customers. Norfolk seemed to attract a rougher crowd. Maybe it was all the sailors coming and going, I couldn't rightly tell you why, but life in a port city sure proved different than life back in Clinchco. Nothing goes in a rush back in Clinchco, you know, no one's in a hurry, and everyone's your friend as like as not. In Norfolk I found I enjoyed studying to be a machinist pretty well and seemed to be good at it. Mostly I just fixed my mind to my work. But I soon found out that even when you're not looking for it, trouble has a way of finding you.

The last weekend in November, me and some guys headed

downtown to shoot pool. The guys wanted to stay late but I had more studying to do, so I started back to the dorm by myself. It was an unfamiliar part of the city and I passed buildings and streets I didn't recognize. When I came near an alleyway, up pulled this car. It dimmed its lights, you know, and at first the guys just rolled next to me with their convertible top down though it was nearly winter. Nobody was saying nothing and I kept walking, quicker now, while counting out of the corner of my eye. Two in the front. Three in the back. Big fellas. None smiling, particularly when they swerved ahead of me and blocked my path. They climbed out and lined up in a row with their backs to the side passenger door, facing me. I considered hightailing it back to the bar, but any help I might receive was some distance away, and they had a car. So I squared my shoulders, reached my hand inside my jacket pocket, and spoke first. "I got no problem with taking you on. All I ask is that you come at me one at a time." In my jacket pocket I always carried a switchblade, something I used for hunting back home, and I pulled the blade out and flicked it open. The sound of my knife echoed with a mighty click off those brick walls.

The biggest fella took three steps toward me, scowled, then stopped. "Why you out here?" he said.

"Studying to be a machinist. Going back to the dorms back at the vocational school."

"Yeah," he said. "I've got a cousin over there."

I nodded again.

"Get in." He kept his scowl. "We'll give you a ride back to school."

I didn't know if it was a command or a question, but I figured if I didn't do it he might change his mind. I closed my switchblade and we all got in. The big fella took the wheel. We started driving and for a while all was dark. Then he switched on his lights again and we started passing more familiar streets. I starting thinking he was going to keep his word after all. The guy next to me handed me a bottle wrapped in a brown paper bag. I took a slug and passed it along, and the liquor relaxed me a bit and I wondered if I might tell some jokes to those fellas. Sure enough, I started telling tales and they started slapping their knees, and once we all got to laughing, everybody loosened up and we started talking. Those city boys had never been out hunting but had always wanted to, so I told them about that. And they told me about the girls they was meeting and about the good places in Norfolk to buy beer. We got to discussing baseball and who Cincinnati was going to put on the mound next spring. That's pretty much the way I was taught to face any fight. I learned that plenty of fellas want to be scrappers, and if they're swinging at you, well, you better swing back and swing hard. But I found out it's almost always better to talk than fight, and when those fellas dropped me off at campus, I reckon we might have almost been friends.

Wish it could've been that way in other parts of the world. A week later the calendar showed December 7, 1941. A bunch of fellas gathered around Popeye's radio that Sunday morning, shocked to hear that Hawaii had been bombed by the Japanese. Pearl Harbor, they called it. The attack came out of the blue. A bunch of our ships were sunk. A bunch of American boys were dead. Nobody could believe the news. A few of the fellows wondered aloud where Japan even was. Shoot, if Japan wanted a fight, America would take it to them, and take it hard. We figured it wouldn't take much to whip a little country like that.

After Pearl Harbor, nothing felt the same. Lots of fellas straightaway quit whatever they were doing and enlisted. Seemed a man never felt more patriotic than just then. Wherever you looked, wherever you went, folks was flying the American flag. This was our country, and if we weren't going to defend it, who would?

December went up and I went home for Christmas break. Even in Clinchco, there was new talk going around town. Boys were signing up, draft or no draft, boys as young as me, and when I returned to the vocational school in January 1942 an uncomfortable feeling traveled up my spine. You'd walk along the sidewalk, and if you were an able-bodied young man and weren't wearing a uniform, people would look at you strange. In the bigger picture of things, that prompted a good feeling. Americans were all in this together, come whatever evil came our way, and nobody questioned what we needed to do. Our freedom was at stake, our ability to make something of our lives. I couldn't quite understand why Germany and Japan wanted to mess things up like they were doing all over the world, but when I got to studying how the situation was playing out, I knew exactly what was required of me. Just didn't know when.

Come next month, I found out. They shipped us all in the vocational school over to the Navy Shipyard across the river at Portsmouth. A big shop was down there, and they wanted us to start working on the ships. Real work, not just schooling work, and we started in on battleships, worked on the USS *Alabama* and made parts for the carriers. The word they used was "essential." We'd never get called up to fight. Working on those battleships was needed for the war effort, they said, and word came that we were all getting frozen to our jobs. It meant that we couldn't enlist, even if we wanted to.

When I found out this job-freezing was coming, I grabbed Popeye by the arm and said, "Now, we don't want to get left out of this war. If we're going to get into it, we'd better do it right now."

So we both went over and signed up for the Army that same day. Later that afternoon, when we came back to the shipyards and quit, the guy in charge really jumped on us. He called the recruiter who signed us up and raised a fuss, but the recruiter said, "There ain't nothing you can do about it. Those boys signed the papers. They're in the Army now." I guess we were the last two people that came out of that Navy yard who joined the service, because they froze it up real tight after that.

Life magazine ran this article about a new branch of the service starting up. Paratroopers, it was called. Some other countries had tried it, and it was met with a lot of success. The paratroopers were like infantrymen except they jumped out of airplanes with their rifles in their hands. Instead of coming at the enemy head-on, they jumped behind enemy lines and created their own battlefronts with whatever enemy they found there. Always ready to fight, the paratroopers were considered elite, like the Rangers or Green Berets are today, and if a fella wanted to be the best, why, he signed up for the paratroopers. It was an all-volunteer outfit. Nobody was bending your arm to make you come in. Why, plenty of fellows wanted to join the paratroopers but weren't tough enough to make the cut. A fellow had to be the best of the best.

Popeye and I got to studying that, and decided that if we was gonna fight, then we'd want to fight with the paratroopers. It took some nerve though, so he and I struck up a little wager. Each of us said that if one of us was gonna back out, then he'd have to pay the other fella ten dollars. Well, that sounded fair. We did a little more studying and found out that the paratroopers made fifty dollars more per month than a regular soldier. Fifty dollars was a lot of money, so that sealed the deal for us, right then and there.

One of my parents needed to sign for me to join the paratroopers because of my age. I had just turned nineteen and you needed to be twenty-one without your parents' permission. I suspected neither Daddy nor Mama would be real happy to sign since the paratroopers was considered dangerous duty. I went home to Clinchco and explained things, and sure enough they weren't happy. But Daddy knew the military and what a young man sets his sights on doing. So he signed my papers anyway, and I was set.

The Army sent us over to Camp Pickett in Virginia for a week where they gave us uniforms and physicals and a heap of shots. They checked us all real close. You couldn't be too tall. You couldn't be too heavy. You couldn't wear glasses. You had to be able to hear well. You had to have so many good teeth. If you had any records of broken bones, they wouldn't take you. I always wondered about that teeth business. I wasn't gonna bite them Germans. But that was that.

I was the first to enlist in our family. A while later my younger brother Jimmy quit school and joined the Navy. My older brother Barney was married by then with a kid on the way, but he wanted to do his duty, too, so he signed up for the Marines. Our youngest brother, Frankie, was too young to join, but I suspected he'd enlist as soon as he was old enough.

Popeye and me passed all our tests just fine. We didn't feel any fear at first, none that we talked of anyway. Course, we weren't paratroopers yet, just volunteering to give it a try. Soon enough they'd ship us out for Camp Toccoa down in Georgia to begin our paratrooper training. That's where the real fun would start.

4

BULLETPROOF

Come nightfall, our train screeched to a stop at the depot. We climbed out and smoke billowed, or maybe dust, except it was too rainy to be dusty. A coffin factory sat alongside the tracks, making a spooky greeting to the town of Toccoa, and Popeye and me were now three states away from home.

Other boys climbed off the train with us, all trying to find our gear, all not knowing where to go. Trucks had stood by earlier, somebody said, but they were gone already. Together we discussed what direction to head and we set out to walk the six miles from the depot to camp. The rain felt warm since it was July already, 1942, but it curled around the collar of my jacket and shivered down my back. The camp was dark when we showed up. Toombs, it was called. I reckoned it wasn't a very good name for a camp for soldiers who are going off to war. But somebody said no, that wasn't right—Camp Toombs had been renamed Camp Toccoa, in honor of the town where the depot was. So Camp Toccoa was what we were to call it from then on. All around me, guys yelled and shouted in the night, and fellas were saying *baRbwire* with that hard R sound, not *bob-wire* like I called it. I didn't know what to make of all this Yankee talk particularly because we were in the Deep South of Georgia.

Popeye and me found some tents and laid out our gear so it might dry. The rain kept falling and we stretched ourselves on some cots and soon were dreaming, I think, although water splashed through that tent like it was coming through a colander in Mama's kitchen. Soon the light was gray and Popeye mucked his boots through the water on the floor and said, "C'mon, Shifty, get up," and we pushed ourselves through the canvas flaps into our first morning at Camp Toccoa.

Nothing looked like much. Just row after row of tents. A bunch of tarpaper shacks huddled along a hillside. Someone said Camp Toccoa had once served as a summer camp for the Georgia National Guard units, but that was before the war had started, and it was getting rebuilt as the new training grounds for the 506th Parachute Infantry Regiment, which was going to be us, if we proved lucky.

Popeye had done some studying about the Army and he brought me up to speed. The 506th Regiment would be about three thousand men in due course, so that's why so many fellas were milling about this morning. We was all coming there to get in. It's also why nobody seemed to know what to do yet. See, the Army was trying something brand-new. Up until then, fellas enlisted in the Army and went to boot camp first, then were all sent to mix with other units. But the Army decided to train a bunch of fellas together at Camp Toccoa as a group. We were going to start at Toccoa together, then go through the war together. And at the end, if any of us came through, well, we'd be together still. That experimenting was maybe why the Army sent us to such a new and faraway place in Georgia. We could've been training at other established bases, maybe Fort Benning, Georgia, for one, I'd heard of that. But maybe the Army wanted us out of the way a spell. If we fell flat on our faces, see, nobody would know the difference.

A sticky mist rose off the red clay mud, and it felt like the rain had stopped sometime before dawn. Off to our right, the sun struggled to climb past the peak of a pine-covered mountain. It was as big as anything Daddy and me had ever hunted on back in Clinchco, and a kid crawled out of the tent next to me and gave a low whistle. Ed Tipper was his name and he didn't like the looks of what he saw. "I bet by the time we're done here they're going to make us hike to the top of that," Tipper said.

All around us, boys were stirring now. All manner of young men had poured into the camp during the night. We was in W Company, somebody said, which stood for Welcome, or maybe Washout, some other kid muttered. Still somebody else said we were in Cow Company, so that confusion proved the general nature of what I felt that morning. Back at the recruiter's office, they'd told me that at six-foot-one-inch and about 185 pounds, I'd make one of the taller, bigger paratroopers. But I didn't know about that. All the fellas I saw this morning were beefy sorts, thick necked, built strong and solid as young coal miners. They lit cigarettes, spit on the ground, and ran their fingers through their hair, grousing about the need for shaves and a wash. A tough-looking Northerner squinted at how I said "Morning," but he shook my hand anyway and said his name was Jim Alley from Washington State. Why, that was clear across America. He introduced me to a friend he had already made, Robert Van Klinken, who lived near the Canadian border in that same region. Van Klinken worked on trucks as a mechanic, he said, and right off I could relate to his working on parts and machinery. He was itching to get married, he mentioned right away, and asked if we had caught sight of any nice-looking young ladies when we stepped off the train. I hadn't seen nobody except fellas, but Van Klinken had turned away already, and Wayne Sisk hiked over and shook my hand. Sisk was on the lookout for girls, too, he said, and beer, or maybe a fight. We were to call him Skinny, and he wasn't a churchgoer, he told me right off, and didn't want nothing to do with their sort of ways.

Burton Christenson pushed his way out of a tent and came over to where we were standing. He went by the nickname Pat and was from California, built wiry like a boxer. He showed us some little pencil sketches he had drawn in a book he kept with him, and I thought it uncommon for such an athletic kid to be that artistic as well.

Warren Muck smiled broadly and told us he hailed from a town named Tonawanda, wherever that was. He asked us to call him Skip and said he had once swum clear across the swift-flowing Niagara River. Now, that was a mighty deed no ordinary man would try, but I couldn't tell outright if he was pulling our legs or not.

Gordy Carson ambled up and began talking baseball with us. He had lettered in five sports back in high school in New York, a natural expert at everything he tried.

Two tough-looking fellas from Joliet, Illinois, Hack Hanson and Frank Perconte, smoked cigarettes and said little. They were older guys, early twenties, and Frank muttered something about how he was dating a woman named Evelyn, going to marry her soon.

Joe Liebgott was tidying up his gear. He was another old man, twenty-five, twenty-six maybe, and tough as a railroad spike. He offered to cut our hair for cheap, seeing as how he worked as a barber back home in San Francisco.

Don Hoobler, Bill Howell, and Bob Rader were three hometown buddies from Manchester who all talked with hillbilly twangs like me. I felt good about that. Bob Rader was one of six children, and he and his older brothers had enlisted in the National Guard in high school so they could eat while the rest of the food in their family went to the younger children. The Guard kicked Bob out when they found he was underage.

Walter Gordon was a fine-featured burly fella who'd been to college already. He was chewing tobacco and had three cigars stuck in his shirt pocket. A Southerner from Jackson, Mississippi, he'd pulled strings and enlisted up north in Philadelphia instead, believing they'd send all the Northern guys south and vice versa. Seemed real smart thinking to me.

About the only guy I didn't like at first was Bill Kiehn, a muscular-looking guy from Washington State who seemed to have a chip on his shoulder. Nobody was going to tell him what to do, he said. Names and faces and stories soon all blurred together, and fellas wondered about breakfast and milled around in the mud, clueless as to what came next.

We didn't need to wait long. Somebody blew a whistle. Popeye gave me a nudge and we formed up. The man up front was part of the old Army cadre, a tough-sounding old bird, and explained that the First Battalion of the 506th Regiment was already filled, so we sorry sacks of dog droppings were all going into the Second Battalion. I guess a battalion was about seven hundred men, and each battalion was made up of one Headquarters Company and three other "alphabet" companies, and we were now in E Company, or

Easy, as he called it. Dog and Fox Companies were also in our battalion, and each company was about a hundred and forty men. We were further told to shut up and look sharp; we were sorry excuses for men and our mamas weren't married to our daddies when we were born.

With that, we were off and running. The first half mile proved fine, since it was all flat ground. The sky was cloudless and I reckoned the day was going to be real hot. We veered off the flats and I noticed an ambulance parked by the side of the trail. "Double time," the old bird yelled, and started sprinting straight up the side of Mount Currahee. Now, that was a surprise. The trail was rocky and steep. Loose stones grabbed at our ankles like the potholes back in Low Gap. About ten minutes passed, then twenty, and on we ran. The fellas groaned now, sweating and puffing, and a kid next to me doubled over and collapsed by the side of the trail. I didn't know if I was supposed to stop and help him or not, but the man up front yelled, "Do not help that man!" so we kept running, always running, and another fellow stumbled and fell in a ball, cussing his turned ankle. The last twenty-five yards to the top were a sheer scramble up shale. I didn't bother to look round at the view, for they turned us around at the top and sprinted us straight down to the bottom. Not quite an hour had passed since we first started running, and when the ground leveled out near the main area they hollered for us to stop. We gasped and held our sides and I glanced around. The ambulance must have been doing some good business because it looked like nearly a fifth of the fellas had quit the program, right from the get go.

The training didn't let up. That first day passed and the next and the day after that. They gave us coveralls to wear at first. When they had roughed out the camp, trees and brush had been bulldozed all over the grounds. They hollered for fifty pushups, and jagged slivers of wood poked up and burrowed into our hands and chests. Mosquitoes chewed our arms and faces. Our instructor yelled to be on the lookout for ticks. Sweat dripped from us, prompted from a thick blanket of heat I wasn't used to back in Virginia. We'd come in at the end of a day, aching, and flop on our bunks, our stomachs hollow, our throats dry. That's when things came clear to me. The Army only wanted the best of the best for this new program. They wanted you to quit Toccoa. Some 5,800 men had piled into the camp, all hoping for the chance at becoming paratroopers. Some 3,000 men would need to fail. That's the way they wanted it at Toccoa. If you were a quitting sort, then the paratroopers weren't for you. I talked to Popeye about this and we both vowed we'd make it to the end.

A West Pointer named Colonel Robert Sink led the regiment at Toccoa, the whole group of several thousand men. I never met the colonel myself, but understood that he wanted his boys in tip-top shape. He made up an obstacle course for us. Every once in a while you'd see him swing by the course, studying the pipe ladder, dreaming up little improvements to make things harder. The course was a real killer. We sprinted the whole way, hand-over-hand at first across a ladder over a ravine. We shimmied up slick plywood platforms, scratching and slivering up our hands and knees. We sprinted across mud pits and climbed like monkeys up huge knotted ropes.

The obstacle course was just one part of the training. A big athletic field sat in the middle of camp, and we duckwalked the length of the field, squatting as low as our knees would take us, hands behind our backs, thigh muscles burning. We lined up flat on our backs, eight men in a row, and held logs above our heads and brought them down to chest level, over and over again, push-up style. They stood us up and had us heave those logs from line to line, throwing through the air and catching them again.

Come evenings they sent us out on hikes—ten milers, twenty-five milers. We carried equipment soon enough, and the gear lugged in our field packs, our water jiggled in our canteens. A fella couldn't drink any, mind you. They wanted us knowing how to push past thirst.

One afternoon we each fixed a bayonet to the end of our rifle and were taught how to thrust it through a man. I had shot plenty of rifles before, but never carried one with a long blade on the end. The thought of what it was there for unsettled me a spell.

Near that time the colonel wanted to simulate some real battle conditions for us, see, so he had the men lug in these washtubs of hog parts and scatter them around the ground. It was a roped course with barbwire stretched at knee length over the top. We crawled under the barbwire through the hog guts—getting sticky from the livers, lungs, and bloody bowels. Machine-gun bullets zinged over our heads to make sure we stayed low. A messy day it was, and it made me wonder at the trouble to come.

Speaking of trouble, leading Easy Company was a tall fella with long arms and jet-black hair who we all got to know real well. Captain Herbert Sobel was his name, although behind his back a few of the boys called him the Black Swan. That was the nicest one of his nicknames, for the other things the fellas called him shouldn't be put in a book. Real hard training with Captain Sobel, real hard. It's not that Captain Sobel wasn't good at taking us raw recruits and turning us into soldiers. He was doing all that, pushing us, yelling at us, hollering "Hi-Yo Silver" and "The Japs are gonna get you." He made us run farther, faster. Long after all the other companies had quit for the day, Easy Company would still be out training. He wanted his company to be the best at Camp Toccoa, and I admired him for that. But I still didn't like the man. Shoot— I reckon nobody likes his drill instructor much, but with Captain Sobel, our dislike ran close to hatred.

It was Captain Sobel's disagreeableness that rankled us so. I never saw the man smile or crack a joke. He shouted with a high nasally voice, and he shouted near everything he said. Why, he'd tear into a man, make him feel as low-down as if he was picking slate. He'd nitpick about things, rules he fashioned just to make you feel mean. It might be the imaginary dust on your rifle he saw at inspection that restricted you to base for a weekend. Or it might be the imaginary lint on your shoulder that put you on latrine detail. The Army calls a man like that chickenshit, there's no nice name for it. It means contemptible. A man who lives by and enforces rules of no consequence. That was our Captain Sobel.

We went on bivouacs, they called them. During the day we might be far off into the woods, but at night we'd be in our tents. Captain Sobel and Sergeant Bill Evans, another officer nobody liked much, went around on these bivouacs trying to steal our rifles. It's a rule you always had to have yours with you. I always slipped mine into my sleeping bag, so it wasn't much of a problem. Well, one night I guess Captain Sobel and Sergeant Evans are sneaking around stealing weapons and they come to this company and it's been a long day and everyone's out real heavy. So they steal the rifles and make themselves scarce. Come next morning Captain Sobel walks up to us in Easy Company and starts shouting that we're worthless soldiers who've lost our rifles. But the men shrug and wonder what he's talking about: everyone's still got his rifle. Turns out the night was too dark, and ole Captain Sobel and Sergeant Evans had stumbled into the wrong company by mistake. They took Fox Company's rifles, and the officers of Fox Company were none too happy about it. We all had a good laugh about that one.

Popeye and me both started out as privates, see, and I think most enlisted men have mixed feelings about the officers who lead them. One night we were practicing infiltration. The Second Platoon was up on a little hill, and all of us in the Third were down a way off. They had dug in, and after it got dark we was supposed to go up the top of the hill without getting caught. Now, Popeye couldn't walk through the woods for beans. We started infiltrating, and he was making all kinds of racket, you know. This guy jumped up and hollered, "You're a prisoner of war. You're caught." Well, Popeye just hauled back, hit him in the eye with his fist, and kept going. Next day we're standing in formation, and this lieutenant came by with a big black eye. Nobody ever told him who gave it to him. Good thing it was so dark.

I'm not saying that was our attitude with all our officers. In contrast to Captain Sobel, we had some fine men leading us. A company is further divided into platoons, see, called the First Platoon, the Second Platoon, and so on. First Lieutenant Walter Moore led us in the Third Platoon, and he was a good officer, an everyday fella. He never pulled rank on you or nothing. Everybody liked him fine.

And Second Lieutenant Dick Winters, the company executive officer. His job was to lead the company whenever Captain Sobel wasn't around. Lieutenant Winters was how you'd picture an officer of an elite outfit to be. In top physical shape, yes, square jawed and a good wrestler, but respectful and kind-spoken, too, always on the lookout for his men. Now and again, Popeye and me enjoyed aggravating Lieutenant Winters. You've always got to call an officer by his rank, you know, but he'd be passing us by and we'd call out real low, *"Why, hello, Dick Winters,"* when no one else was around. He'd brush us off and grin. He could have really busted our chops for that, but I think it didn't bother him because he knew we both respected him so much. I couldn't rightly say, but there seemed to be friction growing between Captain Sobel and Lieutenant Winters, maybe trouble a-brewing. Only time would tell.

Another fella I respected a lot was our platoon sergeant, Amos Taylor, who went by the first name Buck. He was a straight-shooting Eagle Scout from northwest Philadelphia and loved being out in the wilderness, same as me. One time back in high school, he and some buddies went camping in a heavy snowstorm for three days, just for the fun of it. That's the type of man he was.

Sergeant Buck Taylor was no dummy when it came to the men he was leading, and he could see a fella like Bill Kiehn was going to get washed out of the paratroopers real quick if he kept up with that chip on his shoulder. Now, Kiehn was an okay guy. Long after other fellas were exhausted, Kiehn was still going strong. He'd be just the sort of man you could rely on in combat. Only problem was that snarly attitude of his. So Sergeant Taylor pulled Bill Kiehn aside one morning real early, got him out of bed I believe, and taught him close order drill, which he still needed to learn. Well, it was still dark outside, but there was Sergeant Taylor taking extra time with Kiehn, going back and forth, left to right, about face, just the two of them. Sure enough, that extra time won Kiehn over, and he shaped up and became an excellent soldier. That Sergeant Taylor fella, he had a lot of leadership in him, he did.

Round that time they held a race up Mount Currahee for the whole company. Plenty of guys had already quit the paratroopers by then, and the fellas who were left were in excellent shape. I put my shoulder to it and aimed to come in first. But, turns out plenty of guys in the company could run better than me, and I came in eighth. I guess that wasn't bad, considering the group I was in. But I resolved to do better at the next test, if I could.

Sure enough, my time for shining came on the rifle range. We were tested on hitting our targets and everyone had to meet a certain score. Top of the line was a grade called expert marksman, and Captain Sobel said anybody who makes expert rifleman gets a three-day pass. That was real incentive. Me and one other fella, that Sergeant Buck Taylor, were the only ones in the company to make expert marksman. So I was real happy about that. Guess all my practice shooting coins back home had paid off.

Sergeant Taylor was courting a sweet woman named Elaine and had plans to see her with his three-day pass, but there was nowhere I wanted to go except home to Clinchco. I moped around the barracks the evening after I got the pass. Popeye sensed something was up because he asked if I was going home and I said no, I didn't have enough money. "Shoot—I'll take care of that," Popeye said. He got a helmet and walked through the barracks calling to the guys, "Hey—Shifty's got three days off and doesn't have enough money to get home. Everybody chip in. Here—I'm going to start it with five dollars." Popeye placed a bill in the helmet, and everybody else threw in a dollar or fifty cents, whatever he had. Popeye handed the helmet to me. "Count it, Shifty. You got enough?"

"Yeah," I said. "I even got a little bit left over."

Popeye grinned. "Then give me back my damn five dollars." I gave him back his money. I still laugh when I think of that.

Well, I went on my pass, and it was a fine time, then came back to Toccoa. We had some more training, and then our time at Toccoa was done. But there was more training to go through, you know. We had already done a bit of early paratrooper stuff at Toccoa, specific to the jumping out of planes, just jumping from modest heights, maybe thirty feet or so. You'd strap yourself into a harness, "ball crushers" the fellas called them, and fling yourself out. It helped a man squash his basic fear of jumping. We weren't real paratroopers yet, that was for sure, and we sure weren't getting our extra fifty dollars jump pay yet neither. We needed to go over to Atlanta to take our jump training still. We needed to get ourselves to Fort Benning. That's when the real fun started.

Colonel Sink had read some magazine article about these long hikes the Japanese soldiers were taking. They could march all night, you know, real tough customers there. Well, the colonel had a good streak of competitiveness in him, so he figured, my boys can whup their boys at whatever needs whupping—hiking, marching, whatever they can do—and he passed word to our officers: I want you to hike from Toccoa to Benning. That was about one hundred and twenty miles. When Lieutenant Moore called us together in Third Platoon and related the news, I remember a swell kid named Mike Ranney busted out laughing. He couldn't believe it. Neither could I. "Sergeant Ranney, be quiet," Lieutenant Moore said. "We're going to complete the march in three days, and every damned man will complete it on his own two feet." Ranney shut up real quick about that.

We started our march on December 1. It was foggy that morning about seven-thirty when we set off, and gray clouds hung low in the sky. Each of us carried all we needed. After an hour of marching, the rain began. We kept going. A good-hearted farm boy named Dewitt Lowrey noticed a little yellow dog following us. The dog must have been a stray, for he had no collar or identifications, and he kept up with us for several miles. Finally we noticed the dog was limping. Dewitt picked him up and saw his toenails were worn and the pads on his paws were sore. He told us, "If y'all will take the stuff in my backpack, I'll put that dog in my pack and carry him." So we did. The dog rode on Dewitt's back from then on. He became our mascot and we named him Draftee, and he was a fine dog, he was.

We stopped for lunch that first day around noon and ate in the cold and rain, then kept marching through the back hills of Georgia. Blisters bubbled up on our feet and we kept going though it grew colder. We stopped near eight o'clock that night, and the wind whipped fierce through our camping area. We made our fires, heated our dinner, put up our tents, and tried to sleep. I shivered with my one blanket and never could get warm. I wondered if we might all freeze to death before morning.

We didn't. We got up and kept on marching. It was raining again and cold and we kept going straight through the second day until quarter of ten at night. I saw guys fall asleep while walking and head right into the trees.

Third morning, my feet were really sore, but we got up and kept marching. Everything clung to us—wet boots, wet socks, wet jacket, wet pants. Only now we started to feel a little tingle at what we were doing. I guess the national news shows had received word of the march, and it spiked people's interest all over the country. *A United States Army unit was out-marching the Japs*—it was just the kind of hopeful news the nation needed. Late afternoon of the third day we straggled into the outskirts of Atlanta, beat and cold, exhausted, but feeling mighty fine, too. We marched to the campus of Oglethorpe University and it felt like a big parade. That night, those of us who were still able put on our dress uniforms and hit the town. Anything we wanted, the city gave us. Men bought us beers, meals. Girls gave us hugs. Mike Ranney walked into a liquor store and a fella offered to buy him anything he wanted.

More celebrating came the next morning. We marched down Peachtree Boulevard for a civic reception in the heart of the city. Bands played. Folks cheered all around us. I guess one or two fellas from other platoons didn't finish the hike, but every man from Lieutenant Moore's Third Platoon made the hike. It was the platoon I was in, and, as a reward, Third Platoon got to lead the parade. We marched through downtown Atlanta straight to the railway depot on our way to Fort Benning. Lieutenant Winters told us that Colonel Sink was mighty proud.

After the march came jump school at Benning. We swaggered after all we had been through at Toccoa; we felt we could handle anything. Our new instructors lined us up the first morning and said, Okay, you're in the big time now. This is men's country. Anyone who wants to leave right now, no problem, we'll put you in another unit. We said we're fine, let's go.

The first stage of jump school is all physical training, and those instructors led us out on a little run, ten miles or so. It was all flat ground. Shoot, we could run on flat ground all day. About halfway through our first run, the instructor calls one of our men to take the lead. Our man says okay and starts double-timing it. We were hardly sweating, but the poor instructor wheezed like an old tire that'd been blown. Before that day was out, they said no more physical training for you; you're all in good enough shape already. So we went straight into jump training.

They take you up towers first. There's different heights, see, and two hundred and fifty feet is the largest. Popeye and I did fine on those. They teach you how to pack a chute. Later on, we'd have other fellas—*riggers*, they called them—pack our chutes for us.

But at the start, we needed to learn how to pack our own. Well, I packed my chute, then repacked it, and that night I didn't sleep a wink. Next morning was our first real jump, see, so I just tossed and turned. Did I do it right? What did I do wrong? What did I miss?

Next morning they took us out to the airfield. Back home in Clinchco, I had never seen an airplane, much less had a ride in one. So the first time I walked out onto the airfield, I looked at that big old C-47, turned to Popeye, and said. "Heck, I don't need to worry about my chute. They're never going to get that thing off the ground."

But they did. That C-47 rumbled to life with those big engines just a rolling and turning, and we were flying. When you jump, they have what they call sticks: two lines of men face each other on benches inside the plane. I was in the second stick, which meant me and my bench were to jump after the fellas sitting across from us. As we flew I started sweating, you know, really feeling a gulp in my throat as to what we were about to do, and I thought, boy, I'm sure glad I'm not sitting over there in that first bench. They all jumped, and the plane circled over the drop zone again. That meant it was our turn. No quitting now. It was time, and I was thinking, man I wish I had been in that first group.

I stood up and hooked up and shuffled to the door. The jumpmaster took a little extra time with each man for this first jump, making sure you were in the right position. I placed my elbows, arms, and fingers outside of the door. The jumpmaster patted my arm and I stepped out. Over my head, my chute snapped into place almost instantly. My hands were over top my reserve chute, and I swung a bit and looked around at the landscape. The view felt just like I was standing on top of Frying Pan back home in Virginia, looking out over mile after mile. I couldn't help wondering what good that reserve would do come actual battle time. We were jumping from way up, that first practice jump, maybe twelve hundred feet or so, but I heard that in combat they'd take you down to six or seven hundred feet so there wasn't as much time to get shot at. A reserve chute wouldn't do you any good from that low. I guessed it was more a security blanket than anything, something that made a man feel he might have a second chance. The ground came up at me in an instant. Everything happens so fast, you don't really know what's going on. My feet hit the field. I rolled over on my side and gathered the silk. All around me I heard fellas hollering and jumping up and down. We had made it. It wasn't that hard, you know.

We soon learned it wasn't all easy going. One poor fella ripped three fingers off on a jump. Another practice jump, a boy named Forrest Guth stood ahead of me in line. Everybody called him Goody. He was a swell fella and knew a lot about tinkering with weapons, making them more accurate, easier to fire, which I respected a lot. We stood up, hooked up, and they said go, go, go. I was halfway out of that plane, and there lay poor Goody on the floor. You're all running out the door so quickly, you know, pushing against the man ahead of you, so I didn't know what to do. I didn't want to pause and miss the drop zone, 'cause a man is liable to end up in water or on a tree, so I just jumped over Goody and went out the door.

Well, we got down on the ground. The first man I saw was Goody. He looked a little shaken but otherwise fine. I don't know how he got down so quick, because I jumped ahead of him and yet he beat me to the ground. It was a mystery.

Some time passed, and the company made one final practice jump—this, a night jump—and then we were through. We earned our jump wings and pinned them on our uniforms and drank a few beers to celebrate. Those little silver wings meant we were real paratroopers. We now were allowed to tuck our pants into our boots, so anybody could see from a distance what we were. We also got our extra fifty dollars pay, and I was real happy about that. An extra fifty dollars was a heap of money at the time. My first month's pay in the service was twenty-one dollars. Then they upped it to fifty dollars per month. Then, with this extra fifty, that made a hundred dollars a month. If you made expert rifleman, that made an extra four dollars per month. So I was getting one hundred and four dollars per month total. I was rich.

Everything seemed like a breeze after we became paratroopers. Other fellas went into town and picked fights with other units, you know, if they saw some other guy blousing his trousers when he hadn't earned it or whatever. I went to town, too, but I was never one much for fights without a good reason. Still, I walked with a new swagger in my step, too, you know, just feeling like I could do anything I set my mind to. I guess all the fellas felt that way. We were real paratroopers now. We were ten feet tall and bulletproof.

Even Captain Sobel loosened up a bit. Or maybe it was just how I approached him after I became a real paratrooper. We went from Benning to Fort Bragg, North Carolina, for more training. One weekend I went home, borrowed Dad's car, and took it back to Bragg with me to run around in. I was in camp one day going through base and ran a red light right at an intersection. Shoot, it was right in front of the generals' quarters. Well, here came the MPs and pulled me over. "Now, I hate to do this," the MP said, he was really apologetic about it, "but I've got to report it. If this was anywhere except in front of the generals' quarters I wouldn't."

The next day I got a message from Captain Sobel: "Shifty Powers, report to the commanding officer."

Now, my brother had come down that same day to pick up the car and bring it back home. So I walked in the door, saluted Captain Sobel, and said, "Sir, my brother's coming here today. I'd like to have the rest of the day off." I don't know exactly what came over me, but it was the first time I'd ever spoken my mind openly to the captain like that.

You could see Captain Sobel's face go red. He said: "Private Powers, I called you in here to chew you out—and you're asking for time off?!"

Well, he gave me the time off. Musta had a good streak in him somewhere.

Fort Bragg was where I first met a fella who'd become one of my best friends, Earl McClung, an American Indian from the Colville Reservation up in Washington. He had done his jump training at Fort Benning and then been sent to us. Most of the fellas in Easy Company didn't think too much about a man if he didn't start with us at Toccoa, but there was something different about McClung. To begin with, that man could shoot. He and I talked rifles and ammunition, hunting and fishing. His father had an old World War I–era 30–40 Krag that McClung learned to shoot on. Most boys are thirteen or fourteen when they get their first deer, but McClung was eight. While growing up, he trapped muskrats, beavers, and coyotes. The boy could practically see in the dark and knew everything there was to know about the woods. I knew McClung and I were going to get along real fine.

From there we went to Camp Mackall, in North Carolina, for more training. The camp was named after Private Tommy Mackall, the first paratrooper to die in World War II, and seeing the name of that camp brought back to me the seriousness of what we were preparing for. Then we went on some more maneuvers in Tennessee and Kentucky. Everything was more serious now—longer tests, six or seven days out in the open. The tone was changing. Men wore different expressions on their faces. They joked less. Home was becoming a thing of the past, something tucked further back into the corners of your mind, you know. I was able to travel home once during that time to Clinchco, and Bill Kiehn came home with me. It felt funny, mixing the two worlds like that for the first time and having a buddy from the service come home and all, but it worked out okay.

You got to realize, the Army doesn't tell you about nothing. Just after Bill and I went home, we came back to camp, then they shipped us to a new location: Camp Shanks in New York. Shanks was near the Atlantic, and they told us to get set to board a troop ship and head overseas. That meant one thing. They wouldn't be putting us on a ship in the Atlantic if we were going to fight Japan. We were going to fight the Krauts for sure.

5

FACES SET LIKE FLINT

They called this one the SS *Samaria*. Popeye and me and the rest of the fellas chewed donuts and swallowed coffee and walked around the pier the morning of September 5, 1943. We were all waiting, gawking at the size of the ship before us. The *Samaria* wasn't too large as far as ships go, I guess, but it was gonna be the largest ship I had ever set foot on. Only ship, for that matter. An offshore breeze tensed my shoulders, and it was hard to believe I'd been in the Army for more than a year.

The pier smelled of ropes and creosote, that black tar pitch put on wood to keep salt water from rotting it, and I nursed a headache this morning. The strong smell and my headache weren't a good mix. A lot of other fellas probably felt the same way. An enlisted man had laid hold of a cache of whiskey the night before, our last night in New York, and we had all passed the bottles around. I was no stranger to beer, but still unfamiliar with the ways of whiskey.

"You okay?" Popeye asked as I kneeled by the side of the dock.

"Yeah. Maybe I shouldn't have eaten that second donut."

"Nah." Popeye was more skilled in these matters. "It's good to have something in your stomach. Comes up easier that way."

I wiped the corners of my mouth with a handkerchief and stood up just as we got the go-ahead. We hiked up the gangplank, lugging our barracks bags and weapons. It takes a while to get some five thousand men on board a ship, and the rest of that day we hung around on deck, the ship still unmoved from the harbor. We leaned against the rails and killed time, whistling at the pretty girls waving to us from onshore. As the sun set, New York gradually grew dark. Next morning, little tugboats strained at the ropes. Our ship was towed from her berth, and we lined the rails to wave at the people on the passing ferries. I got a lump in my throat as we steamed past the Statue of Liberty as she slowly slipped by. After that, it was all open ocean. I'd never seen a world so vast or bright or blue.

Fellas were crammed everywhere on the *Samaria*, many more than it was built to hold. A bunk was available only every other night, as bunk space was rationed, so Popeye and a bunch of fellas and me slept out on the deck. The showers ran salt water only, and only cold, so a lot of fellas chose to just stink up the joint. Socks and armpits mixed with the awful stink of that chow. I didn't know what was worse. The *Samaria* was an English ship, and I guess the English crew didn't know beans about good eating. Two meals only were served each day, and your mess kit might hold boiled onions and tomatoes, fish soup and Brussels sprouts, bread sliced thin as paper. The thought of finding something good to eat occupied much of my day. Some guys lived on Hershey bars. I ate mostly cookies—breakfast, lunch, and dinner. No, wasn't no squirrel on board. I'd've given anything for some good squirrel stew.

We had duties on ship, calisthenics, nothing worth remembering. Most guys whiled away their hours playing poker. I played a bit, but mostly just yakked with the other guys. Twelve days later we landed in England, climbed on this train with the windows boarded up, and they took us to a little town called Aldbourne. A few hills clustered around it, not as tall as the hills around Clinchco, but even these little hills helped me feel more at home. We were billeted in a bunch of locations around town, some men in stables, some in these little buildings call Quonset huts, some officers with families in the area.

Right away, I liked the British people. Everyone I met seemed sincere, strong-willed, and earnest, relieved we were there. They had caught their share of bombing in the bigger cities, see, and every face wore an anxious look, even through their smiles. Folks in Aldbourne were preparing to be invaded by the Germans, you know, so they had hidden food out in the woods and practiced defending themselves against German soldiers. But I was shocked to see that all they had to fight with were their garden tools—pitchforks, shovels, rakes, and hoes—no guns or rifles. I guess their government had made it almost impossible for the average citizen to own a real weapon. I thought about what a massacre it would be if the German paratroopers ever landed in the English countryside. Those Krauts were heavily armed with burp guns, mousers, hand grenades, machine guns and would have wiped that village out.

Months went by in Aldbourne and we trained more, fine-tuning what we knew. We went on longer field problems. We hiked through woods. We learned new combat exercises. Night operations. Hand-to-hand fighting. Map reading. First aid lessons. Chemical warfare training. We dug foxhole after foxhole throughout the cold, rainy winter.

We jumped, too, on a regular basis. Full gear now, learning to use the risers to guide ourselves so we didn't hit trees or walls on the way down. Easy Company lost our first man during a night training jump. Private Rudolph Dittrich was his name. His parachute never caught the air and he hit the ground hard. I never knew the man personally, but we were all real sobered about the loss. I felt sad for his family, and it caused me to remember the seriousness of what we were doing.

Winter went. Spring came. We picked up a few replacements, guys coming into our unit from elsewhere. I tried to be kind to the replacements, maybe smile at them, but you've always got things to do as a private—potatoes to peel, guard duty to pull—so it's hard to get to know every new guy who comes in.

One replacement, Joe Lesniewski, took a real ribbing from a few guys, maybe because of his slight Polish accent. Joe got in a couple fights and seemed to hold his own pretty well, but he was always alone. One day he was in a room where a fellow was playing a guitar. Joe had learned some Western songs back in the states, and he started singing along with those good old Western tunes. That's when Skip Muck ambled over. Skip was real kind to everybody. Back at Fort Bragg, Skip had befriended another replacement, Alex Penkala, and he was doing really well now. Alex's folks had thirteen kids in their family, and his mama had died when he was real young, so I guess Skip had taken Alex under his wing, you know, showed him the ropes. That day in Aldbourne, Skip Muck went over to Joe Lesniewski and they start singing together. They sounded real good. Alex Penkala came over, too, and they had a bit of a musical group going now. I think making that one good friend made all the difference for Joe, because he didn't have any problems from then on.

Me and Earl McClung were getting to be better and better friends, too. In Aldbourne we went out on the rifle range, twice I remember. A few newer guys were having trouble qualifying, so McClung and I compared notes and got on either side of a guy, then fired at the other guy's targets. Sometimes a guy would know it, sometimes he wouldn't. Maybe the guy would just pull back his target and there'd be a new bull's-eye in it, and he'd think he'd done it himself. These were strong, hardworking soldiers, mind you, younger guys like us, but just city kids who needed some help aiming. I found myself looking cross the range at McClung a couple times when that was happening and thinking, this guy's really a fine friend, you know.

We privates were down on the low end of things. Not much respect for a fella at the bottom. Food was scarce in England, and our cooks, I don't know what they were doing with our food, but it wasn't worth the salt you shook on it. One day I fussed about the food and a cook heard me. I stepped outside the mess hut and that cook hauled off and hit me in the eye. Five other cooks stepped out, and I was all alone against them, so I figured I'd just go my way without saying much.

A day or two later came my chance. I was halfway through a dozen tubs of potatoes along with this other fella, might have been Jim Alley, don't quite remember. It wasn't much fun, that's for sure, and that same ole cook came in and fussed at us for being so slow. When he left, I stood up and stuck a trench knife into the wall, right near the door so he'd see it, but a good distance away from me, too, maybe twenty-five feet. Then, when I heard the cook walking up again, I threw a potato against the wall so it made a loud thump. Well, that cook heard the thump all right, 'cause he came inside the hut, stared hard at the knife sticking out of the wall, and must have figured I'd thrown it there, real accurate just as he was about to come in, which is exactly what I wanted him to think about what I could do if I was aggravated enough. That cook turned on his foot, hurried back outside, and never once fussed at me ever again.

Seems there was unfriendliness going around other places, too. But this fussing had a much more serious bent. The trouble with Captain Sobel all came to a head in Aldbourne. It wasn't that the man couldn't lead Easy Company during our training exercises. It's that the man had no head for combat. When it came to walking through the woods, the man was louder than a tank. When it came to reading a map, the man got us lost. When it came to aiming a rifle, well, the man couldn't throw a rock into a lake and have it come out wet.

Fellas grumbled at first, but then the noncommissioned officers, the real backbone of the Army, concluded that if a man like Sobel was left in charge, more fellas than not would be coming home in a pine box. Captain Sobel had put in for a court-martial on Lieutenant Dick Winters, and the matter was pushed past the breaking point. The complaint was over something stupid, too, not inspecting a latrine on time. Lieutenant Winters had inspected the latrine on the hour he was ordered to, but Captain Sobel had switched the order by fifteen minutes. An order Lieutenant Winters never received. Certainly nothing to lose a fine leader over.

Well, I didn't hear the ins and outs of how the mutiny went down until much later, but it seemed that all the NCOs in our company wrote a note, all resigning their posts. It was a serious offense, up and quitting like that, and could have meant facing a firing squad. But it also sent a clear message for Colonel Sink to see what the men truly thought of Captain Sobel.

Mind you, the colonel wasn't happy about what the NCOs did, seeing how a huge invasion was right around the corner. He chewed them out something fierce for writing the notes, busted one or two of 'em down to privates, and shipped another or two out to other companies. But in the end, the colonel also saw the smarts of the plan, for he reassigned Captain Sobel to be a jump instructor someplace else, put Lieutenant Winters back in his same role, and brought in another company commander to lead us: Lieutenant Thomas Meehan from Baker Company. Lieutenant Meehan was everything Captain Sobel wasn't—fair and respectful—and I reckon under Lieutenant Meehan we became a normal company again.

A number of other leadership shakeups occurred around then. Lieutenant Walter Moore was our leader for the Third Platoon. He was an excellent man, a lot like Winters, but one day Lieutenant Moore was giving an explosives demonstration over in a school nearby, and one of the devices he was handling exploded prematurely. It messed up his face, his hands and eyes, and put him out of the service. He would have been a good man to follow. Lieutenant Fredrick Heyliger became our new platoon leader. He was married already and had a baby son, Fred Junior, born the day we had set sail across the Atlantic on the *Samaria*. The guys called our new platoon leader Moose, on account of his size, I guess. He was strict but fair, and the fellas all liked him lots. As a hobby, Lieutenant Moose Heyliger enjoyed bird-watching, and he could name every tree, plant, and shrub he saw. I was happy to follow such a man into combat.

That March, 1944, I celebrated my twenty-first birthday along with Popeye, Skinny Sisk, Jim Alley, Bill Kiehn, Earl McClung, and a few other fellas. Over beers, we talked about how we'd all developed the same hitch in our craw. We'd been in the Army for nearly two years now, all training, training, and we were anxious for the real thing. Any time we had an off hour, we went to bars in Aldbourne, sometimes caught a train up to London or Swindon, and we were always raring to go. More drinking. More fighting. All symptoms of our anxiousness. It grew to almost a fever pitch among some of the fellas, though we had no idea of what truly lay ahead.

On May 29, we received our release. They ordered us into trucks and we said good-bye to Aldbourne. Chills went up my spine: we were finally on the move. They trucked us over to another camp near an airstrip at Uppottery in southwestern England. It was about ten miles from the coast and I heard seagulls squawking as they flew past. Security was tighter than usual, armed guards surrounded the camp, and everything was real secretive, nobody talked to nobody about nothing.

They crowded us into these big rooms and had us study sand tables, they called them, big maps that showed every bridge and fence along the Kraut-occupied Normandy coast. The Allied Army's mission was to hit the beaches of Normandy full force. We'd throw everything we had at the Nazis. Our specific part of the plan as paratroopers was to come in ahead of time. In the hours before the coastal invasion, we'd land in the countryside and loosen up the enemy, making sure they didn't pour hell down on the boys storming the beach. It seemed simple enough, particularly with all the preparation they gave us. Colonel Sink urged us to strike hard. He promised it'd only take us three days of hard fighting to get the job done. No problem, I thought, a man can survive any hardship as long as it's only for three days.

On June 4, 1944, we got word this was it: the invasion was

set for that night. We blackened our faces, got into our gear, and filled out a life insurance form for ten thousand dollars. A few of the men shaved their hair into Mohawks. A strong wind started blowing that afternoon, and I thought it might be difficult for our planes to fly.

Our gear was really something else. A paratrooper needs to carry everything he needs with him into combat, see, so we had big pockets and crammed enough food into them to last three days. K-rations, they were called. Tasted like sawdust, really, but kept a man going. Everything else went into our backpacks, called musette bags. In there, we'd put our rain poncho, a blanket, cigarettes, maybe half a pup tent, our mess kits, a toothbrush and razor, maybe a candy bar or two, maybe an extra K-ration if you were a chow hound.

Then you wore an ammunition belt. Strung on the belt were two lines of ten clips of M1 rifle ammunition. Each clip had eight rounds, so you had eighty rounds of ammunition total. That felt comforting to me. Also attached to that belt you'd have your entrenching tool to dig foxholes, your canteen full of water, your bayonet, your gas mask, and a small first aid kit with a morphine syrette and a bandage or two.

You wore suspenders, each with a metal ring, and from each ring hung a hand grenade. Strapped under your left shoulder was a holster with a .45 sidearm. You'd keep a trench knife down in your right boot. Next to your collar you had a zippered pocket where you carried a switchblade. If you jumped and got hung up in a tree, you couldn't reach down and get the knife out of your boot, so you'd get your switchblade and cut the cords. You strapped a compass on your right ankle, and strapped a British Hawkins mine on your other ankle. It was a pressure plate mine, not very explosive, you know. It wouldn't blow up a tank, but it'd knock the track off one. If you put two or three of them together, then you could cause some damage.

Of course, you wore a steel helmet, a basic steel pot with a chin strap. You had your main parachute on your back, and your reserve chute on your front. Around your neck went a yellow Mae West lifejacket to be used if you landed in water. I guess the Germans had flooded a lot of the inland areas, real deep water there, so drowning was a real concern. Funnily enough, they called it a Mae West because it inflated and looked like two huge bosoms. The lifejacket wasn't a perfect system by any means. I tried it a couple times in training, and it was almost impossible to get to the handles that opened up the bladders to inflate it. If you did, the Mae West would inflate against your equipment and sometimes pop. Or it'd squeeze the air out of you until you passed out. Shoot—with all the equipment we wore, I doubt a Mae West would have kept us afloat much anyway.

If a man operated a machine gun or bazooka or was part of a mortar squad, he carried pieces of that equipment, too—the base plate, the launch tube, the rockets, and so on. Other fellas might help him carry his ammo or extra equipment. But it was heavy going there.

The British had come up with this new thing, a leg bag, they called it, and some of the fellas were given these leg bags to stow extra ammunition, radios, machine-gun tripods, medical gear, high explosives—anything we might need once on the ground. I didn't carry one, wasn't ordered to, and didn't volunteer. I'd never want to stick my weapon in a leg bag. I always strung it up front through my reserve chute. That way, my rifle was always in my hands, even as I floated down from the sky. My rifle was always loaded, always ready to fire. By the time a paratrooper got all his gear on, I'd guess he was more than double his body weight. It was tough to walk, much less climb into a plane.

We got mail call then, and I learned my younger brother Jimmy had enlisted in the Navy and was being sent to the Pacific. That meant three boys out of four from the Powers family were now in the service. Frankie, the youngest, was still too little, but wanted to go as soon as he was able. Another fella from the company, Bill Guarnere, wasn't as lucky with the letter he received. He learned his brother, Henry, a medic with the First Armored Division, had just been killed in the fighting in North Africa. We all felt real bad for Bill. He took the news hard, of course, and a new, angry glint came into his eyes. He vowed revenge on his brother's death in the days to come.

That evening before we headed to the airfield, the Army gave us the last supper. It was the best meal I'd ever eaten—thick steaks, mashed potatoes, bread with butter, peas, coffee—as much as any man could hold. Even ice cream for dessert. That wind still whipped outside, even stronger now, and as we cleaned our mess kits, word came that the mission was scrubbed for the night. We let out a moan and shuffled off to watch a movie instead. It proved real hard to sleep later on. We knew the wind would die down soon. There'd be no way they'd postpone the invasion twice.

The morning of June 5 dawned clear and bright. We suited up again and were trucked out to the airfield. Each of us was ordered to swallow a motion sickness pill, which we had never needed before, and was given a little slip of paper. On it, General Eisenhower had written a message of encouragement. Bill Kiehn was standing next to me and read it out loud for all the guys to hear: "Soldiers, Sailors, and Airmen of the Allied Expeditionary Force! You are about to embark upon the Great Crusade toward which we have striven these many months. The eyes of the world are upon you. . . . Good luck! And let us all beseech the blessing of Almighty God upon this great and noble undertaking."

It took four extra guys, two pulling and two pushing, to get each man up into the plane. Out of the corner of my eye, I saw most of the company headquarters staff climbing into the same plane together, a different plane than me. Lieutenant Thomas Meehan was with that group, the man now leading Easy Company. Sergeant Bill Evans also climbed aboard, the officer nobody liked much. About a dozen other young leaders climbed into that plane, their faces set like flint. Flight 66. Funny how that name sticks in my mind, even today. A kind young medic named Ed Pepping was set to go on that flight, but they pulled him out at the last minute. Burr Smith, a bighearted Californian, was also set to get on that flight, but he was transferred to another plane at the last minute, too.

It was real dusky inside our own plane as I climbed aboard. Paratroopers shuffled to sit down on the benches lining either side of the fuselage. Behind me in the stick was Sergeant Buck Taylor. He'd be the last man out of the plane and jump just after me. It felt good having a capable leader like him nearby. Ahead of me in the stick was Bill Kiehn; another good friend, he'd jump just before I went out. Popeye was placed in another plane. We promised we'd meet up on the ground if we could.

As our plane's engines roared up and we took off on the runway, I couldn't help but think I was passing from one world into the next. We flew encased in the murky steel tube; the red lights inside the plane gave each man's face a ghostly tint. You'd glimpse the glow from a cigarette tip now and again as men breathed in and exhaled smoke. No one joked or told stories. The engines rumbled with a deafening roar. The motion sickness pills mixed with the adrenaline in my veins, shoving it back to wherever it came from, making me feel far away, like my head wasn't on my body anymore.

Just before my eyes closed, one part of that little paper that Kiehn had read replayed in my mind. General Eisenhower was talking to us. I knew his voice from hearing it over the radio lots of times and I imagined it booming in my ears: "Your task will not be an easy one. Your enemy is well trained, well equipped and battle hardened. He will fight savagely."

Yeah, I vowed silently, and so will we. We're well trained and well equipped, and we'll fight back with all we've got.

Normandy lay ahead, the pills kicked in, and I drifted into an edgy sleep.

6

THE THINGS I HAD NO WORDS FOR

My helmet clanked against the side of the plane, and my eyes flew open. Our jumpmaster braced himself near the gusts of the open door and glanced down at the channel. Word passed along the line of men: dots, he saw, stretching far across the moon-lit sea—battleships, gunships, carriers, destroyers. All churning a beeline toward the Normandy coast. It felt good knowing all that massive firepower was on our side, you know, but still I worried for those boys who'd be storming the beach, come a few hours. Those of us who were going to jump into the middle of the mix would have it rough enough, I reckoned, but those who ran straight at the enemy would have it even rougher. I thanked God I was a para-trooper and not a rifleman down on those ships.

We flew in formation for some time. The only sound was the drone of our C-47. It might have been past midnight, maybe one o'clock, when the dark hulk of the Normandy coastline emerged out the windows. Our pilots—God bless every one of them—had to face all this from another kind of perspective and make huge choices. We hit a cloud bank and dived from fifteen hundred feet to about seven hundred. We were still flying too high, too fast to make a safe jump, but I figured they'd slow down for us later on. The coast was nearly upon us, and I fidgeted in my seat near the back of the plane. Within arm's reach were two fifty-gallon drums of aviation gas, carried as reserve fuel. I hoped to hell nothing would spark it off.

When the first ping hit our plane, I thought we might be flying into a rainstorm. We kept flying and I heard two more pings. Three. Four. I glimpsed flashes of light, then something whammed against the fuselage like a sledgehammer on a railway spike. Our plane lurched as our pilot weaved to miss the next one. The sky brightened then shaded, blazed then blackened. It reminded me of fireworks except we were flying straight through the explosions. Another burst. Another wallop. Our plane shuddered and pitched us about. I heard a thick *rat-a-tat-tat* from antiaircraft fire. Bullets began to zing through our cabin and on through the other side. Another burst. Another flash. Heavy flak slammed against the side of our plane. Our left motor caught and sputtered. My nerves were taut. I writhed in my seat. "Let's get the hell out of here!" Bill Kiehn yelled. I shot a glance at Sergeant Buck Taylor. His fists were clenched, his mouth held in a grimace. The plane made for too big of a target for the enemy. We were trapped inside. We couldn't wait to jump out.

Near the doorway, a red light flashed on, our signal to stand up and hook up. We sounded off, the plane still hurtling through the explosions. Starting at the back of the stick, each man shouted his number then tapped the shoulder of man ahead of him. *Ten okay. Nine okay. Eight okay. Seven okay.* We knew we had three minutes before the green light flashed on, our signal to jump. There came our green light, ahead of time. "Go! Go! Go!" yelled the jumpmaster. The line of men surged forward and out the door. *Too fast! Too fast!* I thought, *the plane's flying too fast,* but I withheld a curse for our pilot. I knew the man was as scared as me. If I'd been him, I'd've done the same thing and kept flying as fast as I could. As I neared the door, our plane began to tilt. The motor must've been hit, all right. The pilot was leaning the plane to its side to put out the fire. *Go! Go! Go!* A few more seconds and the plane would be at a right angle. I'd be crawling up the side of a wall, unable to scramble up and jump free. The door was still about ten feet away. Bracing my leg against the incline, I plowed forward against the back of Bill Kiehn's packed parachute. *Go! Go! Go!* In front of us loomed the crazy hole of night.

The moment I jumped, a tremendous hurricane hit me from the plane's prop blast. For a split second, everything seemed weightless; my body felt lost. Out of the corner of my eye, I glimpsed our plane's left motor flaming in a ball. My static line caught tight and jerked my chute open with a flapping whoosh from behind my head. Abruptly I slowed and swung through the darkness. The sky was full of lead and flak. Bullets ripped up at me, tearing apart my chute's panels. A man on the ground was traversing us with long bursts of fire. How blue it looked, how green. I figured it'd be all red, you know, but it wasn't. I didn't know exactly how the Germans loaded their tracers, but we loaded ours with four bullets, then one tracer, then four bullets, then another tracer. So for every tracer I saw, I knew four more bullets were coming right behind it. I wanted to land, to crouch on the ground, to find a tree and duck for cover, but it felt like I wasn't moving, just hanging stationary in the air.

I almost broke a grin when I glimpsed treetops below my feet. But you don't want to land in a tree, so I yanked on a riser, steering the chute to the side. My boots brushed past branches, scooted over the tops of hedgerows, and I aimed for an open, empty space. Field maybe. Not water, I hoped. I landed with a soft thud. Pasture. Thank God. Adrenaline surged through my body. I slid out of my chute, checked my rifle, and patted my gear to make sure everything was there. All my ammo was still on me, all my equipment looked in working order. The moon had broken through the clouds, and I crouched, not sure where anything was. I stared into the dim light, trying to orient myself. I wondered if I'd ever meet up with Popeye like we had promised. Off in the distance I heard gunfire. I wondered where the other men in my outfit were. I heard the late night warble of a crested lark, probably scared out of its nest. It was just that bird and me. The gunfire died down and it grew quiet. I was all alone.

Well, the enemy could have been anywhere. My eyes adjusted to the light and I found I could make out the shape of things pretty well. Wasn't much to see. Leaves and bushes. Deep shadows for cover. I was happy about that. I had parachuted into an area strewn with eight divisions of Germans, four million land mines, and fields said to be flooded higher than a man's head, but I was perfectly dry and out in the boonies, with no fighting around. Our outfit was supposed to have dropped near a town called Sainte-Mère-Église, but I didn't see no town. No buildings, no roads, no street signs. I got to studying about how fast we'd been flying, and the time it took to get all the men out of the plane. Between the first and last man out, I guess a lot of distance could fly by. I might have been anywhere. I wasn't afraid. I mean, I was. But I wasn't. We had received so much training, you know, I knew that I simply needed to take stock of my situation and do the next right thing. I remembered from the sand tables that we were landing on a little peninsula—Cherbourg, it was called. So Utah Beach would be to the east of me. If I got out my map and compass, I figured I could head down that way toward where the sun would be rising and hopefully find my outfit. I wondered if the rest of the fellas were as lost as I was.

I started walking. I'd only gone about ten feet when a leaf flickered in the shadows of a nearby hedgerow. Moonlight spilled through the branches and I could see the man's face clearly. Sergeant Taylor. He was folding up his map, shaking his head in disgust. I was glad he had made it to the ground without getting shot. I walked closer and he immediately recognized me. "Any idea where we are, Shifty?" he whispered.

I shook my head. "Just glad to be on the ground, Sergeant."

"I think we're off the map," he said. "As close as I can figure, we're about seven miles from where we're supposed to be. We should be able to find a road and be there by first light. Follow me."

The plan sounded good and we set out at a march, all the time looking for trees, buildings, some sort of landmarks to get better bearings. Across the field I noticed another shadow moving in front of a hedgerow. Sergeant Taylor and I crouched to the ground. A silhouetted figure emerged from the end of thicket and started moving across the field toward us. The man held his weapon in the firing position and he moved slowly, glancing all around.

"I'll click him," Sergeant Taylor said to me. "You aim." I nodded and brought my rifle to eye level. The army had given us these little toy crickets that click-clacked as a signal so we could tell who was friendly out in the dark. Sergeant Taylor click-clacked the man. The figure walked closer without any response. He was maybe fifty yards away.

"He's a Kraut," Sergeant Taylor hissed. "Shoot him, Shifty."

Squinting down the barrel of my M1, I could see the man's outline. Forty yards. Thirty. I had a clear shot to his forehead. Earlier back in Aldbourne, I had filed my rifle's sear, the piece that holds the hammer back when the bolt opens, so it made a hair trigger. It would only take a murmur of my finger to make my rifle fire. I steadied my aim. "Let's give him another chance," I said. "Give him the password." My rifle stayed zeroed on the figure's head. The army had also given us code words for signaling. You'd say a word and a man needed to answer the correct word, otherwise you were to blast him. The words changed every day or so. Tonight's were "Flash" and "Thunder."

"Flash!" Sergeant Taylor called out in a hush. His voice seemed to go a mile in the night air. There was no response.

"Maybe he didn't hear," I said.

"He heard all right. Shoot him, Shifty. He's a Kraut. Shoot him, now!"

I steadied the rifle and held my breath. He was maybe fifteen yards away. So this was it. I started to move my finger.

"Thunder . . . ?" came a man's voice. "Jesus Christ, did someone say Flash?—Thunder! Thunder! For Christ's sake, Thunder!"

We recognized the voice immediately. It was Bill Kiehn's. Sergeant Taylor and I stood up and motioned him over. Bill took a shaky step or two toward us and we saw his familiar face clearly in the moonlight. "Shit, Bill," I said, and slapped him on the back. "I come near a hair of shooting you. I'm mighty tickled I didn't."

"So am I," he said, and gave me a wry smile.

Bill Kiehn had lost his cricket signaler in the jump. He was breathing heavy but otherwise fine. He fell in with us, and we took off walking again.

The grass was wet with dew, and we walked for some time without seeing anything significant or any people. Occasionally we heard gunfire, and we headed in the direction it came from. Near a row of trees we approached the figure of another man. He was lying on his side, moaning. We gave him both signals and he didn't respond, so

I held my weapon on him until we got close enough to see his face. It was Private First Class Phil Peruginni, another man from Easy Company. I didn't know him well, but we had talked a few times. He was still harnessed to his parachute, his leg twisted in front of him.

"Broken," he said, as we crouched. "Couple places I think. Hurts like hell."

Sergeant Taylor pulled out his first aid kit and gave him his shot of morphine. "Sorry, Phil," he said, "there's nothing more we can do." He turned to me. "Cover him up with his parachute, Shifty. It'll keep him warm. Medics will find him soon enough."

I hated to leave the man, but Sergeant Taylor was right. We couldn't carry the man in the condition he was in. Shoot, we had no idea where we'd carry him to. I took branches and camouflaged the area he lay in. Phil had a canteen full of water, his food, and another morphine syrette in his bag. We said so long and kept going.

The darkness was turning gray when we stumbled across a two-lane road. It looked like it would lead to where we needed to be, so we started to follow that. It might be safer to follow a road, you know, or it might be more dangerous. But following it was easier than hiking cross-country, that was for sure. We walked along the road and didn't see any Germans, though after a little while we began to see a civilian or two sticking their heads out from behind their haystacks.

The sky began to show pale orange across the horizon, pale blue farther up toward the clouds. Dawn was breaking, June 6, 1944. In a few hours, our men on the ships would be storming the beaches. As we walked, day-old mosquitoes buzzed near our ears, eager for one more chance at blood. Sergeant Taylor, Bill Kiehn, and I made a small band of three as we headed east. We walked as near to the sides of the road as we could, with me slightly ahead of the other two men. As we rounded a curve, I heard voices around the other side. Dropping to one knee, I raised my hand in a fist, the signal for the others to stop. We listened, but the voices had faded, so we scrambled closer into the trees off the road and edged forward. We pushed back branches and caught a clear view of a group of men setting up a roadblock.

"They're ours," I said. "Looks like guys from the 502nd."

Sergeant Taylor nodded. "Let's see if they need help." He took the lead now and signaled to the group. They gave a little start, but recognized the signals and our paratrooper uniforms right off, then went back to whatever they were doing. Sergeant Taylor approached the officer in charge, talked with him a few moments, then came back to Bill and me. "They were dropped in the wrong place. He's already got a bazooka man set up, ready to blast anything that moves on the road."

It was only a minute or two later when I heard the rumble of a truck coming toward us. It was far in the distance at first. I nodded to Sergeant Taylor and he signaled the officer in charge. We could all hear the truck's engine by then and knew it wasn't one of ours. We hit the ditches to take cover. The truck came into full view and swung up the road toward us. It was filled with German soldiers. The officer from the 502nd barked orders at the bazooka man, and he put one in the pipe and blasted it toward the truck. A tremendous blast of earth, fire, and smoke blew up. He'd scored a direct hit.

With our weapons aimed, we headed toward the burning truck. No resistance came on the Germans' behalf. The men from the 502nd got there ahead of us. I walked to the edge of the wreck and paused. A uniformed German lay in front of me, one leg bent near his knee, the other leg extended straight. One of his arms was flopped over his chest, his other arm ended in a bloody stump. The man's eyes were open, but he wasn't breathing. Another German lay a few feet away, facedown, the top of his skull opened. Blood oozed from what was left of his head and pooled around his neck. I tried to take in what I saw. As I shifted my weight, my boot squished against something and I looked down. I was standing on a piece of a man's foot.

Sergeant Taylor moved closer to where I was standing. "C'mon, Shifty," he said. "Let's get going."

I stood unmoving, my face focused ahead. They train you for this, you know. They train you.

"C'mon, Shifty," he said again.

Dead and wounded Germans were scattered all over the road. Some men yelled in pain. Others just sat. I shook my shoulders and caught my mind again. Sergeant Taylor was right, and I understood more what he was telling us to do. The officer from the 502nd outranked him. He had his platoon with him already. We were outsiders. He'd be ordering us to stand guard over the prisoners and wounded for the rest of the Normandy campaign, and we'd come too far already for that. Sergeant Taylor found the officer and told him we were going to head out and keep trying to find our unit. The officer didn't object, so we kept moving down the road.

A breeze blew now, rustling the leaves, and we kept walking, walking. The breeze was making it harder to distinguish movement, and I kept my eyes peeled, my ears open. Sometimes we saw more troopers, but none were from our unit. They might walk with us for a while, but they'd soon veer off again and try to find their own. We walked and walked.

Off to our right, we saw a glider crashed in a field. It was one of ours, and we figured somebody might be hurt or need help, so we hiked over. Wasn't a soul around, but that glider had a jeep in it as cargo. The jeep was stuck fast and reared up on its back wheels, making a corner to the ground. Sergeant Taylor nodded. I had an idea what he was thinking, but I wanted him to suggest it first. Sure enough, he did. "Let's go get that jeep," Taylor said. "We'll ride it to the beach."

I grinned. Well, the jeep had some braces attached to it that were holding it stuck. We wrestled with the braces a bit, but it was no use, so Taylor said, "You know, fellas, if we put a little charge on this here brace, we can blow that loose." We were all trained in explosives, so Kiehn took out a chunk of C-4 and put a cap in it. We ran for cover, and Kiehn hit the charge. It went off with a big *kaboom*.

"Damn," Kiehn said.

"Hmmmm," Sergeant Taylor said. He had one hand on his chin and looked real intent on studying what lay before us.

"Maybe that jeep was leaking gasoline," I said.

"You think?" Kiehn said. "It's a good thing Captain Sobel wasn't here to see it. He'd make us pay for it."

Well, when we blew that charge, everything caught fire, see. So the glider was now burning. And that jeep was now burning. And we weren't riding anywhere. That was for sure.

The afternoon shadows grew longer and we kept walking. Evening approached, and we neared the beach. It might have been more than seven miles that we had walked, but I didn't want to say nothing out loud. We walked on for some more time still, then it grew dark. Off to our right we spotted a little bombed out building. We figured it might be good to hole up there for the night. If we came upon the beach at night, we'd probably draw friendly fire on us. So we pushed back the boards and went in. We ate a K-ration or two and closed our eyes. I don't know if I actually slept. First light we got up and kept going.

When we got to where we needed to be at last, Lieutenant

Winters was one of the first people we saw. "Where you been?" he asked. It was a friendly comment, not critical, though he clearly expected to see us earlier. He pulled Sergeant Taylor aside and said he had some news for him. I wandered over and started seeing familiar faces. A lot, I recognized. A lot of others were from different outfits. Men were trying to get loose ends together and mobilize, getting ready for the next attack we'd make.

Fellas started comparing stories. Everyone had been through different things. Some had landed in trees, some had landed in water, some had been fighting the Germans, some hadn't seen any at all. In the days that followed, we learned that Earl McClung had jumped into the middle of a hailstorm of flak and landed in the town square of Sainte-Mère-Église. He'd fought with some guys from the 82nd for a while but they were never able to successfully take the town, mostly because the Krauts had nine tanks inside the city. He'd received a new nickname during that fight. Because of his scouting skills, the officer in charge had repeatedly sent him back into the city to see how things were. Time and time again, McClung went back and forth, crawling through ditches on patrols. One morning after he had been out on patrol all night, McClung lay down by some bushes, exhausted. Jim Alley and Paul Rogers were with him, and an officer came along and called for the services of a machine gunner. When the officer turned his back, Alley and Rogers lay their machine gun next to McClung, then pointed to him when the officer turned around again. I guess McClung wasn't too happy about waking up and suddenly being made a machine gunner. Rogers wrote a funny poem about it with a line that went, "Who hung the gun on One-Lung McClung?" So the nickname stuck.

It wasn't all fun and games. Far from it. We learned that Ed Pepping, the kindly medic, had been badly hurt and was soon out of the fight. Lots of men weren't around yet, and we wondered where they were. Shortly after arriving where we needed to be, Sergeant Taylor came back to us and pulled me aside. Kiehn had disappeared somewhere into the group of fellows and wasn't around just then.

"No one's seen Lieutenant Meehan," Sergeant Taylor said. That was our company commander. "He's missing along with Sergeant Evans and all the headquarters staff in their plane. We think it went down. Probably no survivors." He turned his head away for a moment. I didn't know what to say. I just had a lump in my throat. They were fine men, all of them. Even Sergeant Evans.

"Lieutenant Winters is now acting as our company commander until we can verify things," Sergeant Taylor added.

I was glad about that.

Sergeant Taylor shook his head as if he had more to say. "Shifty, before we arrived, the fellas led an attack at a place called Brecourt Manor. They broke up the Kraut guns, and their actions helped save a lot of our boys on the beach. But four of our men were lost in the battle. Don't think you knew them. Two more were wounded. Popeye was one of them. He's alive, Shifty. Been evacuated to a field hospital. I don't know how bad he got it. But I thought you'd want to know."

Well, I took all that news with me and headed off to a broken building and just sat a spell. I thought maybe I'd eat something, you know, but I wasn't hungry. I thought maybe I should sleep awhile when I had the chance, but I wasn't sleepy. I wondered how that bullet felt for Popeye. Maybe it hurt him real bad. Maybe he was scared. We had just got here, you know, to the shooting part of the war, and things were happening all around me that I didn't know how to put into words. So I sat. Then I put my head in my hands. Then I got up and joined the rest of the fellas in my outfit.

7

ORDERS

All us enlisted grunts sat on top of a hunk of concrete, smoking cigarettes. It was a few days after D-day, maybe June 10, June 11. Couldn't tell you exactly what town we were near. We shaded our eyes against the glare, laid back, and baked in our uniforms. Sure enough, the lull didn't last long. An officer barked orders to look sharp and move out, and the air filled with the rattle and clink of men picking up weapons and musette bags. Man, those Chelseas tasted like cardboard. They came with the K-rations. Lucky Strikes, my usual brand, carried a certain sweetness with the burn. What I wouldn't give for a pack. I stubbed my smoke and stood up.

We were still regrouping. Guys were coming to Easy Company from all over the peninsula. Some reached us just as this new order came, and they didn't get any rest at all. Just come in, say hello, and get going. We started our march. Couldn't tell you exactly where on the map we were heading, other than to this city that the Krauts had clenched their fists around. Carentan. It was near an important crossroads. Orders were to take it back at all costs.

I guess a lot of other towns had been retaken over the past several days by other outfits. Afternoon turned to evening and we saw fires in the distance. Random rifle shots were heard and far-away bursts from machine guns. We passed blown up vehicles and a bunch of smashed equipment by the side of the road. The man ahead of me stumbled and cursed as we hiked. I looked down and saw he had stubbed his foot on the carcass of a dead horse. Its belly was bloated and it stunk like the back of a slaughterhouse. A short time later the same man ahead of me stumbled again. This time it was over a Kraut. The man lay on his back with one arm sticking up, eyes open, his corpse frozen in place.

Lieutenant Dick Winters was leading the company, and First platoon was out in front ahead of Second and Third, with Lieuten-ant Harry Welsh leading the First. The lieutenants were both fine men and good leaders, but Lieutenant Winters was receiving his orders from somewhere higher up, and that might have been the problem, for it was a lot of stopping on this march, digging foxholes, setting up machine guns and bazookas, then moving out again and hiking some more, only to do the very same thing a short time later. Darkness set in, and you had to crouch down every so often to glimpse the man ahead of you in silhouette against the somewhat lighter sky, otherwise he'd vanish and you'd be lost. Mosquitoes flew up in a frenzy and we slapped our necks against their swampy bites. All that stagnant water was still lying on the land after the Germans had flooded all those fields. I felt a little aggravated, but I wasn't fussing out loud. I was glad we were all together again, most of us in the company anyway, and I felt confident we could handle whatever lay ahead.

Come dawn, I guess we finally got to where we were going, because the order came to stop and take cover behind a little hill. Just before I crouched, I looked down the road and saw the out- skirts of a city. Signs were in French, and a sloped road with ditches on both sides led into town. Trees and field grass were motionless, almost too quiet, and word was hushed along in the morning air to us to get ready to attack.

Funny what you remember that happened in the lulls. A fine officer, Lieutenant George Lavenson, hiked out into the field because he had to do his business, you know. I had talked with him several times. He was the battalion personnel officer and dreamed of owning a canoe camp for kids one day. Well, he was squat- ting in this field with his pants down and a rifle cracked from out of nowhere. In that same second, Lavenson lay sprawled on his side with blood leaking out of his thigh. A medic ran over, and I crouched and scanned the distance but didn't see no movement, so that Kraut sniper must have known what he was doing. Another order came quick. We needed to press forward. It was maybe six in the morning.

We locked and loaded and started double-timing toward the city, you know, when I heard someone yell a long "Look o-o-o-u- u-u-t!" and a machine gun fired up the road toward us, long bursts, *birrrp-birrrp-birrrp-birrrp-birrrp*. Rock and dirt spat up near my face and we hit the ditches and flattened out and kept our heads down. Those bullets kept flying, and I found out that when a bul- let goes by your ear real close it makes a little popping noise. The ground rained upward, and Winters hollered at us to *"Keep moving! Keep moving!"* and charged out of his ditch with those bullets still snapping and glancing all around him. We figured he knew what he was talking about, so we got up and starting running toward the city with him in the lead. I think it was Lieutenant Welsh and his team that threw grenades at the German machine gunner.

More fire spun in at us. I couldn't see where from. Bullets zinged and zanged and we kept running, running. Everything was cussing and men shooting back. I fired my weapon at the buildings in front of me and kept running and fired again and kept running and it aggravated me that I couldn't get a clean sight line on anything. A body lay on the ground and I dodged it while trying to think on the run. I guessed that the Germans were running back into the city, or maybe out the other side. I pushed past the wooden gate of a fence and I was in the city now. Gray buildings loomed up on both sides. The firing started up again. All was shooting and chaos and Dewitt Lowrey took shrapnel to his head and went down. In my mind flashed pictures of Lowrey working his father's farm near Atlanta. Hunting and fishing were his favorite pastimes, just like me. He had carried that little stray dog we found on the march from Toccoa to Benning. After he was hit, I never knew what happened to Lowrey.

I kept running, running, past a little chicken coop right there in the city, and somebody was yelling, and bullets flew all around. Ahead, I glimpsed bursts of fire coming from the upstairs window of a warehouse. I pushed my shoulder against a wall to stop running, crouched, glanced around the side of a building, pinpointed the window with smoke, then ducked back. The shot was mine. I held my breath, glanced around the building again, fired, then ducked back again. Blasts came from another window. Shards of brick sprayed past the corner of the building in front of me. I'd got the sniper. Our guys ran forward past me to the next building. One of our men threw a grenade toward the other window. It exploded off the side of the building in a hail of debris. "We gotta take that warehouse!" someone yelled across the street. "Shifty! Shifty! You okay?!" I hadn't moved since I'd pulled the trigger and ducked for cover, but suddenly I found my feet again and surged forward.

Sergeant Taylor yelled at me to hammer some windows, so I blew them out, then grabbed some cover near a building while more of our men ran up. "Tipper, take Liebgott and start clearing these buildings!" another sergeant ordered. The houses were built in rows, you know, and Tipper ran to the first and threw a grenade through the window while Liebgott kicked open the door. They disappeared inside, then Liebgott ran out and on to the next house. Tipper emerged, his rifle smoking, and paused on the doorstep. A mortar whistled in, and he exploded, or so my eyes told me. Bricks flew everywhere, and when I could see again through the smoke, Tipper was still standing, still holding his weapon. I remembered Tipper wondering on the first day of our training if we'd hike up Currahee by the time we finished Toccoa. He was a fine athlete and a good man. Right now blood poured from where his right eye had been. His head looked swollen like a watermelon. The clothing on his right arm and both legs was torn up. Blood soaked his uniform. More mortars came in, one right after the other, landing all over the street. *Kaboom! Kaboom! Kaboom!* Liebgott reached Tipper first. He hollered for a medic, helped Tipper sit, and cradled him in his arms.

Everything flew at us now—mortars and machine guns and artillery and the blown up sides of buildings. Clancy Lyall ran around a blind corner straight into the outstretched bayonet of a German soldier running the other way. The weapon stuck fast in Lyall's gut. The two men both looked so shocked, I think neither knew what to do. Lyall got his rifle up first and shot the German out of him. The German fell backward and pulled the bayonet out of Lyall as he fell. Lyall was a goodhearted farm boy from Texas. A medic ran over and jabbed him with a morphine syrette. Another of our men blasted the side of a building with a bazooka. A huge hole opened up and a German soldier staggered out. Our man pulled a pistol and shot the German in the face.

Sergeant Carwood Lipton and Sergeant Taylor were acting as a team, leading some of us in Third Platoon up a street. Sergeant Lipton took the right side, hugging the buildings as he ran. He paused and yelled at us to move further along. Middle of his yell, a mortar dropped vertically, landing eight feet in front of him. Smoke and brick blasted up. Lipton flew backwards, maybe ten feet, his whole body airborne. He crumpled to the street, landed, and shook his head as if dazed, blood running from a cut under his eye and a hole in his thigh. Lipton was a dependable leader, one of the few married men in the company, and I had talked with him often about rabbit hunting, which he enjoyed as a boy. Tab Talbert, one of the best soldiers in the company, reached Lipton first, checked his wounds, and threw him over his shoulder to carry him to an aid station. As we ran through a covered alcove, I noticed the body of Albert Blithe crumpled near a wall. Blithe's face was ashen and he was still alive, but his eyes stared into space, as if the man wasn't in his own body anymore.

Another lull came, a longer lull. We ran through the rest of the city, blowing out windows and searching buildings. No one seemed to be around anymore. Our running slowed to a walk. I guess the city was secured, and we had done our job maybe. At least the Krauts were gone. I didn't feel like yelling in victory. Didn't feel like celebrating at all. I had shot at men for the first time ever, shot and killed them, and those thoughts swirled inside my head with no place to land. Just had to keep going. Keep going was all.

I walked down the main street, me and another guy, don't remember who. We kept our rifles up, always looking, always watching. From the distance I heard a *tack-tack-tack* on a power pole. Was a woodpecker hammering for his supper, and I knew the fighting was over then. We walked on for some time, and Carentan grew completely quiet. We reached the other side of the city and stopped, just looking across the fields. We turned around and started walking back the way we had come, looking for the rest of our outfit. We walked for maybe half an hour, maybe an hour. It was hard to gauge time. Maybe we walked in circles.

Off to our side was a store with a sign over the windows that read *"Vin."* The soldier I was with gave me a nudge, scc, and we eyeballed the store closer. "Might well be some Krauts in there," my friend said, one eyebrow raised, and I understood what he was getting at. We opened the door gentle-like and looked around. Bottle after dusty bottle lined the shelves. I didn't know much about wine, but it seemed a shame to leave an opportunity like that untested.

We each found a bottle that looked to our liking, then hiked behind the store and pulled the corks. That first gulp went down sharp and sweet, but no later than by second gulp, a bullet zinged in and hit high over my head. I put a hand over my eyes to shade the dust and looked up. Where the bullet landed seemed harmless enough, so I just kept gulping. Another bullet slicked in all snake-like and found a target maybe five feet from the first bullet hole. Was that the best that sniper could do? My buddy and I chatted away in the afternoon sun and finished about half a bottle each and that was enough for my head. That Kraut sniper kept shaving bullets in on us every few minutes or so, but he was a mile wide of a barn door and bound to leave soon enough, headed the other way, trying to find his friends. So that was that.

We got up, walked back through the city, and found our out-fit. Guys were milling about, the wounded were being carried away, and an order came to eat something while we had a chance. We squeezed canned cheese into our mouths from our K-rations, maybe ate a few crackers and chewed a stick of gum, then another order came through and we stood up and started hiking again.

Before long we were out behind the city. The sky clouded over and started a light drizzle. We left the road and hiked through the fields, always heading away from the town. I didn't know where we were going or exactly why, but we were together again in the company, all of us. Men had dirt on their faces; their uniforms were speckled with blood. Dirt turned to mud in the rain, and water wormed down my neck, and a machine gun burst out on us, a short *birrp-birrrp-birrp*, and we hit the mud and scanned the hill. I reckoned those Krauts had run out of the city, regrouped, and now they wanted to get back in.

We lay a moment, catching our breaths, then the sky opened up and mortar fire fell in earnest. Huge splashy explosions kaboomed all around. We crawled on our bellies through wet grass to get our bearings, then got up and sprinted at a crouch into the trees. A man to my right went down and I didn't see who it was, and another on my left went down and we hit the trees at a full run and broke through branches and found cover. A little ridge was there, with a field in front of the ridge, and on the far end of the field another ridge. We started firing at the Krauts from our ridge, with the Krauts firing back at us from their ridge. I glanced up and fired, then ducked down, then glanced up and fired again. It went on like that for some time, just us shooting and them shooting, and the rain continued to pelt us and the day grew dark and it was night before long, and for a while everyone stopped firing and the rain poured.

We dug foxholes in the dark and crawled into the mud like we'd crawl into bed. We closed our eyes, trading off sleep in shifts, but nobody actually slept. The man I was with had a flask and he pulled it out and we each took a long hit to get warm. I wished I could light a smoke, but everything was wet, and the mud seeped up, and my clothes clung to me like I'd fallen in a river. Another order came to fix bayonets on our weapons. Come first light, we were to run across the field and attack. It rained and rained throughout the night, and I might have dozed but I swear I heard a man scream, just like he had been bayoneted. Someone hollered for a medic. There was moaning, whimpering, but it died down soon enough, and the rain ran down my ears. Maybe I hadn't heard anything after all.

We were studying a map at dawn when the first round of enemy mortars came in. They seemed bigger, whistling in with huge thuds, landing like boxcars being thrown through the air. Earth sprayed up in chunks, and I heard one of our men hollering our position into a radio. Another man yelled *"Go! Go!"* And another man ran up a small hill. His shoulder smoked and he crumpled backward and rolled down what he had just run up. Our mortars opened up, and I crawled up a rise, glanced over the top, and emptied the clip of my M1. Had to find the target. Had to see the shape of the enemy. It wasn't no use just firing like this. Had to see. Had to hear. I glanced up again, took a second to look through the weeds, and spotted the black shape of a shadow high on the opposite ridge. I fired. The shadow fell. I ducked down, glanced up again, and paused. Another shadow moved to the right of the hill's crest. I fired. That shadow fell. A long burst of machine-gun fire shot out from near my head, one of our guys shooting across the field. A long burst returned from the enemy. Branches dropped all around me. Leaves shattered like confetti.

A new, low rumble shook the earth. Where had I heard that sound before? I glanced up over my cover. Far on the enemy's ridge-line, I glimpsed the snout of a long gray pipe. A man's helmet came into view, then the rumble grew louder. Tanks! German tanks! Where had they come from? We were no match for tanks! *"Keep firing!"* someone ordered. So we did. We held the line and pulled our triggers. *Find the flash of light. Find the shadow that moves.* Firing. Firing. Always firing. The spent shells flipped hot from the top of my gun, spinning away from my eyes, spinning, spinning. Lieutenant Harry Welsh ran out into the field with a bazooka and fired at an oncoming tank. Another enemy tank answered him with an explosion that blew a nearby tree in half. *"Medic! Medic!"* someone yelled. We fired and fired.

I wasn't sure how much longer any of us could last when another rumble sounded, but this one came from the hill behind us. Big booms. Beautiful booms. Our tanks were coming up from the beach to meet the Germans. Our boys thundered into view and blasted away. We kept firing, firing. I saw a man step over the crest of the hill, his leg shot out from underneath him. He flipped and turned and fell on the ground. All was smoke over the far hillside. Their tanks started rumbling the other direction. This time I heard cheers. Our cheers.

I stopped firing and sat on a nearby log, then stood again and walked a bit. I pulled out a pack of Chelseas. A few were dry enough by now and I lit one. The smoke blew in ragged trails out of my mouth. The woods grew quieter. I lit another cigarette and smoked that. Then I smoked a third. I guessed the battle for Carentan might be over. I guessed we'd won. An order came through and we packed up and headed out.

Over the next few days, more orders came in. Don't remember exactly what they were. More patrols. More shooting. More holding other lines. More firing. I was often ordered to go out as lead scout. Look around. Listen. See what I could see. Report back. I felt okay about that.

It might have been a week later, we were out on patrol when Lieutenant Welsh asked for volunteers to check out a farmhouse. Albert Blithe was back with us and could see again. He was a good man, more of a fighter than you'd think, and our medic had called what he had developed during the battle of Carentan "hysterical blindness"—how he'd sat and stared into space, unseeing, for a while. The blindness was gone now, and Blithe volunteered to go. Martin and Dukeman went with him. They disappeared into the leaves, and a moment later a shot rang out from the windows near the roof's peak. Blithe had been hit between his shoulder and his neck. Joe Lesniewski ran up, pulled a clean T-shirt out of his musette bag, and packed it in Blithe's wound. We opened up on the farmhouse, firing and firing. After that, all was quiet.

Sometime in that period we hiked back to Carentan and stayed a few days. The Krauts didn't hold the city anymore and it was safe. From there, we went to a field camp near Utah Beach. Got a lukewarm shower there, I remember, and some hot chow. Then we were ordered to leave Normandy. Seemed the best order I'd heard in quite a spell. Those three days of hard fighting we'd originally been promised had stretched to more than a month of fighting in Normandy. We boarded a ship and headed back to England. They gave us steak and oranges and ice cream on the ship and it tasted real good. I guess I had done what I'd been ordered to do, because I got a promotion around then to sergeant and I wasn't a private anymore. Still didn't feel like I knew much about much.

Some of the fellas got to talking about the time we had in Normandy. The conclusion was that we weren't going to survive the rest of the war. I shared the view, I guess. Yeah, I did. Easy Company had jumped into Normandy with a hundred and forty men. Coming back from Normandy, only sixty-five were still with us. You think, shoot, here it's just the start of the war and half our men are already gone. Ain't no way a man's going to get to the other side alive.

Well, we got back to England, and a few things happened there that might not be fit to mention in mixed company, you know. When you're twenty-one and don't expect to live long, you're more likely to do things you might not ordinarily do. I wasn't courting a steady girlfriend or nothing. Sure, I wrote girls back home, and they wrote me, and I guess I knew better than this. But it happened. I'll say it plainly so. We went to London on a pass, McClung and me, and a trainload full of guys. "You're a goddam girl chaser," McClung said as we climbed off at the station, but I don't know if I was all that or not. Within an hour we were brimming with beer and someone said, "Hey, there's a whorehouse down the street," so we were off. McClung carried his M1, and I wondered why the hell he needed that, since we weren't in a combat zone anymore. The whorehouse was this old wooden building with a bright sign blinking out front. A line of soldiers stretched out the door and clear around the side of the building. They were all greenhorns, new recruits coming straight to England, and we took to the back of the line in a bunch.

"Ah hell," McClung said, after waiting a minute or two. "We'll never get in tonight with all these jokers around." Three lights shined red over the porch. McClung elbowed his way to the front of the line, directly past the heys, yos, and watchits. He shouldered his rifle and shot out the lights. *Blam! Blam! Blam!* Well, those new recruits scattered like fleas off a dog in a washtub. Suddenly there was no line anymore at the whorehouse.

We went in and the ladies circled us. One took me by the arm and led me upstairs. She was old as a fossil, with bright red lipstick, and her hair bunched to the side near the top of her head. She hollered for my cigarettes, smoked the one I handed her straight down to ash, then kissed me hard on the mouth. Her teeth smelled like the inside of a rabbit's hutch and her voice rasped low when she asked me what I felt like doing tonight.

I was just about to answer when, from downstairs, I heard another *Blam! Blam! Blam!* I thought the battle for Carentan was on again and sprinted down the rickety steps. There was McClung with his M1, shooting up the insides of the whorehouse. "What the hell are you doing?" I yelled.

He stopped firing and looked at me. "I ain't got no money," he said with a shrug. "Let's go."

"Shit," I said.

McClung hooked his M1 in one arm, pulled out a cigarette, and lit it real calm.

"Shit," I said again.

McClung *kablammed* his rifle again for good measure and laughed. "C'mon, Shifty, let's get out of here."

I laughed, too, and clattered the rest of the way down the landing. We banged through the front doors and got the hell out of there. I don't remember what the ladies said after McClung started shooting. I guess they were all hiding up in their rooms. So that was that.

I went to the hospitals to check on some of the guys who'd been wounded. Popeye was lying on his stomach when I found him. He'd got a purple heart and felt bad for messing up, as he called it, and couldn't wait to join up with the company again. I felt real happy he was going to be okay.

Back at base, this sergeant asked me if I might like a motorcycle ride up to Worcester, where we were going for a spell. He'd found this military bike back when we were over in Normandy, see, and nobody had ordered him to give it back yet. So I said sure and climbed aboard. He gave it a kick start or two and the motor revved up and we varoomed down the road.

It was a fine day with the sun peeking out from behind those English clouds, and as we zoomed by this American convoy we slowed enough for me to hear somebody holler out "*Shifty!*" I never saw who it was or who knew my name. But the man wasn't from our outfit. It must have been somebody from back home in Dickenson County, Virginia, who recognized me from a high school basketball game or something. The sergeant yanked on the throttle and our bike leaped forward. The countryside flew by from the back of that motorbike. For the rest of that afternoon, I held to that thought, home, and grinned like nobody's business.

8

A BLUR OF BATTLES

The rest of the summer of 1944 passed as if in a shroud. Mornings dawned warm, afternoons grew hot, you know, like summer should be, but it was hard for a man to shake his memory of Normandy. A man couldn't wrap his mind around the horrors of what we'd been through, no matter how hard he tried. Trees still grew, squirrels still chattered as they raced between hedgerows, we still did push-ups and jumping jacks and ran five-milers through the English countryside. But nothing seemed normal anymore.

I knew Normandy was just the start of our fighting. We all did. More battles would come, but we had no idea what sort of action might come next. New replacements, wild-eyed killers who couldn't even shave yet, climbed off trucks at our camp and brought Easy Company back up to full strength. Orders were barked. Rumors flew alongside the orders. We were going here. We were going there. Word came down more than once that we were going to jump on another operation. France. Then Belgium. Both missions were scrubbed at the last minute because the battle situations changed. Fine by me, you know. Fine by me.

Then we got word to get ready for Holland. No scrubbing the mission this time. The battle would be bigger even than Normandy in terms of airborne divisions involved. They called it Operation Market-Garden, and the plan seemed simple enough. A long road snaked up the middle of the country, see, straight into Germany. Different allied paratrooper outfits would drop at various places alongside the road and wrestle it back from the Krauts. Then, British ground troops would zip up the road with their tanks and heavy machinery and head right into Germany. The war would be over real quick, and we'd all be home before Christmas. It wasn't going to be an American operation. It was run by the British, see, which meant we'd be catering to them to some extent. Wasn't sure how I felt about that. I liked fighting for Uncle Sam, you know.

One afternoon just before we jumped I ambled out of the lunch line and shaded my brow to look across the horizon. A familiar figure came limping toward me across the grounds, the smile on his face as big as a pumpkin's. Popeye was back from the hospital. We shook hands, and he started jabbering away as feisty and fierce as ever. Seemed the Army had told him that if he stayed out of action more than ninety days, well, they was going to send him to another unit when he got well enough. "But goddam it, Shifty," Popeye said, "if I was gonna let the Army do that to me." So he busted out of the hospital, even though he was still too sore to sit. That's how much he wanted to be back fighting with his buddies in Easy Company. You had to admire Popeye.

My buddy Bill Kiehn wouldn't be making this jump though.

He'd been wounded back in Carentan and they'd sent him to the hospital in England. He was out of the fighting for a spell.

Sergeant Buck Taylor had just come back. He'd been wounded back in Carentan, too. A grenade had flown over a hedgerow, blown up, and caught him in the leg. Wasn't that bad of a wound. He probably should have been evacuated while we were still fighting in Normandy, but he toughed it out until we got back to England, then went to the hospital on his own steam. They fixed him up and sent him right back. I was happy to have him around again.

Sergeant Carwood Lipton was still healing from the face and leg wounds he got in Carentan. He rejoined the outfit in England as quick as he could. They made him the company's new first sergeant. He was probably the best NCO in the whole army, and I was glad he was back.

Well, all the upper brass was really gearing up for this new jump, but somehow to me it didn't feel as big of a deal, you know. Not like the first one. I still felt some butterflies in my gut when the day came and I was heaved into the plane with all my gear. But I was chewing gum this time, feeling loose in my shoulders. Another fella in the stick opposite me read a paperback novel. We were old pros now, heading out with our rifles for another day on the job site.

Our planes took off for Operation Market-Garden on September 17, 1944. I gazed out our plane's window at blue, cloudless skies. Down below, trees already had those red-raw hints of color, and fall was in the air. This time it was going to be a daylight jump, not like Normandy, and when we neared the drop zone, stood up, hooked up, and bailed out the door, I almost grinned. Wars should always be fought with this kind of fine weather.

It was a big jump, you know, the whole regiment came floating down together. Real easy, too. No wind. No swinging around in the sky. Not much anti-aircraft fire coming up at us. Just nice, soft, plowed fields to land in. Almost felt cushy. I bent my knees as the ground approached, landed, slipped out of my harness, and looked around. In the distance was a windmill, a grove of pine forest, and the spire of a huge church. I spotted orange smoke, our company's signal to all find each other, and I set off in that direction. Most of the guys were already milling about in the meeting area. Medics were looking after a couple fellas who'd hurt their backs on the jump. Bill Wingett broke his leg when he landed, so he was out, and he was a fine soldier. But those were the only injuries I noticed.

After we grouped up, we hiked down the main road toward a town called Zon. You'd hear a machine-gun blast aimed our direction once in a while, but it wasn't much. Mostly, we wanted to hightail it to a bridge that spanned the Wilhelmina Canal. That was our first objective, to make sure that bridge stayed safe. For some time all was just the jingle and clump of soldiers hiking down a road. I thought the countryside was a mite quiet. No birds. No wind other than a bit of breeze through the brambles. Maybe too quiet.

One Lung McClung tramped out in front as our scout. Sometimes it'd be me as scout, sometimes it'd be him, but today it was him, you know. McClung walked a quarter mile ahead of us, his rifle aimed along the sandy road. I kept a clear sight line on him in case he hit trouble. McClung reached the canal and ambled across. As he neared the other side I glanced down at the river. It was shining blue and brown, flowing so peaceful, with little crests rippling up from the breeze. The rest of us were still thirty yards from the bridge.

It felt like the air changed—like a storm had been brewing over the hills, and we walked straight into that storm. My eyes shot back at McClung on the bridge, and my jaw dropped. "Hit the deck!" somebody yelled. We heard a huge *kuhBLAM!* then *blam!*— a chunk of firewood landed six inches from my head. Stones and timbers poured out of the sky and thudded in the dust. The Krauts had blown the bridge.

McClung was a goner. A huge lump worked its way up my throat and I fought to press it down. No way he could've survived that blast. We stayed flattened until the sky cleared, then stood up and fought to see past the smoke. Doggone, I nearly burst. There was ole McClung, grinning at us from the other side of the river. He told me later he'd flopped down behind a big ole shade tree as soon as he got across. Wanted to take a little rest, you know. That tree saved his life.

Didn't see no Krauts in the distance. I'm sure they were already running hard by the time the bridge blew. We still needed to get across that river. Gordy Carson jumped into the current, swam to a rowboat in the shallows on the other side, and brought it back. Some engineering-type fellas got in the boat and towed a line across. For the rest of the day we scoured the riverbank for planks to salvage, then built a makeshift bridge. The air turned cool and dusky. We dug foxholes, ate K-rations, and slept in shifts. Next morning, we splashed across. Strike one against us. We were supposed to hold that damn bridge.

Up ahead lay Eindhoven. Our next objective was to make sure the town was secure. All of us in Third Platoon were out in front this time in a flanking position, hiking across open country. A replacement officer named Lieutenant Bob Brewer led the way. He was a big, tall officer and stood head and shoulders above a crowd. Ahead of us lay a stone building, maybe three hundred yards away.

A light wind blew from the southeast. Visibility was clear. Bees buzzed. Seemed peaceful, yet a thin trickle of sweat went down my back.

"We're too exposed," I hissed to Rogers, some distance away.

He nodded. "Need to find some cover—quick," he said.

Crack! The side of the building smoked. Lieutenant Brewer was down. We flattened out, worked our triggers, and scanned the building to find the sniper. It was impossible to get a clean shot. Sergeant Taylor sprinted over to Brewer, looking for life, but the sergeant shook his head and shouted at us to keep going. Brewer bled from the throat below his jawline. We advanced at a crouch, still firing. A medic named Al Mampre must've not been convinced the lieutenant was dead yet, for he ran over, grabbed some plasma out of his kit, and shoved a needle into Brewer's vein. A bullet cracked again. Mampre winced. The bullet peeled the flesh off the medic's leg all the way to the bone. He grabbed his leg above the boot line and dumped sulfa on his wound. We grabbed cover as best we could and shot the hell out of the building. I didn't see anyone inside. Some Dutch civilians ran out with a ladder and carried Brewer and Mampre to cover.

McClung took over as scout and we continued toward Eindhoven. Private Don Moone walked with him. We came out of the field and reached a road. I heard a rumble in the distance. A German weapons carrier full of soldiers roared around the corner and swung into view. McClung and Moone stood dead center of the road and loaded a rifle grenade. The truck seemed to accelerate as it bore down on them. McClung and Moone fired at the truck from about twenty yards. The grenade blasted against the grill and exploded. A direct hit. The truck swerved, its engine on fire, and crashed into a post. Germans stumbled out and zigzagged up the road. We opened fire and scattered gravel. The soldiers ground to a halt and threw up their hands. We took them prisoner and sent them back to headquarters with a guard.

As we neared Eindhoven, an old Dutchman squinted at our uniforms from where he stood alongside the road. He stepped toward us, his gait stiff, his eyes watery. Fishing deep inside his coat pocket, he took out an orange armband, the forbidden symbol of the Dutch resistance, and strapped it on. "I shall never forget this day as long as I live," he said in stilted English, and broke into a huge toothless grin.

That was just the start. As we walked into the city, a strange noise filled my ears. It was a mob, but they weren't angry. I guess the Dutch didn't much like being under Nazi occupation. They'd been that way since the war began five years earlier. Crowds lined the cobblestone roads, waving and cheering. The Dutch civilians held out trays of food for us—oranges, apples, pears, and honey. Did we want some hot tea? Care for a fresh glass of milk? How 'bout a beer? We shook hands and posed for pictures. Young ladies kissed us. We signed autograph books like movie stars. For the rest of that afternoon we were swarmed with people, grateful we had come. We pushed through to the other side of the city, heading northeast.

Some tanks rumbled up, heading to Nuenan. They slowed down long enough for us to scramble aboard. We rode for some time, then it grew dark. Don't remember where we slept. We got up and kept going, still on tanks.

When we reached the outskirts of Neunan, we scrambled off and hit the ditches. Brief fire broke out real sudden. All was yelling and explosions. Our tanks had a short skirmish with some German tanks. When the vibrations cleared, we started hiking through town, looking for Krauts.

Each house had a backyard. Hedges separated each backyard from another. We moved cautiously, with suspicion, running at a crouch, eyeing anything that moved. Far away, two Germans climbed out of a second-story window and moved across a roof. They were closest to another paratrooper, but the other paratrooper's rifle didn't fire. Quickly, he field stripped his rifle on the spot and fixed the problem, but by that time, the Germans were gone. At least now we knew we weren't alone.

I hiked through a cemetery, jumped over a wooden fence, and hit the ground at a crawl. As I pushed through a hedgerow, I heard a German machine-gun burst a few rows over. Robert Van Klinken was pelted in the chest with three bullets and went down. Those closest to him pulled him to safety, but his face was ashen; he'd soon be dead. I hardly had time to notice when it happened, but later I remembered how I'd talked to him lots of times, and that he was a young mechanic from Washington State. All he wanted to do was go home, get married, and have a bunch of kids. Robert Van Klinken was kindhearted, always laughing, and then he was gone.

Far away, I heard the rumble of more tanks. Johnny Martin yelled to watch out. He'd spotted a German tank hidden in the hay no more than a hundred yards away. Martin ran to an approaching British tank to warn him about the trouble that lay around the corner. The British tank commander stood with his head and shoulders exposed. I saw the tank commander shake his head. The British tank revved up and continued forward. Martin climbed off just in time. *Wham!* The German tank hit the British tank square on. It caught fire. Most of the crew scrambled out, pulling the commander out with them. The tank commander's legs had been blown off.

I didn't have time to think. A machine gun cut loose in front of us, biting into the dirt to my left. More fire to my right came from a rooftop. Still more fire came, but I wasn't sure from where. I ducked for cover, glanced up, fired my weapon, ducked down, glanced up, and fired again. Nearby chugged a driverless burning tank. It plowed into a power pole, knocked it flat in a shower of sparks, and kept going. I emptied clips, one right after the other. A man went down to my right. Another man ran to help him. He was gunned down. The town seemed ablaze in noise and explosions. From somewhere, an order came to fall back.

We dashed to the outskirts of town, found the backs of some idling trucks, climbed aboard, and rode back toward Eindhoven. Fellas sat with their hands on their knees, panting, spitting. I lit a cigarette, my hands shaky. Four dead, someone muttered, eleven injured. When I looked back at Nuenen, I knew that the Germans had overrun the town. I didn't like retreating.

Things went from bad to worse. That night, from our foxholes far outside the city, we looked down the road the other direction at a fiery orange sky. The Germans were bombing Eindhoven, the city we'd passed through earlier with so much celebration. It was a very, very bad night.

We picked up and went on. Next came a little town called Veghel; that was a hard day for us, mighty hard. We were on both flanks of the British when the Germans attacked. We fought back with all we had, but the Krauts came at us with all kinds of stuff— half tracks, artillery—I don't know where they got it all from. We fired and fired, then sprinted into an apple orchard next to a crossroads, dug slit trenches, and took shelter behind trees. That proved a mistake. The Germans shelled us with huge iron blasts. The sky rained jagged pieces of red-hot metal. Shrapnel sliced and burned through branches, and the branches clumped around us. Holes in the ground proved little cover against artillery like that. After six hours of shelling, black craters dotted the earth. Finally the sky grew quiet. I felt helpless and shaky. Dusk hit, the air turned cold, and a light rain began to fall. Our grimy uniforms turned wet. We were cold and miserable.

I guess around then is when things started to become fuzzy for me. What I mean is I never lost my sense of hearing, never lost my sense of eyesight, but I lost a sense of how one day flowed into the next. I'd wake up in my foxhole, eat a K-ration, make sure my rifle was clean, get orders, and go. Sometimes we gained a foothold. Sometimes the enemy did. At night I dug another foxhole, ate another K-ration, closed my eyes, and tried to sleep. Life became a blur of battles. Rain continued to fall, and we all knew the main road wasn't secured. The British weren't sailing smoothly up to Germany like we'd hoped. The war wouldn't be ended by Christmas, that was for sure.

Weeks passed. Nights grew frosty, and the earth was hard in the mornings when we got up. We'd been fighting in Holland maybe six weeks when a jeep came through with a mailbag. I was happy to see my sister's familiar handwriting, but the first part of her letter nearly stopped me cold.

My brother Jimmy's carrier, the USS *Gambier Bay*, had been sunk over in the Pacific, she explained. My sister first found out about the disaster in the newspaper. She didn't want Mama or Daddy to find out and worry, so she hid the newspaper between the mattress and bedsprings. A few days later, the family was out shopping. When they came home, the postmaster had let himself in the house and propped a telegram against the sugar bowl on the kitchen table. The postmaster knew everyone well enough in Clinchco to let himself in like that. Everyone in the family saw that telegram and suspected the worst. I stopped reading the letter long enough to wipe my eyes, then kept reading. Fortunately, Daddy opened the telegram and Mama read it aloud. It contained one line, probably the most beautiful phrase the family had ever heard:

BE HOME ON SURVIVORS LEAVE. STOP.
JIMMY. STOP.

I let out a huge lungful of air. He'd spent two days in the open sea before being rescued. My brother was still alive. The letter came as a welcome respite from all that was around me. It had other bits of news in it, too. The basketball scores from the last few Clinchco High School home games. News that Mama had decided to decorate for Thanksgiving anyway that year, in spite of three of her sons being away at war. Home. I read the letter over and over, but day-to-day life on the battlefield continued to blur. They trucked us to this place called The Island. It wasn't really an island, more a bunch of dikes set up with grassland between them. Lots of fighting there. Lots of patrols. A man never had a chance to change his clothes or take a bath. We all stunk.

You always needed to move after dark in Holland, because it was mostly level country, see. One night, don't know where we were, a lieutenant said to me, "Sergeant Powers, you get two guys, run across that dike over to the edge of that field, and set up a listening post." Now, a listening post is so you can hear what the enemy's doing. If trouble's afoot you can call back to your unit and let them know.

I got two guys, younger replacements, and we went out in the dark. We scrambled over some barbwire fences, cursed our way through nettles, waded across a ditch filled with scummy water, and got to where we needed. "Watch the bushes, and see that they don't move," I told the guys. I sat down only to jump right up again. One of the younger fellas was jumpy and had fired his M1—*pow, pow, pow*—making a heap of noise. "Where are the Germans?" I asked. He pointed to three bushes. "That's just bushes," I said. "Grab your gear."

We were in trouble now, and ran to the other edge of the field. We jumped into another ditch, and sure enough, the Germans had figured out where the gunfire had come from. They fired a few artillery rounds right where we'd been. I told the fellas to shut up from now on. We patrolled around another two hours or so, but never did see any Germans. So we went back.

Another evening, McClung and me went out on patrol together. We heard some German tanks rumbling around so we decided to get the hell out of there and report back to our outfit. As we hiked along, a German plane came down low, strafing all around. Darkness was setting in, but it was still light enough to see. That pilot took a pass around, and McClung said, "Damn it, Shifty, I'm getting sick of this." He aimed his M1. The next time the plane came by, McClung shot a bunch of holes in him. Now, an M1's a fine weapon, but there ain't no way a man could shoot down a plane with it. Still, I'll swear to this day that McClung shot down the Red Baron. That was getting one on base for us.

A week or two later we came up to this little town. It was late in the afternoon. The Germans were holding the town, and our aim was to take it back. The officer in charge decided we needed to wait until daylight to do it. It wasn't absolutely dark yet, and a jeep with two American soldiers busted through our lines on its way to headquarters. Up the road, the Germans stopped the jeep and took those two soldiers prisoner.

I was down in my foxhole when all this happened, and one of my guys came over, explained the situation, and hollered, "Shifty, two Germans are walking down the road holding two Americans. Come get 'em." So I went up to take a look and oh, it was a turkey shoot, you know, real simple shooting to take out those Germans and set those Americans free.

I lay down on the ground, aimed my rifle, and took a bead on the German on the right. I figured, I'll shoot him first, then switch over and shoot the one on the left. Then I got to studying the situation. If I shoot those two Germans, the Americans will be out in the open, and the town's filled with Krauts. They're bound to hear the shots, see their men down, and they'll shoot the two American prisoners before they can run to cover. So I just debated and debated, and watched them walk out of sight.

Well, the next day we took the town, and drove out the Germans, killed a few, and got some American prisoners back. I hoped that some of those released prisoners were the two Americans I saw on the road. But I never knew for certain.

A while later it was my turn with my squad to go up on the dike and watch all night. A levee ran between there and the river, and we needed to keep our eyes glued to it to make sure the Krauts didn't come across. Well, before it got dark, I memorized everything in front of me, left to right. Two willow trees. Three. An old stump. A little shoal of rocks. Five clumps of shrubs, and so on.

Next morning I rubbed my eyes, looked, and looked again. A tree had appeared that wasn't there the night before. I called back to the command post, and of course they told me to go check things out. So I hiked over real quiet and saw German hobnail boot tracks and a place in the mud where a machine gun had been set. That new tree had been set up to camouflage a German outpost. Fortunately, the Germans had come and gone during the night, so the upper brass decided to let it go. Once the Krauts found out that we knew about it, they weren't going to come back.

About that time, maybe it was earlier in the fighting, Sergeant Taylor got into a motorcycle accident on Hell's Highway, that road that snaked up to Germany, and got sent to the hospital again. Along came a new officer to lead us in Third platoon, Lieutenant Ed Shames. Now, some of the fellas didn't care for the new lieutenant on account of the way he barked orders and liked things kept shipshape. But Lieutenant Shames had received a battlefield commission after Normandy and knew his stuff. We got along okay. Lieutenant Dick Winters got moved up to battalion headquarters right about then, so he wasn't around as much, which I didn't enjoy. Lieutenant Fred Heyliger assumed command of Easy Company, but he was shot on Halloween night by one of his own men who mistook him for the enemy. A highfalutin officer named Lieutenant Norman Dike assumed command of Easy Company. The fellas called him "Foxhole Norman" behind his back, because he was gone so much. Him being gone a lot was fine by me.

Must have been a week or two later, Lieutenant Shames said to me, "Sergeant Powers, get your squad and go down this road. A German patrol is supposed to come through here tonight." So I got the guys ready, took our machine gun, and went out. A squad is normally twelve men, but a few of ours weren't around. If I remember correctly we had eight men, maybe less. We got to where we were going, set up the machine gun, sat there all night, and never did see any Germans.

It got daylight, but we were too far away to safely make it back to the command post with that cold sunlight making plain our every movement. A big old farmhouse sat in a nearby field, so I told the guys, "We'll go over there and spend the day, then come dark, we'll head back." They liked the sound of that, so we hiked over to the farmhouse, checked things out, and found a bunch of guys in the basement already. They wore American GI uniforms, spoke English, and appeared friendly enough, so it seemed okay.

We spent the day near a wall lined with dusty Mason jars, all empty. There was maybe twelve, fifteen of those other soldiers hiding out in that basement with us. Sort of twitchy guys, I thought. Kept to themselves. Only one or two ever said anything. None sat down, and they weren't walking around either, pacing, you know, like men would ordinarily do while waiting. My squad was tired after being up all night, so we just sat down, ate K-rations, and dozed.

Come half an hour or so before it grew dark, I was listening closer to the way these fellas shifted their weight as they stood, see, and something didn't sound quite right about their boots. I nudged my squad. "Let's go," I said. One of the fellas asked what the rush was. It wasn't fully dark yet. I brushed off his question and told them to move quick. I kept my thoughts to myself, but I remembered that Germans were known to capture or kill American soldiers, then dress up in their uniforms so they could hike across enemy lines and see what's what. Now, I don't mind fighting a man when he's across a field from me, but in that little basement with twenty-five men all with rifles, a battle would've been a slaughter. Those fellas in the basement with us were Krauts. I'm sure of it.

One day near the end of our stay in Holland, it might have been eleven, twelve at night, and a lieutenant told me, "Sergeant Powers, get nine men and take a combat patrol out in the area. There's a report of a German combat patrol in the area and they have twelve men. Anybody you see, shoot him."

Now, I don't know why that lieutenant figured our ten men was better than their twelve, but that's the way it was gonna be. It was absolutely black dark, you know, so black I couldn't see the hand in front of my face. I lined my guys up, and we headed out. I left my M1 back at the command post and took two pistols because I couldn't see the end of the barrel with the M1.

We walked down this road a way. I was out in front of my squad, and I heard footsteps coming the other way. We all hunkered down on the ground. "Cover me," I whispered, aimed, and got a bead on where the figure was coming from.

"Shoot him," the man behind me whispered. "He's a Kraut."

I ignored him and peered closer into the night. The moon was just peeking out from behind the trees, and I could see his outline real clear now. My adrenaline pumped. I steadied my breathing and got ready to shoot. The man's silhouette came clear. I had a direct sight line to his forehead. The man was taking his time coming close. I said that night's password out loud, just to give him a chance, but there wasn't a response. My finger went to move on the trigger.

"Shoot him, Shifty!" came a whisper. "He's a Kraut for sure."

I said the password again.

"What? Hello!" came a voice from out of the darkness. "For God's sake, don't shoot. Don't shoot! I don't know tonight's password!"

It was Bill Kiehn. That same boy I almost shot on D-day. He'd been wounded in Carentan and gone to the hospital in England. He'd healed, and they'd put him in a replacement depot where the

Army threatened to send him to another unit because he'd been out of action so long, he explained when he got closer up to us. So Kiehn had busted out and gone AWOL and came back to our unit on his own. He had stopped down the road and picked up a box of supplies for us and was walking back to camp. Twice I'd come near a fly's whisker of shooting Bill Kiehn. I sure did. Both Bill and I were mighty tickled I hadn't.

The rest of our days and nights in Holland weren't as happy as that story. Wish I could remember more details, but I can't. Maybe I don't want to. I remember that Joe Lesniewski, the replacement who'd been befriended by Skip Muck and Alex Penkala, caught the blast of a German potato-masher grenade while out on patrol. He went to the hospital all bloodied up, but he lived to rejoin us later. Lieutenant Buck Compton, everybody's favorite officer in the company, took a bullet while charging up a ditch, but he came back to fight another day. My good buddy Jim Alley got blown to the ground by a blast of shrapnel that left thirty-two wounds in his side, face, neck, and arm. He lived, too.

Others weren't so lucky. I remember their names. Faces. The way a fellow might have told a story and made you laugh. Bill Dukeman didn't make it. Nor did James Campbell. Vernon Menze died. James Miller. Ray Schmitz. James Diel. Bill Miller. Robert Van Klinken. Dead. We had jumped on September 17 with 154 men. When we pulled off the line on November 25, we had ninety-eight.

I wasn't sure how I'd clear my blurry head, even as orders came through and we climbed aboard trucks, heading to France for a rest. I tucked my thoughts away to sort through later. Many of the fellas talked about how Operation Market-Garden was a failure. It might have been. Me—as I slouched low in the back of that truck, I looked forward to hot showers and eating real food and not looking over my shoulder every moment, wondering if a bullet was heading my way. Had to shake out the cobwebs. Had to keep going. Maybe a couple nights of good sleep would help. In spite of Operation Market-Garden's bleak outcome, I was still holding out hope that the war might be truly nearing its end. Oh, I hoped. We bounced around in the back of that truck heading for Camp Mourmelon, but a little twinge down my spine told me that what I hoped for was still a long way off.

9

CRAZINESS

All was dark and drizzly when our trucks pulled off the road into Camp Mourmelon. I lurched in and out of wakefulness. We'd been riding for thirty-six hours. The truck's motor hushed, and I stumbled off the tailgate and blinked. The first look around the camp was anything but reassuring. The Krauts had used the camp before we got there, don't know what for exactly, but it looked like they'd been boarding horses where we were about to sleep. Barracks were dusty with hay. Boards were hoof-kicked. The whole camp smelled musty and rotting. It was the most beautiful place in the world.

We stowed our gear, staggered to the showers, and scrubbed soap and hot water all over our filthy skin for the first time since jumping into Holland. For chow that night we gorged on roasted chicken, white bread with real butter, steaming vegetables, pie, and hot coffee. Best tasting meal the army ever served. It almost made me forget the wormy apples we'd been plucking off trees, the odd loaf of stale bread we'd scrounged. Even a K-ration had been a treat in Holland toward the end.

We found bunks and fell asleep. Couldn't have been more than an hour later I woke up and sprinted to the latrine. I heaved one way, then squatted the other, then stumbled back to bed past a line of squirming guys headed to do what I'd just done. I guessed none of us could handle real food yet. Twenty-four hours later I was up and grinning. Forty-eight hours later I was as good as new. Twice in a row now I'd slept all night without being ordered out on patrol. I'd slept on an actual mattress. I'd got up in the morning and nobody was shooting at me. This was the life.

Rain kept falling, and they put us on some light duty hammering loose boards on the barracks, tossing gravel on the muddy sidewalks, digging drainage ditches. It felt good to hold a shovel in my hand when I didn't need to dig a foxhole. We trained a bit, too, did some marching, some runs. Nobody felt like doing much, and for the first time since I'd been in the army, everybody above us seemed okay with that.

Now, right about then is when I started having serious doubts about Earl McClung. When we were out in the mud and cold and shooting, the man was as fine a soldier as ever was. But when it came to garrison duty, ole One Lung was probably the worst soldier that ever wore the Army's uniform. We celebrated Thanksgiving at the end of November and swished turkey meat with canned cranberry sauce around in our mess kits. Then word came down right away to look sharp for a full retreat parade. The whole company busied itself with polishing and shining. Guys grumbled and moaned. Plenty of men didn't have all their gear anymore. Plus, it's hard to spit shine your boots when they've been rained on the past three months. But we did what we had to do. If even one man wasn't slicked up, then the whole company would get gigged. That'd mean no passes.

One Lung's bunk was a couple over from mine. He lounged on his wool blanket and thumbed through a dog-eared copy of *Field & Stream*, one toe sticking out of a hole in his socks. I knew he wasn't going to move, so I ambled over. "Hey, Mac, gimme your boots," I said. McClung tossed them my direction and I started shining them for him. Kiehn caught what was going on. "Hey, Mac, gimme your pants," he said. McClung tossed them over. Someone else yelled for McClung's shirt. Another hollered for his web belt. Someone else took care of his garrison cap and tie. We got ole One Lung looking like he was going to a wedding. "It's a damn good thing you can shoot straight," I said. Sure enough, One Lung hated anything that smelled of refining. After we did that parade, we went back to the barracks. McClung skulked in, took off his pressed trousers and kicked them under his bunk. He took off his freshly ironed shirt and kicked it in a corner. I bet he didn't come near those fancy duds for the rest of the war.

Well, glory. Passes were issued all around. Want a pass? You got one. Here, take two, and have a good time. It was never like this in any Army I'd been part of. I think it was the first of December, and it must have been the whole damn company that bustled on into Rheims, ready to cut loose. A bunch of jokers from the 82nd was already prowling the city by then, and it seemed like all any fella wanted to do was cuss, guzzle beer, chase women, shout aggravations at other outfits, and fight. It was a short season for blowing off steam, and it seemed we couldn't think of how to do it except by misbehaving. We all went a little crazy that night. We rightly did.

We swung back on into camp and did a little whatnot, then were handed more passes. Well, glory times two. Popeye, McClung, and me hopped the first train heading to Paris. Wanted to see the big city, you know. We swaggered into the first crowded pub we saw, elbowed our way up to the bar, and slapped down our cash. Big Band music pounded through the smoky air. The rafters were really swinging. It was gonna be a night.

Now, I'd known from previous times that Popeye could be a bit ornery when he so chose. It was good-natured orneriness, mind you. Still, that boy had a powerful streak of misbehaving in him. He did.

A bunch of Navy guys lined the tables in the back of the bar. They were hollering at us, hollering at the waitresses, hollering at the wall, hollering at everybody they felt like. We ignored them and started drinking. The beers slid down the counter to us in bottles, and we sucked 'em down and lined up our empties. I counted seven bottles in front of me before long, eight in front of McClung, but none in front of Popeye. I gave him a nudge as he swilled the last drops from the bottle he drank from. "Whatduya got going?" I asked.

Popeye sniffed. "Goddam Navy jokers." He waved his hand nonchalantly and flung the empty bottle over his shoulder. I kept my eyes focused ahead. It was too loud to hear where the bottle crashed.

"Shit, Popeye," McClung said and glanced our direction. "You been doing that long? I reckon it's about to get warm in here."

Popeye grinned.

Five Navy guys walked up. I guessed they'd figured it out, because none were smiling. "Paratroopers, huh," said one. He cracked his knuckles and made a fist. Another, his neck as thick as my thigh, started working his jaw as if he was about to say something smart. He didn't get far before Popeye hauled off and punched him in the nose.

We all scrambled. A fella went for my chin and I blocked his fist and hit him in the stomach. He doubled over and somebody caught my right ear with a jab. The blow stunned me as a chair flew by and crashed into the bar. I squished my fist against the nearest Navy man's eye. He heaved over backwards while someone caught him and shoved him forward. I pushed him off me, ducked, sprung up, walloped another man in the head, then ducked again, only this time too slow. When a fist caught me just above my eye, I decided to go down and stay. The whole bar was fighting now. I crawled along the floor as beer glasses sailed through the air. A man thudded next to me. He was out cold. Everything across my sight line was a jumble of bodies punching and fighting. I peered around the corner of an overturned table and glimpsed a familiar grin. Popeye crouched under the table across from me. He offered a wry salute, and I scuttled over. "Just wondering," I shouted, "how many bottles did you toss at those Navy boys before they figured out who threw them?"

Popeye shrugged. "Every goddam one I drank."

Figures squalled near the door. All was a bustle as uniformed military police burst their way into the bar and started busting heads, blowing whistles, breaking guys apart. McClung's belt floated across my sight line. I ducked my head up just as McClung leveled his last man then crouched down to Popeye and me. "We better make a run for it," McClung said. It was a peach of an idea. We pushed our way to the door and sprinted down the street.

We ran three, maybe four blocks before we decided the coast was clear. My eye'd started to swell, and Popeye bled from a gash on his cheek. McClung asked me for a handkerchief, wiped his knuckles on it, and handed it back. We checked our wounds and knew nothing was serious, so we began to pay attention to our growling stomachs and talked about how a hunt for food might be in order. Come near the fanciest restaurant we found, we swung through the doorway and landed in a booth by the window.

A bunch of soldiers sipped cocktails around the room, fine-looking dandies all fancied up with girls at their tables. None were from the Navy, which I was happy about. A starchy looking fella in a black suit sidled over and jabbered at us in French. He balanced his bow tie between his finger and thumb, then when McClung roared "*Food!*" he turned his nose up in the air and stomped off. We shrugged and noticed our thirst, so Popeye decided to roam a bit, then came back shortly with three bottles of wine he'd liberated off various tables when their owners weren't looking. We poured ourselves big tumblers, kicked back on our chairs, and put up our feet.

My, that waiter. He hurried back over, one of his arms bent in a crook, see, with a towel wrapped over that arm. He snapped off the towel with a mighty fuss, whipped our table clean, then hauled back to the kitchen with a loud snorty sniff.

"What a joker," Popeye said. His boots were still on the table. "Some fancy joint this is—they can't even keep out the cats."

It was true. Maybe it was part of the highfalutin tone they were trying to set in this restaurant, I don't rightly know, but big ole French cats yowled up and down the floor, fat and sleek from lots of milk, I reckoned, and brushed up against our legs. It seemed the craziest thing. One old marmalade leaped up on my lap and settled in. I rubbed its furry belly, and she stretched out with a purr.

The uppity waiter strode back. He waved his arms at us again, slobbering all the while in French. He was sure mad about something.

McClung raised his hand like a sergeant slows down his troops. "Yeah, we got it," he said to the waiter, "but where's our goddam food?"

The waiter crossed his arms and tapped his foot. He didn't move.

"I reckon this fella wants us to leave," I said.

"I reckon we've had enough of this joker," said Popeye. He scooped up the nearest Tom and, before anyone could blink, threw it into the waiter's face. The cat shrieked. So did the waiter. He ran hollering around the restaurant while the cat landed on his feet. It slid calmly out the front door when we held it open for him. We followed closely, letting the door slam behind us. If you ask me, I think getting out of a joint like that was a smart move for the cat.

We grabbed food from somewhere else, then sloshed back to base, fell asleep, and nursed hangovers the next morning. Seemed all the enlisted men out on passes had been cutting as loose as us, for the passes tightened up after that, and they started sending us out on five-milers to get the aggravation out. It wasn't all bad stuff that we did. They organized baseball games, basketball, football. Boxing matches. Healthy things for a fella to do. They set up a couple movie theaters around base. An NCO club opened and we had a good time there. A big football game was planned for Christmas Day—the Champagne Bowl, somebody named it—us against the boys from the Five-Oh-Deuce. Lieutenant Buck Compton had healed up from the bullet he took in Holland, and they made him coach of our team. He'd played football for UCLA before he was in the Army and had even played in the Rose Bowl. He knew what he was doing. Joe Toye, the toughest man in Easy Company, watched the practices from the sidelines. He'd just returned from the hospital and was still healing up. Joe Toye could have been a professional athlete if only the war hadn't changed his plans. On a good day, Joe Toye would have charged up and down the field like a man with two legs on fire.

Well, the atmosphere around Camp Mourmelon started seeming right festive. We figured nobody would do any more fighting until the weather turned warm again in spring. Maybe we'd jump into Germany then. Maybe head into China and take on the Japs. It didn't matter. We got paid a few times. It felt strange to have money jingling in our pockets again. I guess if a fella wasn't out on a pass, he didn't have many places to spend it around Mourmelon, so a lot of gambling started up. I was never much of a poker player, though I enjoyed it now and then.

One night maybe six of us sat around in an old barn playing poker. Now, when you're playing poker, you've got to concentrate. I was working on a baby straight when a grenade popped off the vest of the man next to me and rolled on the floor. "Live grenade!" I hollered. We were all still twitchy from Holland, and everybody dived anywhere he could. Our card table turned over. Money and cards flew everywhere. I kept expecting a huge blast, but none came. It was a dud.

Well, I got to studying what had just happened, and I guess it was all a big joke. The fella had taken a hand grenade, screwed off the top, then poured out the powder. He'd put the grenade back together, then loosened the pin. I didn't say nothing. No harm done, I figured. Of course, nobody stole the money when we scattered— if a man did, the guys would catch him and he'd get whupped.

A couple nights later I was nearing a full house at a different poker game when somebody tried the same thing. "Live grenade!" someone hollered. We all hit the floor, and sure enough, that grenade was a dud, too. I guessed that was how it was going to be, because a couple days later, it happened again. It didn't matter how many times different guys tried the joke, the results were always the same. If someone hollered "Live grenade!" we took cover. That's the way we were wired.

Lot of craziness happened at Mourmelon. Come halfway through December I was sitting in the sergeants' barracks late one evening when Johnny Martin and Bill Guarnere swaggered in with two cases of champagne. All the other sergeants crowded around, and Martin popped the corks. We held out our canteen cups, and he filled them to the brims.

It was the first time I'd tasted champagne, and, well, it felt to me like sweet fizzy apple juice. Why, that stuff slid down as easy as soda pop, and I guess a lot of fellas were thinking the same thing because we guzzled the first case and started in on the second. There we all were, drinking champagne and laughing away, and I don't know who said something aggravating at first, but another guy mouthed back, and another fella said something similar, and pretty soon the first guy walloped the second guy over the head with his canteen cup. Then it all broke loose and we all got into it, tossing guys into the walls, beating each other over the head, smashing our fists against each other's chin. Wasn't too long before First Sergeant Carwood Lipton hurried into the barracks and yelled at us to knock it off. All the bunks were broken off the walls by then and he was real mad. "You guys are supposed to be leaders," he hollered. "A bunch of sergeants doing all this! Clean up this mess, then you can sleep it off."

It sounded like a wise plan, so we did. Next morning we fell out for chow call, our heads still woozy, and Lieutenant Dike, our company commander, wore a grave look on his face. I figured he'd chew us out, too, at very least make us run a few miles, but all he said was "After breakfast, stand fast."

Stand fast. What did that mean?

We cleaned the barracks again, then all stood fast. Afternoon stretched into evening. Some guys went to see movies. Some played cards. Some went to sleep. Other fellas acted like it was business as usual, but I felt a strange uneasiness in the air.

Seemed like it was the middle of the night, December 17, maybe early morning the 18th, when someone hollered for us to "*Look sharp! Get up! Get going!*" We bolted out of bed. Word had come in that the goddam Krauts were throwing everything they had at us over near a town called Bastogne. "Where the hell's Bastogne?" somebody mumbled. "*Just move!*" came the reply. "*Grab your gear!*" "What gear?" the man said. "I ain't got nothing."

He was right. Few of us had anything except the clothes we'd worn into camp. Some of the fellas didn't even have weapons anymore—they'd turned their rifles over for repairs. We were supposed to turn in our ammo when we got to camp, but I never did, so fortunately I still had that. But it wasn't much, and I knew there wasn't much ammo around camp at all. Mourmelon didn't even have an ammo dump—I'd checked into that one off afternoon.

"Bastogne's in Belgium," Sergeant Taylor said. He walked into the barracks and started packing his gear. He always did have a clear head. He'd healed from his motorbike wound and joined us back in camp, and he continued, "It's near the Ardennes Forest, and it's gonna be cold up there, so grab all the warm clothes you can find." He put on a hooded sweatshirt that his parents had sent him back in Holland. He was one of the lucky ones. Warm clothes?

What were they? Our boots weren't felt-lined. We didn't have any long underwear or thick wool socks. We had our combat jackets, but they weren't meant for winter. Some of the replacements didn't even have helmets yet. Joe Lesniewski had turned his boots in for repair and was running around in his stocking feet. I packed a change of underwear into my sleeping bag along with a change of socks and my pistols. I still had my M1. But that's all I had.

We bust out of our barracks and loaded onto a bunch of trucks, their engines already idling. "Shove on over," somebody yelled, and more guys crowded on. There was no room to sit, so everyone stood. The trucks ground their gears, and as quick as that, we headed off into the night.

We rode for some time, the trucks lights blazing. Every once in a while the trucks stopped and we jumped off the tailgates and pissed on the sides of the road. We climbed back on and kept going. The wind blew all around us, and we shivered and snapped our lighters, trying to smoke. It started raining, then stopped, then started again. A few men had K-rations and we passed around crackers and gum. The roads were potholed and we jostled against each other. A few times the roads got so steep and slick that the trucks got stuck in the mud. We all got out and helped push them over the hills. Must have been a mile or two outside of Bastogne, our truck stopped for good. We jumped out, pissed again, stretched, formed up into columns, and started hiking toward the town. I heard distant rifle shots in the hills.

As we marched down both sides of the road, we started seeing figures coming toward us, American soldiers, all with their heads down. When they came closer, we said hello and they looked up, their eyes wild. "Don'tchall go up there," one man said. "They'll murder the lot of you." I didn't know what he was talking about. "Ya gotta run," said another. "Krauts are armed to the teeth—tanks, bombs, artillery. You'll never make it out alive."

This puzzled us, this behavior. These men were retreating from the very place we were marching toward. We scuffed along in silence for a minute or two before one of our men had a good idea, "Hey, how about giving us some of your ammo," he called out. "Yeah," said another. "We'll take everything you got." The other troops started handing it over—their hand grenades, their bullets. It wasn't much, but I figured it would see us through for a while.

As I hiked toward Bastogne, I shivered. I was wet and cold and hadn't eaten much for a day and a night already. But the gnawing in my gut wasn't chief in my mind just then. I was wondering at what kind of craziness we were heading into. Nobody had any idea, I guessed, except the soldiers hiking the other way.

10

ONLY SAFE UNDER THE EARTH

From out of my foxhole I peered down the twiggy corridor into the murk. The pine trees were planted in rows, gridlike, you know, and they cast eerie shadows in the twilight. I peered closer. I'd never been afraid of trees at night, not really, but these ones glared like they had eyes. The Bois Jacques woods, they called these trees, and I remembered nights back in Clinchco when we hiked to Dave's Ridge and slept next to that abandoned schoolhouse that folks said was haunted. The feeling I got up at Dave's Ridge was as close to the feeling I had now as I'd ever had. But even that wasn't close. A fella couldn't sleep thinking a ghost was nearby. You'd stare all night into the blackness, wondering when the devil was gonna reach his bony fingers around your throat and drag you away.

I tightened my arms around my rifle, and pulled my sleeping bag closer around me. Twisting my shoulders against the frozen side of the foxhole, I tried to find a mite of comfortableness. My feet ached. I wished I could rub some life into them, but I dared not take off my boots for long. My teeth chattered. My whole body was tensed against the cold. A smoke would taste good, but I wouldn't risk a flame. I wished for a drink of water, but the inch or so I had left in my canteen was a block of ice. From somewhere out in the dark forest, a branch snapped. My finger went to the trigger and my eyes darted to the sound. I listened, my neck taut. Nothing more moved except the snow that sifted down in small silent flakes.

I couldn't grumble much. I knew other soldiers were feeling the same misery as me. We were all huddled in our foxholes, a few here, a few there, stretched out thin in a defensive line against the enemy. In my mind I retraced the picture I'd drawn of the landscape in front of us. We were far back in the trees, but nearer to the edge of the woods the landscape formed a little inlet, almost like a river when it gets wide and turns on a corner. On our right and left were long lines of trees that formed two broad sides of a cove, and in the middle of that cove was a field. We couldn't see the field from our holes, but we had set up outposts on the edge of the forest. Whenever our turn on outpost came, we'd head to those further foxholes and look out on the field then. It sloped down to a little town called Foy, maybe a mile away.

The fellas had been talking, see, and nobody at my rank knew exactly how many of the enemy we were facing. We just knew there were lots, and that they were plumb aggravated to see us. We were pretty sure the Krauts were camped in the trees to our right. We guessed they also stretched ribbonlike in front of us toward the north, holding the line between us and Foy. Well, shoot, somebody said the line of Krauts stretched clear around the town of Bastogne, and I didn't doubt it. The word was that we'd come up to fight eight divisions of German troops. That was a heap of men. This was a mighty important battle, it was. If the Krauts could take Bastogne, well, then they could take the seven roads that led in and out of it. We all knew those roads were mighty important. Getting them was probably key to the Krauts' last hope of victory. We were all that stood between them and the roads of that Bastogne.

My feet felt dead and I flexed my toes in my boots, trying to push blood around my body. I shivered, peered out of my foxhole again, then settled back and looked over at Popeye, who dozed with one eye open. Maybe I should try to catch a few winks, too. My head nodded. Was I dreaming? *Hold the line at all costs.* That was the only real order I remembered hearing. I guessed I was doing that. Doing my job. Sitting in my foxhole in the snow at night. My stomach growled. I pushed on it, trying to hold back the sound. My last meal had been yesterday morning. I patted down my pockets, hoping I'd missed half an old Hershey bar somewhere. Nothing. I wondered what the weather would hold for the morrow. During daylight, the skies so far had proved too overcast for planes to fly in and drop supplies. If we were ever going to make it, we needed to see some blue sky soon.

Another twig snapped. I rolled over in a flash and peered out into the dark. The wind was beginning to pick up. Maybe it was only that. Far off to my right, a branch moved. Didn't look like wind. I brought my rifle up, put my finger on my trigger, and aimed into the falling snow. I wondered if I should call out. Couldn't remember the passwords. Maybe it was Bill Kiehn again. A gust of wind blew. Blackness grabbed out at me. I wheeled around. Popeye had me by the ankle.

"Get some sleep, Shifty," he said. "I'll stay up for a while."

I felt the tension all through my shoulders. "Yeah. Yeah, maybe you're right." I cradled my rifle near my chin and shoved my hands up into my sleeves.

It felt good knowing a man like Popeye had your back. There were plenty of good men just like him joined in this fight. Easy Company wasn't alone in the woods. Far from it. Lieutenant Winters had set up battalion headquarters behind us some distance, at the south edge of the woods. That thought was comforting—having a good officer and his overall command so close. Then, I knew the fellas in Dog Company were some distance south of us. They were real hard fighters, too. All the men in Third Battalion were dug in north of us, and I think the men from First Battalion were over near a town called Noville. We were all of us surrounding the town of Bastogne, maybe ten thousand Allied troops total. That was the picture—surrounded. We were around the town, and a larger ring of Germans surrounded us. Someone guessed it was four to one odds in favor of the Germans. But that didn't bother us none. As paratroopers, we were used to being dropped smack-dab in the middle of the enemy.

I could just make out some of the features of Popeye's and my foxhole. We'd made it real good. It had a little shelf and we'd put some logs over it for artillery cover. We'd strung up boughs over the logs to keep out the falling snow. Every time we breathed, our breath came out white. Icicles pointed down from the roof of our foxhole. Digging a hole in the Ardennes the first day we had arrived proved rough. That ground was so cold, you know, it was hard to get your shovel through. But it's funny how quick a man will get his shovel moving if he thinks he's about to be shelled. Nothing came at us right away that first day, but we could hear the rumble of artillery in the distance, the crisp *rat-a-tat-tat* of a machine gun from time to time. Earl McClung was some distance away letting a guy named Don King dig the foxhole for the both of them. Bill Kiehn and Sergeant Taylor sweated nearby on their holes. Skip Muck, Alex Penkala, and George Luz had built a giant foxhole beyond us a ways and it was a fine sight to see. It seemed like forever ago we'd started in on those foxholes, but it was only a day or so back.

A twig snapped again. No mistaking it this time. Popeye tensed and brought his rifle up. I slithered out of my sleeping bag and brought my rifle up beside his. Our eyes darted through the forest. The wind shoved the branches around. It was getting close to daylight. Another twig snapped. "Who's there?" I said.

"Shifty, Popeye, it's me," came a hushed whisper. Sergeant Taylor crawled over and slid into our foxhole, bringing a shower of snow with him. "Breakfast is here. Cooks brought up some soup from Bastogne. It's over in a jeep near headquarters." He looked around our foxhole with an admiring eye. "By the way, Lieutenant Shames reminded us to tell you guys to save your ammo. No firing at anything, except to repel a major attack. Got it?"

I nodded. The sky was just growing gray. Popeye had slumped down against my sleeping bag. He was breathing into his neck and looked like he might doze off again. I slapped his shoulder, and we slid out of the foxhole and hiked silently back through the woods to where the jeep was parked. A few other guys milled around, rifles in hand. We fished out our mess kits, and the cook ladled out a scoop of soup into each cup. "Sorry," he said. "All you get." The beeflike broth had a few beans in it and went down cold as I drank it. Joe Lesniewski finished his soup just after me. I glanced down at his feet, remembering he'd left Mourmelon without any boots. His feet were wrapped in burlap bags.

A guy named Frank Mellett bumped my shoulder on his way up to the chow line. I was about to say something when he turned at me and scowled. "Waddayou staring at?" he snarled.

I don't know why that boy aggravated me so. He was a fine soldier and one of the original Toccoa men, but our personalities didn't mesh. Mellett was from up North, Brooklyn, I think, and we talked different. Others liked him okay—he was a good friend of Hank Zimmerman, and Hank was a real swell kid. It was just that Mellett went his way, and I went mine. That's the way we liked it.

I decided to keep quiet and head back to my foxhole. Popeye followed, blowing into the openings near the wrists of his thin GI gloves. The wind picked up even more as daylight dawned. A great icy blast flew through the corridors of the trees. Nearly cut a man in two, that wind. Snow had stopped at the chow line but started falling again, and the wind erased our tracks as we hiked. We crawled back into our foxhole and peered into the woods. Branches swayed against the wind. I reached up to scratch behind my ear and brushed off an icicle from a pine bow over our hole. The icicle slid down my neck.

"My hands are damn near ready to fall off," Popeye said at a whisper. "I don't know if they'll ever get warm again." I looked over at my friend. Popeye's arms were crossed and his hands were under his armpits. He uncrossed his arms and slapped his knees twice. "Shifty, did you hear a British pilot was shot down over Bastogne last week and captured by the Krauts?"

I shook my head, shivering.

"Yeah," Popeye continued. "So the poor fella survives but really gets messed up on the jump down. The Kraut doctor who treats him in the prison camp has got to hack off one of his legs."

I rearranged my back against the foxhole and eyed him closer.

"Well, the Limey must be really studying the situation," said Popeye, "because he says to the Kraut doctor, 'After you take my leg off, can you have one of your bombers drop it over London on your next raid?' The Krauts think he's a real loony but say okay. A few days later, gangrene sets in and they got to cut off his other leg. The Limey pilot asks the same thing, and the Krauts agree. Poor fella's really had it, and next they got to hack off an arm, and he asks the same thing. Again, the Krauts agree and drop his arm over England. . . . Hold on, Shifty, I got an idea, I'll be back in a minute." Popeye crawled out of the foxhole. I glanced up. He had his fly open and was urinating on his hands. He crawled back in a few minutes later and shot me a dirty look. "Goddam, Shifty, but that cooked my hands up real nice. You gotta give it a try."

I shuddered but almost grinned. "You were telling me about that pilot fella?"

"Ah yeah," Popeye said. "Finally, they have to amputate his last arm, and the Limey asks the same thing. But this time the Kraut commander comes to tell him off—" Popeye screwed up his face and puffed out his chest, doing his best imitation of an angry German officer. "'Nein!' says the Kraut commander. 'Ve cannot do zis! Ve suspekt you are trying to escape!'"

We both sniggered.

A twig snapped again. We grabbed our rifles in a flash and peered into the gray light. "Glad you got some chow," Sergeant Taylor said, as he crawled into our foxhole. His face was grim. "It's been too damn quiet out there this morning. Let's go cross over the road and see what we can see." Popeye and I nodded. I didn't know how much sense it made to go looking for a fight, but Sergeant Taylor was always levelheaded in these matters. The three of us crawled out of the hole and started working from tree to tree over to the area where we guessed the Germans were.

The snow was crisp, you know, and I worried about the little crunch it made every time we set a foot down. I was out in front as scout and we were some distance away from our foxhole when I noticed movement ahead of me that didn't look like wind. Working closer to another tree, I ducked down, motioning for the others to do the same. A man with a hooded padded parka shuffled around in the snow, maybe a hundred yards away. With his right hand he carried his assault rifle at the trigger. Over his left shoulder he'd slung a Panzerfaust 60, a big rifle-like tube able to shoot a hole through a tank. Two other men milled about nearby: one sitting and smoking, one standing and fidgeting with his ammo belt. A group of five other Germans worked near a clump of trees maybe fifty yards back, hauling boxes of ammunition and supplies, I guessed. I'd seen enough. I worked my way back to Popeye and Sergeant Taylor.

"So, that confirms it," Sergeant Taylor said slowly, after I'd told him what I'd seen. "The Krauts are our next-door neighbors, all right." We turned around and headed back to our hole, expecting the worst.

We went on more reconnaissance patrols that afternoon. Didn't see anything then except some smoke in the distance. That night me and another fella were sent to the edge of the woods, to the outpost foxholes. He'd sleep for a spell while I listened, then we'd trade off, and so on, every two hours throughout the night. It got miserable cold in that listening post. That boy I was with, well, might have been two in the morning and he decided he's gonna have a smoke, so he sparked up his lighter. Nearly lit up the whole sky, and

I dang near walloped him. I'm sure the Krauts were watching us, but nothing happened. Maybe they were taking a nap.

The next morning greeted us with another scoopful of soup by the jeep, a little less food than the day before, a little colder. Another patrol happened that morning. Another that afternoon. A few days went by that way. Patrols in the day. Outpost at night. Sometimes we'd see some Krauts and they'd see us. We'd fire a bit and they'd fire a bit, but it wasn't much. Sometimes at night they started up their tanks. They didn't sound like they were moving anywhere, just rumbling the engines, trying to scare us.

A few mornings later there was no soup by the jeep, just a box of K-rations per man. I ate my crackers and Hershey bar with a gloved hand then headed back to my foxhole and tried to nap. Ten minutes later I got sent out on a patrol and heard a rifle crack but it wasn't nothing. A few hours later I came back. I kept my spare change of socks around my neck so they'd dry from body heat. Snow had melted into the leather of my boots, and my feet were soaked. I took off my wet socks and put on my dry ones. Even my dry ones were a little damp. For a moment I got to studying my feet, sockless in the snow. They were bone white, with little hints of black beginning at the toes. I put my socks and wet boots back on and lay down. I didn't sleep.

A few hours later, Sergeant Taylor slid by and told me to go out on patrol again. I never dreamed of refusing an order, you know. I grumbled a bit, but I never refused an order. I hiked out into the woods with a few other guys, listening for every snap of a twig. Don't know what was wrong with my head this time. Every few feet I kept shaking the fog out of my ears. My eyes wanted to close. Sounds buzzed all around, but it wasn't nothing important. I fought to stay alert. We kept hiking. We heard a few shells every once in a while, a few rounds from a rifle. But it was mostly quiet.

Some days passed. I don't remember the date, mid-December maybe, but me and two boys were out on patrol. The mercury had dipped even lower. Coldest winter in Belgium's history, said someone, and I guessed he was right, because that winter wind sliced straight through our jackets as we worked our way through the woods.

We were some distance from our foxholes when we heard a sudden snap and a buzz through the air. I knew a German 88 shell had been fired our direction. There were no holes near us. No good cover to speak of. We flattened ourselves against the snow and mashed our faces into the frost. The shell landed twenty feet away with a thud. It stuck into the ground and stayed there, straight up and spinning. Must have spun for five minutes. Then all was quiet.

A huge swallow went down my throat. I stood up, brushed off the snow, and glanced at the other guys. The shell was a dud. They stood up after a bit, and we kept going, working our way through the trees again. I got to studying about that shell and wondered who'd made it in the factory. Probably slave labor, I figured, and maybe some person had made that shell into a dud on purpose. That thought almost got me to grinning. Wherever that fella was, he'd done the one thing he could to help out, you know. He saved my life, whoever he was.

Days came and went. Most seemed the same, you know. Bitter cold. Constant shivering. Dark skies. Aching feet. I lost track of time. A shell came in now and again in daylight and burst in the trees, raining splinters, limbs, trunks, and pieces of metal down on us. The Krauts also liked to shell us at night, you know, just every so often to keep a man awake. It was strange: after a while it felt like I could sleep anywhere I wanted. But when I tried to sleep, I couldn't. The aggravation was enough to send a fella shaky. You'd hear of a man now and again who'd shoot himself in the foot, just so he'd get sent off the line. It seemed like we were all becoming a little that way. One morning I walked past a man's foxhole, and a German corpse lay over top of it, frozen stiff. The GI wormed his way out, his eyes blurry, and gave me a level stare. "Made damn good insulation last night," he said with a shrug, and hiked over to the jeep for a K-ration.

One day we were just sitting in our foxholes when the clouds parted. It was such an unfamiliar sight. All around us gleamed bright, cold, blue sunlight. In a few jiffies, some of our planes flew overhead and dropped supplies. We ran out to the field to get them, dodging bullets that came our way. Not much food. Not much warmer clothes. I think each man got two boxes of K-rations. I hadn't eaten in about a day and wanted to wolf both of mine, but didn't know when food would come again, so I figured I'd make things last. At least some fresh ammo fell out of the sky. I guessed that's mainly all we needed. We were in business again.

It seemed funny to think that Christmas was only a few days away. Wouldn't be any presents wrapped with a bow this year. Instead, we hiked out to another spot near a road. Not a lot of trees around this time. We knew the Germans were on one side of a road. We were on the other.

Walter Gordon, the smart fella from down South, crouched behind his machine gun, a huge towel wrapped around his head to keep out the cold. His assistant machine gunner was a new fella; I couldn't remember his name. McClung and Sergeant Taylor were nearby. Hayseed Rogers and Jim Alley lay crouched in the snow. We were all listening, all frozen stiff, all staring at the other side of the road to where the Germans were.

Crack! A bullet whizzed over and Gordon collapsed, shot through the shoulder. We opened up into the other side of the road, searching for the sniper with our triggers. Mortar fire. Machine guns. Artillery. Whatever we had, we gave them.

Rogers and Alley rushed over to Gordon, hauled him out of his hole and dragged him back into the woods where it was safer. Out of the corner of my eye I saw Sergeant Taylor and McClung sprint across the road, probably in the direction they'd seen men running, probably searching for a better sight line of fire. I still saw targets from where I was, so I stayed put. We whaled bullets into the trees for some time, shooting everything that moved. I know I got a couple. Then it was quiet.

McClung and Taylor hiked back a short while later. McClung sat down beside me. "Didn't I tell ya I was a fast runner," McClung said. "I ran so fast I plumb outran the Krauts."

Sergeant Taylor crouched beside us. He slugged McClung in the arm. "Ole One Lung ran so fast, he ran straight by this one guy. Then he realizes what he's done, stops running and turns around, and the German's standing there with a thirty-round machine gun pointed at his head."

"Misfired," McClung said. "Otherwise, I'd be a goner."

Sergeant Taylor nodded. "I was behind a little ways and saw what was happening. We finished him off. Then we hiked over to his machine gun to take a look. The German's gun's chamber had rusted. The bolt only went halfway in and stuck on him."

McClung grinned.

"Looks like you guys did okay, too," Sergeant Taylor added, but he wasn't smiling when he said this part. "Just before we came back over, we counted twenty-three German bodies on the other side of the road."

I didn't quite know what I thought about that. I was mighty happy that McClung was still alive. We'd done our jobs, sure. We were holding the line. But I didn't know what I thought about the rest.

On Christmas morning we trudged back to the jeep and held out our canteen cups. They'd found some old brown beans and made a stew. Must have found 'em in a cave in Bastogne somewhere, because bugs crawled around the bottom of that stew. Well, it was something in your stomach.

A note went around that day from company headquarters. Seemed the German commander had sent a message to our general, telling him to surrender. Real pleased about himself, he was, like he was doing us a favor or something. Our general was so aggravated by the German's message he didn't rightly know what to do at first. Finally he sent back a runner with just one word: "Nuts!" Well, I'm not sure if the German commander could interpret what that one word meant or not. But any of us could see plain as day it was one man's way of telling another man to go to hell. We all got a good kick out of that, we did.

A couple days later I was out on patrol near Noville and spotted a tree that hadn't been there before. It was maybe a mile away, but I'd memorized the line of foliage the day before and knew what I saw. A little gully ran down left-handed, you know, and I could look off to my left and see that gully and a fence line. Well, that tree was brand-new. So I went back and reported to Sergeant Lipton. He brought out his binoculars and studied the spot. Sure enough, the tree moved. Krauts were bringing in gun barrels—88s, the sergeant guessed, big artillery pieces, firepower that could bring down a plane. Sergeant Lipton got on his radio and described the target to some upper brass back in Bastogne. They gave the okay, and we brought in our artillerymen. They gave a few blasts and scattered those big German guns. Pretty soon the place where that new tree had been staked was completely deserted. I felt fine about that. Maybe saved some lives. I don't know.

New Year's Day 1945 came, and for a few moments sitting there in my foxhole in the snow I got to studying if maybe it was the last New Year's I'd ever see. Then I shook that fool thought out of my head and went out on patrol.

The snow stood about knee deep that day, and anywhere a man hiked proved a real chore. We took the odd shelling now and then, just random, you know, enough to make us all tense. We hiked around in circles. Come evening, a few Kraut planes flew over and dropped bombs on us. Wasn't much. Joe Toye took a piece of shrapnel in his wrist and went to an aid station. We all knew a man as tough as him would be back before long. Sure enough, Joe Toye hiked back to his foxhole a while later, his rifle tucked under one arm, his other arm in a sling.

I wished I could sleep, you know. But I never really did. My head started feeling funny most every day, all day and all night. My body felt elsewhere. I kept having these dreams, I think, powerful, angry dreams in the midst of the occasional nap. Ghosts were in the woods. They were floating around, murmuring to me with nonsense words, making me feel all hollow inside. I was carrying my rifle in my dreams, but if I'd have been a little boy, it was the type of fright that would have woke me and sent me running to my parents' bedroom. I wanted to burrow like a rabbit; be snug in a den underground. I never wanted to leave my hole, you know. It was only safe to be under the earth.

A few days later we'd been out on patrol for some time and were all feeling mighty miserable. If only we weren't so tired, you know, maybe it'd be easier to think straight. We were hiking back to our holes in the woods above Foy, all us in Second and Third Platoons, when whoever was calling the shots decided to hike back through an open field as a shortcut, hoping to make it back to our foxholes before dark, I guess.

I started thinking this wasn't a good idea, you know, us all walking across an open field like that. But on we went. It felt spooky out in the middle of that field. I thought back to Lieutenant Brewer and how he'd got shot by a sniper in that open field just before we went into Eindhoven. I slowed my breathing, focusing on everything around me. My eyes were peeled. That was the way I always hiked in a combat zone. Through my head ran a list of places to go. A little rise was over to my left. An old log stuck out of the snow near my right. If the shelling came, where could I duck? Where could I hide? As I passed each point, I picked out the next.

We were nearly to the edge of the woods when I started thinking we were going to make it. I felt happy for a moment, then I almost slapped myself. We weren't safe. Why didn't the man ahead know that? Those Krauts could track our positions all across that field and zero in their artillery. What were we thinking? We were just so damn tired, you know. So damn tired.

I was still thinking this when Popeye and I crawled into our foxhole. I noticed George Luz some distance away and wondered what he was doing. He wasn't in a hole yet. My eyes closed. If only we weren't so tired.

I didn't hear the first shell coming. It exploded off a tree off to my right and sent down a firestorm of splinters and lead. Another shell raced in like a boxcar, hit the ground and exploded. The sound was deafening. Terrifying. One by one they followed. *Whisssst-bam!* Over and over again. All around me, the ground rocked and pitched.

All was quiet. Very sudden-like, the shelling had stopped. A man moaned from somewhere. "Medic," he said. "Medic." It was Joe Toye.

"I'll get ya!" came a yell. Bill Guarnere was going after him. My tongue felt tied in a knot. I wondered if that was exactly what those Krauts wanted us to do—think all was okay and crawl out of our holes searching for survivors. That way they could shellac the lot of us. Guarnere and Toye were too far away to hear me yell.

Kablam! The earth shook. *Wham!* Another shell hit. *Crack!* A tree burst into flames and fell over. I heard yelling. Screaming. I wondered if George Luz was still out there. Again and again the shells flew in. *Whissst-bam!* One after another. I glanced up. The sky was alight with enemy artillery fire. Must have been thirty thousand mortars and rounds in the air, everything all mixed together. It was like someone had been lugging around a coal car of fireworks and it suddenly caught fire. For the next chunk of time, everything went off—88s and naval guns, grenades, and screaming meemies, those rockets bundled together that screamed so loud it pierced your ears. The sky rocked and heaved. The ground shook. There was nothing to do but sit and take it.

When the smoke cleared, I sat for a moment, dazed. Popeye and I crawled out of our hole. I didn't know whether to holler or run or start shooting or go back in the ground. What struck me at first were the trees. It was like some giant drunken logger had slashed over our heads with his chainsaw. He'd torn through trees at random, busting them in half, setting others on fire. They smoldered frozen in the winter air.

I took a step forward, trying to listen. Were there any more shells? What was coming next? I took another step. Another. I saw men lying on the ground. Blood pooled on the snow. It soaked out in a circle, red and black.

Joe Toye lay on the ground with his leg blown to bits, just hanging from his body. He was bleeding from the chest, head, arms, and saying, "I'm hit. I'm hit," in this real soft voice. Bill Guarnere lay some distance away. He was a mess of blood. They were both conscious and calm, no screaming or yelling. Joe was shaking, you know, and Bill was trying to light a cigarette even though his leg wasn't there anymore. I saw Lipton, Malarkey, Heffron, and Doc Roe run over. I felt out of it, you know, stunned. I didn't know how to rightly sort it out. I found my head finally, and we worked for some time, there in the snow. Stretcher bearers took Joe and Bill away.

Right after that is when Lieutenant Compton was evacuated to the hospital. Well, I didn't ask why. A few rumors flew that maybe he'd gone shaky. But I didn't believe that. An officer as good as Lieutenant Compton would never have snapped under the stress. Even as bad as it was. I think the man's feet just got to him. They were hurting him awful bad. That's what I believed.

A few days later we were clearing the woods west of Foy and resistance seemed light. We hiked to where we were supposed to be and dug in, then the Krauts started shelling us almost immediately. It was the same sort of horror. Huge bursts. Whole trees falling over. The air awash with flames.

After the smoke cleared, someone called for Skip Muck. He didn't answer. Someone else called for Alex Penkala. He didn't answer either. George Luz usually shared a foxhole with them. Maybe it was his voice I heard. Maybe he had dived for cover in a different hole this time.

I crawled out of my hole and worked my way through the trees. The voice was still calling, still looking. *"Skip! Alex!"*

George Luz was digging. He was on his knees in the snow with his helmet off. He was using the helmet to scoop away dirt. There was franticness to his motion. He stopped digging, sat back on his heels, then looked to the side and held his gaze away. His eyes were ringed with dark circles. His hands were filthy and bloody. He picked up something from out of the dirt, but I couldn't see what.

"Luz?" I said.

He shook his head. Others gathered around. They knew.

"Luz?" I asked again. I looked closer. In his hands he held a small corner of a sleeping bag.

Sergeant Taylor came over. "Shifty," he said. His voice was husky. "C'mon. Help me out over here."

There were no bodies. Just a few parts. A shell had flown in and landed directly on Alex and Skip's foxhole. Everything was gone.

A man can't quite get that through his head. No. He can't.

I thought about Skip Muck, the heart and soul of Easy Company. When we were back in Aldbourne, he had taken Joe Lesniewski under his wing and made him part of the group. I thought about Alex Penkala, how you'd often see him writing little letters to his sisters. He'd read me one of them once. It was a cheery note, you know, asking his sisters to send him cookies, promising he'd write again soon.

I helped out doing whatever I could do for a while. Then I brushed away the snow and sat on a stump. I thought about praying, but I didn't know how to put anything into words. I wished I could go home. I wished we all could.

Then I went back to my foxhole in the woods in the snow in the ground. My feet were aching and frozen. My stomach hollow and tight.

11

FOY

Another cold front skulked in, and Captain Dick Winters nicked the skin of his neck. I shook my head in disbelief. It was twenty degrees below zero, and the man was shaving. From where I stood near the chow line, I watched him shiver under a tree, wiping lather and blood off his face, and I got to studying that. I reckoned an officer who kept his face clean shaven during Belgium's coldest winter in thirty years must want his men to know he's still the toughest son of a gun around, you know, that his resolve is still strong and you can still follow him anywhere he goes. He probably also wants his men to realize that they're all going to be staying in that location for a while, as miserable as it is, so they should make the best of it. I scratched the stubble on my chin as the cook sloshed half a cup of bean soup into my steel cup.

Dawn was breaking and the wind bit us. We'd been outside in the snow for a month, maybe five weeks, I didn't know. Time didn't mean much to me. I finished my soup, hiked back to my foxhole, peered around a bit, then headed out to the edge of the forest and slid into an outpost hole.

I stuck an unlit cigarette in my mouth and came near to grinning at the thought of my morning routine. From where I sat, I looked out across this big open field and could see about a mile. Cold green trees and little scrubby brown and reddish trees poked their ways out of the snow. It was not a nice bright red, the color of those trees, but a dead, cold red.

Sure enough, there he was. Every morning like clockwork, far off in the distance, a German crawled out of his foxhole and hiked around a knoll with a bucket. Every morning he did the same thing. The snow made everything hazy and I squinted, dull even as the gray light was. I could barely see the man. But he was there again. Maybe he was going to get chow. Maybe he was going to do his business. I didn't rightly know, but it didn't matter. He'd disappear before long, I knew that much. But there was always about ten good seconds where he was wide open.

This morning, I figured he'd grown too comfortable. I wasn't grinning at that, mind you, because I knew what I needed to do. As far away as he was, I brought my rifle to my shoulder anyway and got me a bead on his position. He walked toward the knoll. I fired. The bullet took forever. I stuck my head out from the side of my rifle and watched it fly. A soft *pop* hit the snow maybe twenty yards in front of him. I'd shot too low. I don't know if the German even noticed the bullet hit.

Well, he was gone in a jiffy, so I watched for a while longer, then worked my way back to my hole. For the rest of the day I chewed on the angle of that bullet, the distance it needed to cover. We weren't doing much that day besides: a patrol here, a patrol there, we fired a few rounds at them, they fired a few rounds at us. All day long the wind whistled around our ears. It seemed like everywhere you hiked these days, you'd see a dead body. Ours, theirs. A civilian once in a while. Horses. Cattle. Death was all over. Men just moved around the corpses and kept going. Everybody in the company seemed scabbed over by now, pretty shaky, you know. This one replacement had been crying in his foxhole ever since that last night of hard shelling. I didn't blame a kid for feeling that way, but I feared all the noise he was making. I felt like bawling myself sometimes, but somehow I just kinda picked up and kept going. I don't mean all that bloodshed hadn't affected me. But I took each day as it came, you know, doing the one thing ahead of me that needed doing. That was all I knew to do.

The next morning I got up, hiked to the edge of the woods, and, sure enough, the same German crawled out of his foxhole. I took my rifle, aimed twenty feet above the top of his head this time, fired, and peered around the edge of my rifle again. Well, that German jumped, squiggled, and took off flying. I couldn't rightly say for sure that I'd hit the man, but the next morning after that when I hiked to the edge of the woods, he wasn't there.

It seems like a man will do anything when he's tired and hungry enough. One afternoon McClung shot a jackrabbit and cooked it. It stunk like hell, but we were all starved so we passed it around. Lieutenant Shames had just come in from a patrol, and McClung gave him a real big piece because he was so cold. He was glad to have it.

Our exhaustion and hunger acted out in different ways, too. One night Popeye needed to shake me awake for fear of the noise I was making in my dreams. I lay there afterward, my teeth chattering, the dark closing in around me. I hated this place. These woods with their icy wind. So much killing. So much dying. I'd never felt so strongly aggravated about a piece of God's green nature before, and I was sure it must be green sometimes, but I plumb despised this snowy hellhole we were in. All I'd ever take from this place was cold memories, a lot of miserable memories, the kind of memories that a man shoves out of his mind if he can.

Then there was this: one evening after it grew dark, word came round to get ready because we were taking the town of Foy the next morning. Popeye and I figured we'd catch some winks before the action, you know, so we covered our foxhole with pine boughs, same as always. It seemed only an instant, I don't know, but I was gone far away from my foxhole, far in the darkness, walking in one of those dream countries where everything looks exactly as you know it. Same pine trees. Same frozen creeks. Same shiver down your spine.

Frank Mellett, that fella who'd bumped my shoulder in the chow line, lurked behind a tree. He popped out, real slow, brought his rifle up to eye level, and pointed at me. He shot first, but I ducked. I scrambled around, searching for my rifle in the black-ness. I couldn't find it. When Mellett slunk out from behind the tree again, I gripped my pistol with both hands, aimed between his eyes, and pulled the trigger. *Blam!* He fell over in the snow. *Blam!* I shot him again. He didn't move.

Morning dawned, and I crawled out of my foxhole, looked around, but couldn't see a soul. It shook me a minute. Maybe we'd been attacked during the blur of sleep, and I was the only man left standing. It had snowed again, and in front of me were huge mounds of white. It looked like I was standing in a cemetery. In a few minutes, Rogers popped out of one of those mounds like he was coming up out of a grave. At least I knew then I wasn't all alone. He hiked over. "Who was doing that shooting last night, Shifty?" he said.

"I dunno. I didn't hear any shooting."

He shrugged and started hiking over to the jeep. I stood motionless, my heart in my throat. I'd brought with me up to Bastogne a little old 7.65 pistol, and when Rogers was out of sight, I pulled it out of its holster and looked at it. Rounds were hard to get for those, so I knew exactly how many I had. Two were missing. Sure enough, I'd fired my pistol twice during the night. It was for real.

My forehead got scrunchy and I started breathing hard through my nose. I shook my head, trying to get a clearer picture of what had happened. Maybe I'd been sleepwalking. I might have jerked that old pistol out and shot it unaware. Then a horror gripped me—I'd killed Frank Mellett in my sleep. It hadn't been a dream after all. I'd killed one of our own men.

Some distance away, the pine boughs parted and a familiar figure slid out of his foxhole. He scowled my direction and slunk back through the woods. Frank Mellett wasn't bleeding anywhere. He was just as alive as I was, so I guessed I hadn't shot him after all. I let out a big sigh of relief. I didn't know what exactly had happened during the night, but I was sure tickled to death to see Frank Mellett up and walking.

Well, we grouped up and headed toward Foy the roundabout way, you know, so it wouldn't be obvious to the enemy. It was still early in the day, and Third Platoon moved forward in a line through this wooded area. Another platoon was ahead of us and came across a big log-covered bunker. We caught up and looked around, reckoning it was a German sentry outpost, so we crouched low. A couple fellas from the other platoon musta reckoned somebody was sleeping in that bunker, so they threw a couple hand grenades in.

I saw Sergeant Taylor slowly moving toward the bunker, his rifle raised. Something to my left moved. A German crawled out of a foxhole near the bunker. *Bang!* Sergeant Taylor's rifle went off. *Bang!* It went off again. The Kraut was dead.

We scouted the bunker. The dead German was the only one around, so we grouped up and prepared to continue through the woods. Sergeant Taylor walked over to where I was, a curious look in his eye. "You know, that wasn't such a smart move on my part," he said in a hush. "A dead soldier isn't going to tell you an awful lot. I should have kept him alive and sent him back for interrogation. Then we'd know what we were up against."

I nodded. That Sergeant Taylor was a smart fella. He was doing his job, but he always wanted to do it better. We moved on through the woods. It remained very quiet as morning grew to afternoon.

Maybe an hour later, Sergeant Taylor and I hiked over to the side to our right flank to see what was going and met up with some troopers from another company. As we stood there talking, a couple shots rang out at random. Sergeant Taylor winced. His leg buckled. Then he sat down hard. The bullet had peeled the flesh back, looked right to the nerves. We hollered for a medic.

"I can't feel my foot," Sergeant Taylor said with a grimace as the medic dumped sulfa on his wounds.

"It's a million dollars," I said, "this one's for sure."

He nodded, knowing what I was saying even before I did. He'd been wounded before, at least twice that I remembered, but he'd always healed to come back and join us. This one was his third strike—and he knew he was out. That bullet had really torn into his leg.

It dawned on me what I was saying, and what this truly meant. My voice went low. "Well," I said, but what I wanted to say wouldn't come out. I swallowed hard. "Say hello to Elaine for me," I choked out at last. That was his girlfriend back home. He'd told me about her plenty of times before. They loaded him on a stretcher to take him back to an aid station. I patted Sergeant Taylor on his shoulder. He gripped my hand a moment. He'd been there fighting alongside us since the beginning. At least Sergeant Taylor was going home alive.

The plan to take Foy seemed simple enough. The town was chock full of German tanks and artillery. All we had to do was charge across an open field, shove our way into the town, and throw grenades at every enemy we spotted. There was no great cunning involved.

Easy Company was picked to lead the attack. First Platoon got the order and started running across the field. We were close behind. We needed to get in there quick before the German mortars and artillery could come down on us. Halfway across the field I started to sweat. I hated open fields. We needed to keep moving. Whatever happened, we needed to get into the town. Bullets started winging in. You could hear the zing and the zang. There was nowhere to go but forward. The guns in First Platoon started getting mowed down. I heard men call for a medic. I saw Burr Smith go down. Frank Perconte lay in a pool of blood. Lieutenant Dike had stopped the platoon behind two haystacks for cover. Haystacks?! The lieutenant signaled for the Second and Third Platoons to hold up. It was the closest I've ever felt to receiving a suicide order. Why were we stopped?! We sat like fish in a barrel. Fire came at us from every window. The closest burned in from a building with a caved-in roof. It was too far away for me to find the sniper. We needed to get mortars on the roof of that building. We needed to keep moving forward.

Lieutenant Speirs was there. Real sudden-like. He was shouting orders. Getting things done. I didn't hear about this until later, but I guess Captain Winters was watching the carnage from up on the hill. He'd grabbed his M1 in his hand and begun to run toward the mess, but higher brass stopped him. He was a battalion man now, not someone who led the charge from the front. So Winters thought fast and relieved Foxhole Norman of his command on the spot. He put Lieutenant Ron Speirs in charge. This was the same lieutenant who'd been rumored to have shot twenty prisoners back in Normandy as they calmly smoked cigarettes. Lieutenant Speirs ran over to the haystack, took charge, and got the mortars humping, the machine gunners laying down a base of protective fire. We went forward.

Artillery set up a smoke barrage in the field. We were scattered out now, different squads going in one direction, others going another. There were maybe six or eight of us in my group. We ran forward into the town under smoke.

A horse barn lay in front of us. We ran up, made sure it was clear, and ducked inside. We had a good view from its windows. We could see most the rest of the town. It was up a bit on a hill from where we were. Another brick building squatted some distance down the street. A tiny puff of white breath, visible only because of the cold, blew from around the corner. It blew again. A flash of German coat sleeve showed, then ducked back. The breath blew again.

Jim Alley crouched next to me. He was a fine soldier. We called him Moe.

"Moe," I yelled. "We can get this guy. When he sticks his head out there again, you tell me." Moe nodded and took out his binoculars. I aimed at the spot the white puff came from and held my breath.

"He's there!" Moe shouted. "Now!"

A little flash of coat sleeve. A little flash of cheekbone. I pulled the trigger. The German crumpled in the snow.

We left the barn and sprinted up the side of the hill, through a vegetable garden and up toward town. We crouched from building to building. Small arms fire could be heard all through the town. We reached the side of bombed out building and glanced in the door. It must have been empty for a while. Ice stood where the floor used to be.

Most of us herded in and took cover while I stood near the doorway and two of our guys worked their way alongside the side of the building. They'd gone maybe thirty feet and had at least thirty more to go when it dawned on me how exposed they were. Come to think of it, I didn't have great position either. *Bang!* One of our guys went down. The next bullet was aimed at me. My feet flipped out from under me on that ice, and I slid right up under a window. More shots rang out. I glanced up then down again. The other man along the side of the building froze. The sniper kept firing. Our other guy didn't stand a chance unless we could get that sniper. I ducked up again to get a bead on where the sniper fired from. He was about sixty feet away, shooting from around the corner of a brick building. I ducked down again and propped my M1 up on the window ledge. Seven rounds were left in my clip. I didn't have time to properly aim. I fired from instinct, seeing in my mind the corner of that building where I guessed the German's head to be. *Blam. Blam. Blam. Blam.* The dust flew off the brick at the corner of the building. I fired all seven rounds.

No sound came from where the German sniper was. Our man found his feet again and checked the other man on the ground. The first man was dead. But the other was just fine. "Okay," I said with a nod. I thought maybe I saved that man's life. It felt good.

We left that building and came to a barn area. A big square yard sat to one side. McClung stormed through the door. Inside, the building was a shell, just roof and logs and a few partitions, but not finished. A lone German wheeled around, his hands up. He looked like a company clerk, and before anybody could get to him, he dived for the staircase and flung himself down. McClung followed. At the bottom was a door. McClung wrenched open the door, flung a concussion grenade inside, and slammed the door shut.

When the smoke cleared, we took twenty Germans prisoner. Two were dead. The basement was their command post.

More fighting came, more shooting. We took the town. I felt okay about that, but later, after we regrouped, Frank Mellett was missing. Someone asked where he was. The answer came. He was one of the ones who'd been mowed down when Lieutenant Dike was hiding behind that haystack. Frank Mellett was dead.

You know, I never liked the man, but I was awful sorry he was gone. I got to thinking that maybe if I'd actually shot him for real in my dream, oddly enough, maybe just winged him in the leg or arm, maybe he'd still be alive. But I couldn't think about that too much before another order came, and we needed to keep going.

Battles blurred after that. We were so tired by then, so hungry, so cold. More little towns, more fighting. Day after day. Noville. Rachamps. I saw some crazy sights. A German tank came up the road, and Lieutenant Shames and Moe Alley were out in the middle of that road looking like they were going to stop that tank by hand. They held their ground, under fire, for what seemed an impossible time. Finally, they moved back and let the tank go up. One of the bullets had gone through the stock of Alley's rifle. Then a P-47 zoomed down and knocked that tank out. That was a good show.

In Rachamps we huddled for a night in a convent. It was the first time we'd slept indoors since leaving Mourmelon. The sisters had a choir there and sang for us. Hymns. Spiritual songs about better places, better times. Their voices echoed off the walls while candles flickered in the warm indoor air. Most of the men sprawled on the pews, quietly munching on K-rations, listening. Me, I stared straight ahead. The sound in my ears was the sound of angels, so different from the gunfire we'd been hearing for so long. So different. I wanted the night to never end.

I guess near mid-January, maybe it was toward the end, the battle for Bastogne and its surrounding towns was declared over. This time we'd won. We got into trucks and headed back through Bastogne, down the road toward a train station. It didn't take many trucks to hold us. Numbers were thinner in every platoon. A platoon is usually forty men. Only eleven were left from the First.

We were going to Alsace, to a little town called Haguenau, about a hundred and sixty miles away on the border of France and Germany. We'd get a little time off, maybe get a shower and a change of clothes, but more fighting was right around the corner.

They put us in boxcars for the rest of the trip. The sun was breaking through the clouds, and straw lined the boxcars, but it was still very cold. Hayseed Rogers was platoon sergeant then and we shivered as we pulled into a little French town. "We got to have some heat," Rogers said.

Inside the train station was a fuddy-looking guy sitting around a big ole potbellied stove. McClung glanced at Rogers, turned to another guy, and told him to put on his gloves. They jumped out as the train chugged slowly along. They ran over to the station, marched right up to that stove, pried it loose, and lugged it back to our boxcar. It was still going full blast with the coal still in it. The fuddy-looking guy just sat there with a confused look on his face.

My, but that stove warmed us up nice. We were the only boxcar in that whole train with a potbellied stove. A little later the train picked up speed. A while after that we screeched into a railroad yard. Our stomachs were growling something fierce. McClung climbed out again, looked over the cars, and picked one he reckoned had good potential. He leveled his rifle and shot the lock off the railway car. Well, glory. It was stocked with 10-1 rations. Bacon, ground coffee. The works. He lugged a crate back to our car and we licked our chops. We hadn't had a good meal in nearly two months, but now we had a hot coal stove and bacon and coffee and we were still alive. We rode like kings all the way to Alsace.

12

MAYBE WE'LL ACTUALLY LIVE

Well, we kicked around on reserve for a short while, did our laundry, stood under lukewarm showers, ate some real chow, things like that. Then in early February 1945, we moved back to the line. We were defending this city called Haguenau, and I confess I didn't feel like doing much. Mornings, I'd get up, you know, light a smoke and eat some stew and run a toothbrush over my teeth, then clean my rifle and head out for outpost duty. I'd sit in the upper window of this building and peer out the broken glass at the enemy on the other side of the river and try to be alert, always looking, always listening. But I felt run-through, plowed, like a man after a hard day's work who only wants to climb the stairs to his porch and sit a spell.

Haguenau was maybe twenty thousand residents. It was French now, but depending on which war you'd been in, it'd been swapped back and forth between Germany and France a couple times. It was a strange way for us to hold the line. We camped in old houses on the bank of the Moder River, which ran between the two countries. Easy Company occupied the buildings on the south bank. The Germans held the position on the north bank. Shots were fired back and forth across the river, but mostly we were surrounded by this unsteady quietness.

I doubt it was an uncommon feeling, this weariness, at least among us old-timers. You'd notice exhaustion in the way men moved. Maybe a subtle groan when a soldier shouldered his rifle. A slower glance before a man crossed the street. The war was winding itself down. We were sure of it. We'd beat the Germans at Bastogne. Broke the enemy's back. And because of that, we all walked more carefully now than ever before. I think even the Germans felt this way. Didn't seem like they had much fight left. For us in Easy Company, a new hope stirred. It wasn't a carefree hope, one that fills a man with energy. But an undeclared hope that drives a man to caution. It's when you sense you might actually come through this thing alive.

Skinny Sisk fit this profile. I watched him out of the corner of my eye for a day or so and he acted more leery than I'd ever seen. Food wasn't real abundant for us in Haguenau, and one day Skinny came across a chicken, sprinted back to the bombed out house we were staying in, and we cooked it in the backyard over an open fire. We'd had a shipment of beer trucked in from somewhere, oddly enough in spite of the scarcity of food, and three bottles each was the ration. Skinny and me both sucked ours down, pulling apart that chicken, and I asked him why he had such a faraway look in his eyes. He spat out a chicken bone, eyed the question guardedly, and said, "Well, the man upstairs and me had words."

"Who—McClung?" It was One Lung's turn to watch across the river.

Skinny shook his head. "Nah, it was during all that shit we took in Bastogne. Shifty, I told God if I ever made it out of there alive, I'd become a rev'rund." He took the last sip of his beer, then opened another bottle.

Well, that was almost funny to hear. When I'd met Skinny back in Toccoa, he'd been the most foul-mouthed, hard-drinking, hard-living reprobate ever to enlist in Easy Company. I had a hard time ever picturing him as a preacher. All I said was "You?"

"Yeah. Why not?" Skinny poured the rest of his beer down his throat and wiped the grease from his hands on his pants. "Someday I'm gonna keep my promise to God." He frowned and added, "If only I could get some goddam sleep first."

I knew what he was talking about. Skinny had been a fine soldier all during the fighting. Back in Holland he'd led the charge a couple of times. He'd killed a lot of Krauts, seen a lot of blood. Experiences like those had a way of weighing heavy on a man's mind, I knew it for fact, especially at night when sleep was hard to come by.

Sergeant Carwood Lipton had changed, too, although his experience wasn't religious. The first day we got to Haguenau, I'd seen Sergeant Lipton sweating and chalk-eyed. He was running a powerful fever. There was talk floating around that they were gonna send Sergeant Lipton to the hospital, but he shook his head, you know, poured back some Schnapps, and said he was gonna go get a good night's sleep. Well, next morning his fever had cleared. Doc said he could stay on the line if he wanted. I was happy, because you hate to lose another good man, even to the hospital. Shortly after that, Captain Winters and Lieutenant Spiers gathered us around and gave Sergeant Lipton a battlefield commission. Made him an officer. I felt right proud of him, I did. Sergeant Lipton had always been there for us when we needed him. When Foxhole Norman was off looking at trees, Sergeant Lipton was the glue that held Easy Company together. No one deserved a battlefield commission more than him.

That was happy news, but I started sensing something different about Bill Kiehn, something unfamiliar and not so happy. He was an only child, you know, and maybe the tension of so many months on the front line was worming its way inside his head. He'd said more than once that his folks would be beyond devastated if anything ever happened to him. One morning he sidled into the basement where I stayed and handed me three potatoes. He'd found a sack somewhere and was passing them out to the men.

"Shifty, you make sure you keep eating," Bill said. "You're not looking healthy."

It was true. The day before I'd caught a glimpse of myself in a broken mirror in the house. My eyes were sunk into my face. Wrinkles ran up and down my forehead. My skin looked pasty and cold. I guess war ages a man. I was only twenty-one, but I looked about forty-five.

"Much obliged, Bill," I said, and took the potatoes. "These will make a real fine supper later on."

He eyed me suspiciously, almost like a mother might do when worrying about her son. "I mean it, Shifty," Bill said. "You be real careful, you hear. We're almost at the end of this thing."

Something caught in his voice when he said *careful*, but I couldn't quite put my finger on what he meant. I thought back to the early days at Toccoa, when Bill Kiehn started out. He was real ornery then. Came in with a chip on his shoulder. But Sergeant Buck Taylor had taken a little extra time with him, helped him out, you know, and Bill straightened out and settled in. He'd come home with me on leave that one time, back to Clinchco. When the fighting started, he'd become a man you could trust with a rifle. He fought with the company at every major battle we'd been through. By Haguenau, Bill Kiehn was one of the most dependable soldiers in the outfit, and I reckoned he'd become one of my best friends.

Well, one day stretched into the next. It snowed the first few days, but the snow didn't stick much, and soon trees branches showed bare against the gray sky. Roads grew muddy and wet. Buildings looked bombed and crumbling. Sounds from artillery fire could be heard sporadically from across the river, but there wasn't much action. The whole place was dismal. It was a paradise compared to Bastogne.

My squad was mostly stationed in this house with two stories up and a basement below. We always kept somebody on observation duty, always watching across the river. Upstairs, we darkened the background so nobody could see us, and whenever our turn came, we climbed the stairs and peered out the window, looking for things that needed looking for.

One morning from upstairs I saw a flash across the river, so I called the guys in artillery on the phone and told them a shell was coming. That shell exploded a street or two over but didn't do much damage. We fired back a round. About the time we fired our round, the Germans fired another. This one flew in and crashed in our backyard. No harm done, I figured, so I kept watching. I saw another of our shells explode on the other side. The guys in artillery phoned back and said, "How's that for range?" I told them it was fine. The Krauts were firing over and we were firing back. Nobody looked like they were hitting much of anything important, because both sides kept firing, so I guessed that it was a good day's work for everybody, come this strange season in the war.

A few days went by, and the Germans must have trucked in this big ole railway gun from some place, because one day when I was upstairs they fired something that didn't sound like anything I'd heard yet in Haguenau. See, when an 88 shell came through the air, it whistled downward, sort of like *fhwee-eee-eee-ee*, you know. But this new shell spiraled in with a *whoor-whoor-whoor-whoor*, like a truck starting up. It came slow, too, so slow I had enough time to run downstairs to the basement before it hit. It was safer in the basement. We all knew that.

The Germans must have liked that ole railway gun, because as soon as I got down to that basement and all was safe, I climbed back upstairs, and right away another big ole shell started flying my way, *whoor-whoor-whoor.* I sprinted downstairs again. This one hit the street behind us and exploded. No worries, so right back upstairs I went. I watched for another while, and still another big ole shell flew in. Back down the stairs I ran. It exploded in the next-door yard. Right back upstairs I went. That went on for most the rest of the afternoon. Me just running up and down the stairs, laughing and cursing at the ceiling every time the ground shook and the plaster rained down.

One night we got word that the upper brass wanted to send a patrol across the river to capture prisoners. None of the fellas were much happy about this. I didn't say much, 'cause I figured they'd probably pick me whether I said anything or not. But McClung got picked as scout instead. So I felt sorry for McClung, but knew he could handle himself. About fifteen, sixteen men total were going, and most of the rest of us were ordered to help out alongside the river. Fine by me.

As soon as it got black outside, a rope was stretched across the water. The men climbed into rubber boats and started to pull themselves across hand by hand. One boat capsized, and the fellas in the frosty water made a bunch of splashing noise. I had my finger on the trigger, aimed at the other side, but nothing stirred over there.

The rest of the fellas got over okay. Wasn't more than five minutes later we heard a rifle grenade. Explosions. For about a minute gunfire burst all over the place, then I saw the team hustle back into their boats and begin to paddle back. Everything opening up around them. Machine guns. Huge blasts. The Krauts weren't none too happy, and we fired everything we had back at them across the river.

As soon as our men reached the bank, it looked like they'd got their two prisoners all right. They were stern-looking suckers with tight mouths. McClung gave me the thumbs-up sign as he scrambled up the bank, but he shook his head, too. One of our men was hurt bad. There was a lot of yelling and shouting and they carried him up: Private Jackson. His face and chest were covered with blood and he was screaming, "Kill me! Kill me! Christ, I can't stand it." It looked like he caught a grenade fragment in his head. Doc Roe ran up, stuck a morphine syrette in Jackson, and tried to get the bleeding to stop as we started carrying him back to the outpost. He twitched for twenty or thirty feet, but was motionless before we got him indoors. A man covered the dead man's face with a wool blanket, and we put away the stretcher. I thought about how Eugene Jackson was just twenty years old. He'd lied about his age to go into the Army. He'd been a good soldier with a lot of life ahead of him, and now he was gone.

Our guards took the prisoners back to battalion headquarters. I hoped those prisoners would say a lot, but somehow I doubted they would. A man at my level isn't paid to think, but I got to studying that situation and I concluded that patrol had been plumb useless. Two prisoners for the life of one of our men. And what were the prisoners going to talk about? How the war was winding down? How they were sorry they'd been captured? How they'd had cold coffee and stale bread that morning for breakfast?

We were right angry when word came around the next night that upper brass wanted more prisoners still. None of us relished the thought of yet another patrol. We sat around in our basement for a while cursing the Army. Men smoked and ate stew. I cleaned my weapon. I was pretty sure I'd need to go out on this patrol tonight. I wondered if I should try to doze a bit, but my adrenaline was running high, so I walked around the basement, you know, trying to get my head clear. I ate a canteen cup full of stew and lay on a bunk for a while, but I wasn't sleeping.

The clock ticked near the time we were to go. Dick Winters came in to brief us. He'd become a major now, and I was real happy for the man. I knew such a stupid order as the second patrol had never come from him. We ten-hupped, thanks to the bushy-tailed ways of a new officer who was going out with us on the patrol as an observer, then stood at ease. Major Winters walked around the basement a moment. He took off his helmet and cleared his throat. "Colonel Sink is proud of the patrol that went on last night," he said. "Real proud. So proud we'll need to go further into town this time, since the outpost on the edge of the river was destroyed last night."

I looked around the room. The men's faces were alert. We were ready to go of course, but eyes registered weariness, and maybe some of the stuff we'd been thinking after last night. I lit a cigarette.

Major Winters must have been looking, too. Or maybe he'd already thought through his plan long in advance, because he sort of rubbed his forehead with his hands, then said in a husky whisper: "Here's what I want you to do. Go get some sleep. In the morning you will report to me that you made it across the river to German lines but were unable to secure any live prisoners. Understand?" He looked around the room again. A few eyebrows lifted. A few grins twitched. Mouths hung open.

"Yes, sir," someone finally said on our behalf.

Major Winters turned to go, paused, then turned back to us and said, "We're moving off the line in a day or two. No sense anybody else getting killed at this point."

I caught his full meaning. I think we all did. Major Winters could think things through plainly, and he was always looking out for his men. That second patrol never happened. Word came back to us the next day that a bogus report had been written up. None of us would ever say a thing about it, that was for sure. I felt a new sense of optimism, thinking we might all make it home alive after all.

It was maybe our last full day in Haguenau. Maybe we had another day to go. We ate some breakfast, and Bill Kiehn had come off duty. He said he needed to take care of some things, then maybe later he'd take a nap in the basement of one of the empty houses. I don't think I said much in return. It was just part of a normal conversation one man might have with another when he comes in from duty.

I finished up whatever I was eating and climbed the stairs in our house to take my shift on outpost duty. For some time I didn't see or hear a thing. I peered out the window at the quiet enemy on the other side of the river. Morning stretched toward midday.

When an artillery shell flew in, it seemed like any other normal shell. It blasted a building down the street a ways. I radioed our artillery guys and told them where it had come from. Guys were hollering down on the street. I didn't know what all the noise was about. It was just another shell. I peered out the window again and saw Paul Rogers running toward where the shell had hit. Other fellas were running, too, but Rogers had an uncommon look on his face. My forehead scrunched up and I started breathing hard through my nose. I was putting two and two together, you know, and I grabbed my rifle and flew down the stairs.

The fellas had dug him out by the time I got there. He was covered in plaster, debris, and broken bits of wood.

They were carrying him out of that bombed out house. The artillery shell had come straight through the front door and flown down the steps, and the ceiling had collapsed right on top of him.

He had decided to take a nap in the middle of the day. He'd gone down to that basement. It was an empty house.

Bill Kiehn was dead before Doc Roe even heard the call for a medic.

We all stood around, our helmets in our hands. Then we went back to whatever we needed to do.

13

AT WAR'S END

We rode in boxcars back to Mourmelon. Fellas swung their feet out the door of the train as we jolted through France, waving to farmers, taking pulls on Schnapps bottles. We were going into reserve for a while, a place where there'd be no more shooting, no more killing, no more dying.

I hunched in the straw near the back of the boxcar. My knees were near my chest, and I rested my elbows on my knees. My rifle lay some distance away. I'd got a new one and it was a piece of shit. My old rifle was just fine. It had been with me from the beginning, you know, back in Toccoa. But somewhere along the line I'd got a pit in the stock, and some chickenshit officer was always gigging me during inspection due to that pit. I was plumb sick and tired of getting gigged. A fella didn't often think about his rifle the same way he'd think about a friend. But when I thought about how my best rifle was gone forever, well, a big ole tear splashed down my face. I wiped it away with the back of my hand before anybody would see. How stupid of me. How plumb stupid. To be crying over an ole rifle.

I stood up, brushed the straw off my pants, and steadied myself as I walked toward the door. Hayseed Rogers stood with his shoulder braced against the boxcar's side, looking out at the country. He'd been standing there a long time. Rogers fished out his cigarettes, handed me one, and stuck another in the corner of his mouth. We both lit smokes and inhaled deeply. I sat down, blowing smoke out of my nostrils, and swung my legs over the edge. Rogers sat beside me. Afternoon sunlight streamed toward us. It bounced back at our faces, and the air of that warm French countryside felt good as we click-clacked along.

"See that farmer in that field over there," Rogers said, pointing. "The one who's wiping sweat from his forehead with that red bandana. You see him, Shifty?"

I nodded.

"That farmer doesn't have to be in that field right now."

I nodded again. "Maybe being out in that field is his choice," I said.

Rogers grinned. "That's exactly what I'm saying. If he wants to be out in that field, then he's a smart man. But if he wants to be a shopkeeper, no one's telling him otherwise."

Rogers was from Kansas and a champion of farming ways, but I sensed he was getting at something deeper than stumping for field work. I ground out my cigarette on the boxcar's edge and was about to fish around in my pockets for one of my own, but stopped short when it dawned on me what Rogers meant. The last few years it hadn't been that way for a farmer in France. Or for farmers in

Belgium, for that matter. For farmers in Holland. Poland. Austria. Czechoslovakia. Denmark. Norway. Luxembourg. Yugoslavia. Romania. Hungary. Lithuania. Latvia. North Africa. Greece. As I thought about all the mess we'd been through from the perspective of fighting for a man's freedom, well, it put a lump in my throat. Back home in America, we'd never had bombs fall on our cities other than on Pearl Harbor, and I doubted if folks back home could grasp what war was truly like, you know, really grip the atrocities of it. Unless a man's had his freedom wrenched away from him and then fought to get it back, it's hard to know what war's like.

I lit my cigarette anyway and handed one of mine to Rogers. He lit his and smoked another, too. We kept staring at the countryside as it passed. So warm. So sunny. Shoot, I knew it wasn't my ole rifle I'd actually been crying about. Bill Kiehn had died so a French farmer could work his field without some Nazi soldier ordering him around. That was the connection Rogers was pointing me to. I knew fighting for freedom was important, but even then, I didn't understand it all either. Maybe I never would. Maybe someday it'd all come together for me and I wouldn't hurt so much, like I hurt right now. In the meantime, I'd file away that picture of the farmer in my mind.

Well, we arrived back in Mourmelon and kicked around. They housed us in twelve-man tents this time, not in old barracks like last time, but Mourmelon was still sort of a divey place. New recruits came in again, and I guess Major Winters didn't want any horseplay this time, like what had happened after the Holland campaign, so he made us all run and do calisthenics, day in day out. No boozing it up in Paris this time. No throwing cats at waiters. It felt a little silly to me, hiking through the rutabagas in the French countryside right along with the new recruits. This was the only time I was actually aggravated with Major Winters, making us old-timers train like that. But I didn't say anything.

We had a few parades around about that time, and General Eisenhower came by and gave us a speech. He also gave our whole division the Presidential Distinguished Unit Citation for what we'd done at Bastogne. I guess it was the first time in history a whole division got honored that way. So I felt proud about that.

After that unit citation, things loosened up, and passes were issued. We all scattered and went to England, the Riviera, Paris, and Brussels on longer passes. If we had an evening pass, we'd head over to Rheims for beers. Things didn't seem wild, this time. Maybe we were all too tuckered out to raise Cain. I celebrated my twenty-second birthday on March 13, 1945, while we were in reserve. Things were quiet.

We kept hearing we were going to do one last jump on Berlin. Really squash the Krauts once and for all. But in the end, the jump went to a different paratrooper division as well as some British troops, so that was fine by us. Those Krauts were fighting to the end.

Near the end of March 1945, orders came through for us to head into Germany by another route. They lined up trucks, and we loaded up, headed for the Rhine. We had full gear this time. Full rations. Extra clothes. Our ammo supply was good. I know some of the fellas were disappointed we weren't making one last battle jump, but it didn't aggravate me much. We'd be heading into Germany with the upper hand. The enemy would still be fighting back, but for the first time we'd see on their turf just how strong they were. I wasn't worried. If we could handle Bastogne, we could handle anything.

Shifty as a toddler with his mother and older brother.

Shifty Powers: always a baseball fan.

Shifty as a teenager.

Practicing shooting.

Shifty in uniform.

Shifty (right) and brothers Barney (the Marines, left) and Jimmy (Navy, middle).

A young Popeye Wynn.

Buck Taylor in uniform.
Photo courtesy Buck Taylor.

A young Earl McClung.
Photo courtesy Earl McClung.

1946 reunion in New York (L to R): Bill Guarnere, Popeye Wynn, Shifty Powers, unidentified, Babe Heffron, unidentified. The '46 reunion included all men from the 101st, not just E Company, so the unidentified men might not be from Easy Company.

A young Dorothy Powers.

Dorothy and Shifty, newlyweds.

Family man in California. Margo Johnson is in pigtails.

Dorothy Powers.

Shifty with his son,
Wayne.

Shifty with his family of origin—brothers Barney, Jimmy, Frankie, mother, and sister Gaynell.

Shifty, working man.

Shifty walking in woods.

Shifty and Dorothy at home.

Shifty and Dorothy with C. Carwood Lipton.

Shifty and his daughter,
Margo Johnson.

Shifty and Popeye.

Target practice off the front porch.

Denver reunion 1999 (L to R): Buck Taylor, Earl McClung, Shifty Powers.

Shifty showing Peter Youngblood Hills a technique for aiming a rifle.

Shifty joking around with Paul Rogers and Earl McClung. The family loves this picture of Shifty, the look of happiness on his face when palling around with his old friends.

ABOVE: Shifty talking to Steven Spielberg.

RIGHT: Shifty with McClung and Tom Hanks.

BELOW: After the celebrations. Shifty with Wayne Powers and Peter Youngblood Hills.

Back at Toccoa.

Running Toccoa with grandson Jake Johnson and his wife, Dawnyale.

Shifty at Skip Muck's grave.

Photo courtesy of Peter van de Wal, Eindhoven (The Netherlands)
website www.abandofbrothers.info

Shifty in uniform. *Photo courtesy of the Coalfield Progress.*

Well, we didn't see much resistance and heading into Germany proved pretty easy, at least at first. When we went through the towns, you'd see a dead German or two along the road, but as far as Nazi troops with guns pointed at us, there weren't any. We were billeted in German homes. We'd show up in a town, knock on doors, and tell the folks they had fifteen minutes to be out for the night. Mostly, they left real nice, although some were aggravated at the inconvenience. We didn't care much for their fussing after what we'd been through. But we didn't destroy their homes or anything. After we left, the homes were always more or less intact.

Most all the homes we stayed in were real nice. I don't think Germany had felt much of the brunt of the war, at least the sections we traveled through at first. What we saw was nothing like what the British in London had gone through. One night we were in this one house and they had a ton of sugar in the basement, and sugar's supposed to be scarce. So, things weren't all that bad off for the folks in this house, anyway. Now, I'm sure in other parts of Germany they'd had it rough, and I know that a soldier goes through mud and blood no matter who he fights for, but I got to thinking that the German people were more like us than any of the other people I met while we were overseas. That was my opinion anyway. Sure, they'd been snowed by Hitler and that Nazi business. When you saw those newsreels with Hitler out there, and the German people are all out there, men, women, civilians, with their arms in the air, hollering Heil Hitler, why, you realize that he had them brainwashed. But the homes we were in looked to me like regular middle-class homes. German folks were neat, clean, and tidy. Sometimes we'd meet a German civilian and try and talk with him a bit. No one understood each other's language, but as long as a man wasn't pointing a rifle in my face, why, we got along fine.

There were a few patrols in here, a few shells flying at us during the night, but no small arms fire that I ever heard. Weeks stretched by and we went from town to town. Mostly, time just dragged for us. We began to have daily rifle inspections. Bunch of military fiddle-faddle. Other than that, the replacements went out on guard duty, and the rest of us hung around and played cards. Sometimes us old-timers went on guard duty, too. But we weren't doing much. Three hot meals a day. Hot showers. Beds to sleep in. Being in Germany was the best conditions we'd ever had during the war.

On April 18 we were guarding a displaced person's camp near a town called Dornmagen. Wasn't much action going on. Just us staring at barbed wire and barracks and beet soup and black bread. I got to studying that, and it was troubling, all those people in that camp—men, women, babies, teenagers. They hadn't done nothing wrong. Czechs and Poles, Belgians, Dutch, French—I lost track of all the different nationalities I came across, all taken prisoner from different parts of Nazi-occupied Germany. They'd been put in prison because they'd been teachers or thinkers or artists or bankers, or maybe just because they looked at some Nazi soldier the wrong way. Most all were separated from their families, they'd not received word if anyone they knew was still alive or dead. They were in the camps because the Nazis wanted them there. It was as simple as that. When the Nazis held the upper hand, the Nazis did whatever they wanted to do. I guessed the Nazis needed the displaced prisoners' labor. Whatever the reason, the Nazis had sure caused a lot of aggravation for a lot of people.

We went through this German city called Cologne, and it was really bombed out. Every window was broken. Every street blocked with rubble. But you'd see the German people picking up bricks, sweeping up, boarding up windows with hammer and nails. Folks were starting to rebuild. It was another indication to me that the German civilians themselves were regular folks like the rest of us.

Near the end of April we loaded up in railway cars again and headed for the Alps. Most of the German armies had surrendered by then, but not all. I guess the upper brass thought that Hitler would try to make one last stand at a mountain town called Berchtesgaden. He'd built a sort of hideaway for himself there called the Eagle's Nest, this big ole high and mighty house of his. The thought was that he'd hole up there and arrange for guerilla fighters to come down and harass whoever they could from that position.

Nearing this location, we saw more destruction from our boxcars on the train. The German railway system was messed up, so we needed to take the long route through a couple countries to get where we needed to be—Holland again, Belgium, Luxembourg, and France, I think. It looked like a lot of those countries had been hit hard. Finally we swung back into Germany again, then hopped off the train and boarded these funny-looking vehicles called DUKWs. They looked like steel boats on wheels, and they could go through water without any problems. Those DUKWs had good rubber tires and rode good on land, too, so it was smooth sailing for us down the road. We hit a big highway called the autobahn and headed east. All the while we traveled, German soldiers marched toward us on the sides and middle of the road. Huge column, six abreast sometimes. They'd all surrendered, and they were heading back to their hometowns, I guessed. They weren't shooting at us this time. We weren't shooting at them. I think that's when I first realized the war was about over. With all these soldiers surrendering, there was no way Hitler could try any more of his foolishness. The soldiers marched on past, no threat, no danger, and we just waved.

We stopped for a night or two near a town called Buckloe. The Alps were real close, and those tall, snowy mountains looked fine. Some of our fellas went out on patrol, but they returned in a big hurry. Seemed they'd found something that didn't look like nothing a man had ever seen before. I guess Major Winters and some battalion staff went back to look at what they'd found, then they called us to go in.

All I saw were prisoners hanging on a fence. The fellas in other platoons went inside, but our platoon didn't go in, at least the squad I was in. That was fine by me. Those prisoners hanging on a fence were like no prisoners I'd ever seen before. Just skeletons in striped pajamas. Their arms were the size around of my rifle barrel. Me and the fellas I was with were ordered to keep going, so we went through and set up an outpost on the outskirts of the area. Other soldiers helped out inside the camp. When the men came back from that duty, few of them talked much about what they saw. It was too hard for them to put into words, I guessed. General Taylor declared martial law all through the area, and he ordered the German people from the nearby towns to go into the camp and clean it up. So the next day we saw German civilians headed down the road with shovels and rakes, going to clean up the bodies in that concentration camp. I didn't know what to rightly think of those two days. From what some of the other men told me, I was relieved I didn't see what they saw. But then again, these horrible things happened, you know, and it benefits a young man to know what the world is actually like—both its good and bad sides. We got word around on April 30 that Hitler committed suicide. He wolfed down some cyanide and shot himself in the head. So I guessed that one evil man who'd caused so much aggravation for so many people all over the world finally got what was coming to him.

It must have been early May when we headed up the road toward Berchtesgaden. It felt like sort of a race. Other companies wanted to get there first. Other Allied armies. We drove up and up these winding roads. Looked a bit like the roads around Clinchco. Finally, a big pile of rubble blocked the road, so we stopped. The Krauts had blown up the road ahead of us the day before, somebody said. They figured we'd be coming.

We blasted the roadblock with some artillery shells, but that didn't do much. So we sat in the sun waiting for the engineers to come up and figure out how to move the mess. Berchtesgaden was up above the roadblock, and McClung and a few others figured they'd climb up the rocks to skirt the roadblock and get to the top. So they did. I thought about going with them, but I'd had a few beers the night before and didn't feel like a climb, so I stayed put.

Well, the roadblock got cleared and the rest of us finally got up to Berchtesgaden, and there wasn't anybody around except us. Certainly no Hitler and none of his henchmen. Berchtesgaden was a real nice town, you know, with these snowcapped mountains all around. We secured some places to stay. Major Winters set up guards around town.

Then the party began.

Did a man need a set of wheels? Well, help yourself to a car. Did a man want a watch? Here you go. Want a bottle of booze? Well, plenty of men helped themselves to those. Looting from civilians was frowned upon, but helping yourself to something from an abandoned SS barracks was something else. We'd been sleeping in muddy foxholes a considerable time now, and we figured the Nazi government was responsible for all the fuss we'd had to go through, so I don't think any of us felt sorry for helping ourselves to a few things.

A few days later, someone found Goering's liquor stash, and, boy, you'd think a fella would have never seen a bottle of booze before. They passed out cases of the stuff, and we all got busy celebrating. The officers helped themselves to most of the finer drink, but few of us enlisted men cared about that uppity drink. Want a bottle of whiskey? Here, help yourself. Have two. Take a case of gin while you're at it. And how about a bottle of wine for later on? We had food and drink and warm houses to sleep in, and nobody was shooting at us, so we drank ourselves silly, we rightly did. On May 7, word came around that all the German armies had surrendered completely. May 8 was declared V-E Day—Victory in Europe— and we popped some more champagne corks and went outside and fired our pistols, and whooped and hollered and generally got right noisy. I don't remember much more about the specifics of how we celebrated. Only that I staggered up for reveille the next morning wearing only my underwear. My head hurt and I had an empty bottle of champagne in my hand, and when I looked around, I appeared to be about the best functioning man in the outfit.

Well, we rolled out of Berchtesgaden a day or so later and headed out for Zell am See, maybe twenty miles away or so. It was in Austria, and it was such fine country to be in. It was really a good time then. The fellas were all hanging out in the back of trucks, singing, drinking, playing cards, telling jokes. We got to some real nice barracks and settled in. Zell am See was a beautiful place with that big ole lake in the center of the town. Roads, houses, everything was nice and clean. We settled in and prepared to stay a spell. Occupation duty, they called it. It was a fine way to be a soldier, I thought.

One morning we went out for a swim, and I got to thinking about the men who were still around. Popeye. McClung. Skinny

Sisk. Hayseed Rogers. Moe Alley. Carwood Lipton. Joe Liebgott. All good men. All good friends. I grinned at the thought we'd made it through. But then I got to studying about how there were so many who weren't around anymore, you know. It was that sad thought of all the guys who were missing that wouldn't let me grin long.

Well, weeks stretched on, and we didn't do much. That's when word came around that the points system was being instituted, and most all the old-timers would be heading home soon. By the end of June, every veteran of Normandy would be gone. Except me, you know. I'd fought on the front lines of every battle since Normandy, but I'd never been wounded. Being good at dodging bullets meant I wasn't going home. Not enough points.

Sure, it bothered me. There was still a war in the Pacific, and I'd go fight there if I needed to, but the fellas fighting over there were real capable, and none of us doubted that they'd soon clean up there. The feeling I had was sort of like when that shell hit right in front of me way back in Bastogne, that day me and a couple of fellas were out on patrol. The shell was a dud, you know, probably made that way on purpose by some prisoner in a factory somewhere. He'd done his part in helping out the war effort. Probably done a lot more than that. But that was how I felt in Zell am See, like I'd done my part in helping out the war effort. And now I wanted to go home.

Well, right about then is when Captain Speirs led us in a troop formation and I noticed one or two of the old-timers with unmistakable twinkles in their eyes. Captain Speirs drew my name out of a hat. I'd won the lottery.

I gathered my gear. Hayseed Rogers took me over to that supply building, and I picked out two of the finest pistols I'd ever seen.

I went and talked with Major Winters, asking him about that

question that had been gnawing at me for some time, the question about explaining things when I got home to Clinchco, and he told me I was a hell of a soldier and didn't need to explain anything.

So I shook hands all around and said my good-byes and climbed up in the back of that truck that was heading toward headquarters. We started winding back down that road, and that's when that truck got in a wreck, see, and I got my very first real wound in the war—right when I was headed home. Everything got swirly for me as I lay there on the side of that mountain road and a nurse stuck me with a morphine syrette, and for a long time these were the only things I remembered: that my name was Sergeant Darrell C. Powers and I won General Taylor's lottery.

Next thing I knew I woke up all groggy in a field hospital and another nurse was taking my clothes off. I opened my eyes for a few seconds and saw her take off my paratrooper boots. When she got to my pants, she jumped back and let out a great big squeal. I had bloused them with condoms like we always did. That's all I remember before I went back under.

I guess they took me to the operating room and worked me over and put me in the hospital tent. That's when I woke up again. I was beat up, black and blue all over. My arm was broke, my pelvis was broke, my head was all busted up, and I just laid on that bed and felt sorry for myself. I'd been away from home for so long, and now this. It didn't seem fair, you know. It just didn't seem fair.

Well, I looked over cross the aisle, and there was another soldier lying there wrapped from head to toe in a plaster of Paris cast. All you could see was his one little hole for his mouth, another hole for his nose, another for his eyes, and the tips of his toes. Right then I quit feeling sorry for myself. That poor fellow laying there couldn't move at all. I considered how fortunate I was.

I was in a hospital bed for some time, and one of the fellas who'd been in the accident wheeled a chair around to where I could see him and told me that he'd lost everything, but he'd checked on my stuff and it was still there. I was happy about that and described to him all I had in my bag. But about a week later, he came round again and said, "Shifty, I was mistaken, your stuff's all gone." Well, I couldn't move to go check myself. I'd taken those two fine guns off and put them in my musette bag because I didn't want to go into headquarters wearing pistols. So I lost everything I had in that accident. All my guns, all my equipment. I was pretty sure where it went.

That's about all I did day after day. I lay around, healing up. Months went by, the Japs finally surrendered, and then the fighting was over for everybody. At the end of November 1945 I heard the news that the 101st had been officially inactivated. Easy Company and all the rest of the outfits in the division were no more. I guess all the rest of the guys in the outfit came home before I did. Finally I came home on a hospital ship, landed in New Jersey or New York or somewhere up in that area, and got put in a hospital there a week or two, then they shipped me down to another hospital in Nashville. I was in Nashville a couple, three weeks, but at least I was back in America. I was still in the Army, mind you, but a fella in that condition, particularly at the end of the war, can get a lot of furloughs and passes, so I hunted up a good long pass for myself, and that meant I could finally head home to Virginia.

The morning was sunny and I hobbled up onto the bus, and my heart started racing at the thought of heading back to Clinchco. I wondered who I'd talk to first. I wondered how things might look different around town. I wondered what my mother would serve up for supper that first day I got back. I was still wearing a uniform, and I found a seat and sat down. On my face was the biggest grin I'd had in three years.

14

THE DIFFERENCE AT HOME

When the bus door swung open at my stop near Clinchco, I limped down the steps and looked around. Hills, you know. Trees. Woods. The air smelled like fir boughs and soil, a good kind of Christmassy smell, and there was water burbling down in the river nearby. Far away came the screechy hoot of a train approaching. A lone car passed in front of me on the road, shifted gears, and wound its way up the hill. I was the only passenger to get off at this bus stop, but I didn't feel alone.

Nobody in my family knew exactly when I was coming home. I hadn't told them because I hadn't known myself. When I got my extended pass, I didn't want to take time even to place a telephone call. I grabbed my gear and went.

I tucked in my chin and started limping down the road. I buttoned up the top button of my uniform against the cold. It wasn't far to walk anyway. Stowed away carefully in my duffel bag were presents. For my sister, Gaynell, I'd brought a silver bracelet and a watch. Mama had written me earlier. Gaynell was getting all A's in high school, and they told her they'd get her this watch if she kept up all her grades. Mama figured it would really tickle her if the watch came from me. Well, Gaynell skipped one class in shorthand and got one B, but there was no way in heck I wasn't going to get my sister that watch.

Our old house stood in front of me, quiet. It was almost suppertime. Lights shone from the front windows. I took off my hat and stared a moment. The whole placed glowed warm and bright. Daddy would be reading the paper, I guessed, sitting in his favorite chair. My brothers Barney and Jimmy wouldn't be home from the service yet, but my little brother Frankie would be a whole lot bigger than when I saw him last. The porch stairs creaked as I walked up to the front door. I didn't know whether to knock or go right in. They were all home from work and school. I decided to go right in.

Sure enough, Daddy was sitting reading the paper, and when he looked up and saw me he gave a little start. Mama gasped from the kitchen and came running, her eyes shiny with tears. Sis sprinted right over with a squeal and gave me a long hug. Frankie was right behind her. Everybody piled around, and we all held tight for a long time. We let go and took a step back and looked each other up and down. Everybody started chuckling, like someone had told a funny story with bits of punch line that ebbed out every so often. There was more hugging, more backslapping. Sis squealed when she saw the watch I brought her, then everyone noticed the time, and Mom and Sis grabbed my arm and pulled me to the table. I sat, and they all sat around, and Mom fussed about and cut me two thick slices of bread and slathered on real butter. She loaded up a plate of ham and beans with a scoop of her famous potato salad on the side. Along came a big ladle of home-canned corn, steaming and buttery. A tall glass of fresh milk slid down the table. A hot cup of fresh brewed coffee followed. "If only I knew you were coming," Mama kept saying, "All I've got are these corn muffins, but I could have whipped up some banana pudding." But she was smiling. We were all smiling.

More plates were piled on the table and we all ate supper together. The cloth on the table was red checked, same as I remembered, and we talked and laughed around that old table. The clock struck nine o'clock and ten and eleven, and near around midnight, Daddy was the first to stretch and say he hated to end things, but there was work tomorrow and he needed to head for bed. One by one they gave me hugs and followed. Soon enough it was just me and Gaynell, and she poured me another glass of milk, but I was so full I couldn't put anything more in me. Finally we said good night. I brushed my teeth in the bathroom, padded down the hall to my bedroom, hung up my uniform, and crawled under the sheets of my very own bed. My room looked just like I'd left it. A basketball in the corner. A couple of old math notebooks from high school. Two pairs of jeans and a bunch of T-shirts in the bureau drawer. My Sunday shirt and slacks still hanging up in the closet. Outside my window, I could hear the chattering of a chipmunk high on the hill. I let out a deep sigh. It was so good to be home.

That night I slept a dreamless sleep. No nightmares. No tossing and turning. When I got up the next morning, I smelled bacon frying. Everybody was out the door already except Mama. She piled a big bowl of oatmeal in front of me as soon as I got to the table, and poured me a fresh cup of coffee. The Army would serve up oatmeal once in a blue while, but it always tasted like the inside of a cook pot. This was thick oatmeal, not a lump in it, with cream and brown sugar. Alongside of it came a big plate of fluffy biscuits with home cooked gravy. Then there was the bacon. It was sizzling crispy, and Mama knew I loved bacon, because there was more bacon that morning than any man could hold in his belly even if all he ate was bacon three meals a day every day for a week. I ate and ate, then licked my lips and let out my belt and ate some more.

After a long while, breakfast was over. I didn't know quite what to do then. Mama was watching me real closely whenever I got up and walked. She was fussing over my limp. For once, I was listening to her. It pained me to walk very far and I knew I was still healing and couldn't do much yet. That morning I walked around the yard a bit. That afternoon I studied my fishing poles in the garage. I did a push-up or two and almost laughed at the thought of Captain Sobel making us do push-ups by the hundreds. It seemed like Camp Toccoa was a lifetime ago. My good friend Pete was home from the service, and he screeched up on the road in front of the house a while later and we sat on the hood of his car and jawed about times before the war.

That's how it went for those first few glorious days back home. A lot of eating. A lot of lazing around. I wished things could be exactly the same as they'd always been, but I started to see that they weren't. It was maybe two, three days after coming back, Mama was out and I told my sister I was going over to Clintwood to go see friends. I hopped in Dad's car and started driving. The town is only fifteen miles down the road, maybe less, but after about five minutes behind the wheel, my heart started pounding something fierce. My hands grew clammy. My stomach did flip-flops. I swerved the car over onto the road's shoulder, took it out of gear, and sat, idling, breathing, trying to slow my pulse, trying to take stock of what was happening in my head. I remembered once as a little kid I'd gone camping with a buddy. We were real young. Maybe seven, eight. The two of us were within hiking distance of home. We had flashlights and our sleeping bags and two sandwiches each in case we grew hungry during the night. I'd never been afraid of the woods, and I wasn't afraid then, but it was a similar feeling out alone in the tent to what I was feeling now by the side of the road. If a fella isn't any braver, he thinks about packing up his gear and heading inside for the night. Well, I looked down the road toward Clintwood. Then I put Dad's car into gear, pulled a U-turn, and headed back home.

Gaynell saw me pulling up in front of the house. She walked outside. "I thought you were going to Clintwood," she said.

I nodded.

"So, why are you back?"

I shrugged. "Too far away, I guess."

"You're joking, right?"

"Nah, I got up to Fremont but figured that was about as far away as I wanted to go."

"Darrell, you can't be serious."

"Yeah, I'm serious, Sis. I just wanted to be home again."

Sis was real understanding about things, but I doubted even she'd grasp what I was getting at. All those years of me being away in the war, I never had such a feeling of security like I did when I was back home. Even when I became a paratrooper. A fella feels confident when he's in uniform and surrounded by his friends. He feels like he can do most anything he sets his mind to do. But when I got home, well, it's hard to fully put those other feelings into words, the not-so-good feelings, how I felt in Europe so many times. So cold. So hungry. So scared. There wasn't enough distance yet between me and those awful feelings, and I didn't want to give up the good feeling of security I was soaking in at home, even for a drive down the road.

That was how it went. One week stretched into two. Two weeks stretched into three. As long as I stayed home, I didn't feel aggravated at all. Now, you would think that after being overseas in the war for such a long time that a fella would crave eating a certain thing that he wasn't able to get while away—maybe cheeseburgers or milkshakes or steak. Well, it struck me funny, but the main thing I started craving was dill pickles. A nearby store stocked barrels full of them, and it was close enough that I could drive on over and help myself. I ate them out of barrels and bought them in jars, too, and sometimes I sat in my car in the parking lot and ate a whole jar full. Even drank the juice. That went on for some time, and I didn't know where that strange craving came from or why it was so powerful. The store owner started seeing me so often that he joked I was pregnant.

Well, I wasn't, that was for sure, but strictly speaking, I was still married to the Army, so before long I managed to get myself over to Fort Pickett, this little camp near Blackstone, Virginia, and got discharged for once and good. It wasn't like I was doing anything for the Army then anyway. I drew a small disability, but that was about the only real connection we were having. There was still a lot I couldn't do. One month stretched into two, and two months stretched into three. I still visited the hospital now and again. All told I was in the hospital about a year. When the weather warmed up in early spring, I tried to paint the house for Mama and Daddy, but because of my arm and wrist still being messed up, I couldn't do that. So I just lay around mostly, going on little walks in the woods, fishing some. Eating lots.

By mid-summer 1946, my body felt mostly better, so I figured

I'd get a job. My machinist's credentials were still good, but nobody in Clinchco was hiring machinists right then, so I got hired on picking slate for the coal company. I hated the gritty work, and it felt like a step backwards, you know, so I quit before long and figured I'd think of something else to do. I didn't know what, but I was confident I'd sort things out sooner or later.

In the meantime, I figured I'd look up some old girlfriends to see what might be what. Mary was real sweet and I'd known her since elementary school. Well, I looked her up, but shoot, she'd gone and gotten married while I was in the service. So that wasn't going to do. Another pretty girl, her name was also Mary, lived over in Newport News. We'd corresponded a bit when I was overseas. She came out to visit us in Clinchco but acted all scared of the mountains, so that wasn't going to do either. She became more a friend of the family. Well, Pauline was a friend of my sister's and a lot of fun. We went on a few walks, saw a few movies, but, I don't know. A man knows for sure when he knows. And I didn't know for sure with Pauline. So that's how things were, and after a while we stopped going on walks and going to the movies together.

Seemed like everybody was growing up, growing older. A lot of my buddies from high school who had gone into the service were married now, starting families, the ones who came home anyway. Most of the girls I knew back in high school were married with kids. Depending on the day, I leaned between feeling real old and real young. My father encouraged me to use the G.I. Bill to go to college, but on the days when he suggested that, I always seemed to be leaning toward feeling old. College was for kids, and I wasn't a kid anymore. At least in my mind. I probably should have listened to Dad.

It felt different being around my parents. You've been through something that you can't describe even to the people closest to you. My parents were the same people they'd always been, always kind, always loving. But things with me—their kid—weren't the same anymore. I loved my home. I loved my family. But I wasn't much sure how I felt about anything else. Before I went into the service, Dad used to tell stories of when he was in World War I. He'd tell funny stories mostly, never the gory ones. Once, when he was going overseas on a ship, he got real sick, and the only thing that saved his life was grapefruit. He always ended that story the same way. "And I've liked grapefruit ever since." Well, I guessed I had my own war stories now to tell. But I didn't tell any of them. Not even the funny ones.

I was still talking to God, you know. Heading that direction in my own private way, I guess. Mom belonged to a church, like everybody does in the South, but she seldom went except back when we were kids. Dad belonged to a different church over in the country where he grew up. His church didn't hold services every Sunday, but they had what they called quarterly meetings. They'd gather everybody together and preach all day, three or four different preachers all belting out a message, strong and sweaty. You'd sit outside in the shade and fan your face, and kids would be running in and out and around. Everybody sang songs. We'd have a big potluck supper later. Fried chicken and fresh baked rolls and Jell-O salad with fruit in the mix. Dad's extended family belonged to that church, cousins and whatnot, so he always considered that his church. It was as much a family reunion as a church service, and I usually didn't mind going when I was a kid. It was good to see all those folks and to eat real well, but after the war I found I didn't want to go to that church as much. Couldn't rightly say what it was. I loved being around all the folks I knew so well. But things were different—when it came to church, as well as much near everything else. That's as much sense as I could make out of things.

I got to thinking maybe a fella my age should move out on his own. I didn't know what to do about it, though, and money was always tight. One day I figured it would be good to go see a buddy on the other side of the state. I didn't tell anyone what I wanted to do, but I got talking to my dad and he was saying how there was a coal show in Cincinnati, an event where they display all the new machines and equipment for mining and such. Dad was real eager to go, but he needed a new suitcase and didn't have money for one. So I took the money I was going to spend on my trip and gave him the money for his trip instead. Dad never knew about that, or else he wouldn't have put up with it. Well, my sister caught wind of this and pulled me aside and pushed some bills into my hand. She'd been saving a bit, and she wanted me to go on my trip, too. Figured it would do me good to get out, she said. So I got to go on my trip, too. I guessed some things never change, and I was real happy that the closeness our family felt for each other was one of those things. I loved my dad and would do anything for him.

Both my living-arrangement and career problems seemed to be solved one day when Bob, one of my buddies who'd also been in the service, came by and said he was thinking of buying a restaurant over in Clintwood. He asked if I'd like to be business partners with him. I had a little bit of savings from the service that I wasn't touching for nothing except the future, so I said yes. The place was called "The Grill," and it was popular with everybody, especially the high school kids. We didn't know much about hiring cooks or running a restaurant, but we learned quick and started serving up short order foods: burgers and hot dogs, ham and beans, fried pork chops and whatever. In back of the restaurant was a room where kids could dance, and the joint would really get hopping on Saturday nights. Upstairs of the restaurant were rooms to live in, so I moved out of my parents' home and moved in there. Bob moved in, too, and it was good to have company. We were good friends and talked about a lot of things together, but I don't know that we ever talked about our time in the war. A man didn't talk about that.

We didn't run the restaurant long. A couple of months maybe. We weren't making much money, nothing to look to the future on anyway. So Bob decided to go into the coal mining business with his dad, and I decided to go back to the coal company. A machinist position opened up right about then, so we sold the restaurant and I moved back in with my mom and dad.

It was good to be back. I hadn't been sleeping real well upstairs in the restaurant, and I hoped I'd sleep better when I got back to my own room at home. I kept having these dreams, you know, these memories. Some of those thoughts were apt to drive a man crazy. One night, those dreams were circulating round my head, you know, so I got up and went out drinking. Real late I came home. My sister, Gaynell, was still up and I sloshed in and sat down in the living room, and she gave me a long, hard stare.

"I've never been so drunk in all my life," I said.

She shook her head and said, "Darrell, you're not drunk." She must have been thinking of pictures she'd seen in a book or something about fellas who're drunk, because my hair wasn't disheveled, my clothes weren't sloppy-looking, and I wasn't staggering around. But I was most certainly drunk.

"Sis, I don't know if I can rightly get upstairs," I said.

A few minutes later, I guessed she believed me. The bathroom was at the end of the stairs, and I ran over and spilled everything I had inside of me up into the toilet. I got to studying that, leaning over the toilet as full of mess as it was, and it dawned on me that this wasn't me, you know. I'd never done this sort of thing before I was in the service. I didn't know why I was doing it now.

Well, Gaynell was a real peach about the matter, because the next day she didn't say anything when I told mother it was from some cashew nuts I ate. But other things kept aggravating me, pulling up devils I didn't know were there. My youngest brother, Frankie, had joined the service, and one day he came home on leave. He and some of his buddies went out to a beer joint in this little town called The Pound. Frank was driving that night, and I guess they stopped somewhere and he stepped out of the car. Three guys came along, jumped Frankie, and knocked him out cold.

My oldest brother, Barney, was married by then, and one of the guys ran over and found Barney and told him what happened. Barney got so mad. He came around and found me, and I pounded my fists together and looked around for a baseball bat. I was really seeing red. The two of us decided we were going to hunt down those boys and tear their hides off.

Mother caught wind of it. I've never seen a sterner look on her face. She stepped between us and our car and held up her hand for us to stop. We were all feeling sorry for what happened to Frankie, she said, but none of her boys were going to get thrown into jail, and that's what was going to happen if we carried out what we were planning to do.

Barney and me stomped off somewhere and drank some whiskey, and I got to studying my actions. Mom was right. I'm not sure if I'd ever got that angry about things before the war. Sure, I got aggravated about things, but not devil-mad, like I'd just been. I didn't know where that came from.

Well, one year stretched into two, and two years stretched into three. In 1948 I was twenty-five years old and working at the mine. One day near the start of sports season, Pete and me volunteered to coach the high school basketball teams, just for fun. Pete was drinking quite a bit then, and could raise quite a fuss when he got that way, so we had drifted a bit in our friendship, but we were still close, you know. He'd been in the war as well, and that's how some fellas chose to cope, I guess. Still, he could be mighty aggravating when he'd had too much to drink.

Anyway, he was on a dry run for a while and things were okay, so Pete decided to coach the boys' team with me coaching the girls. There was this one girl on the team, Dorothy was her name. Such a fine-sounding name. Dorothy. Now, she was a fine-looking young lady, just seventeen years old, a junior. I'd known her around town for years, but she'd always been a kid, you know. Still, I got to watching her run up and down the basketball court, and I thought to myself, Shifty, that girl's all grown up.

Well, I started winking at her, you know. And I started talking to her, you know, about more than just basketball stuff. I asked her out on a date, and we went to a movie. When it got good and dark in the theater, I kissed her. After the movie was over, we went out driving and parked up on the Ridge. That's when I kissed her a lot more. She kissed me back, and I told her she was real pretty, the prettiest girl I'd ever seen, and that I liked her just fine. She said she'd had a crush on me ever since I got back from the service, that I was the most handsome young man she'd ever laid eyes on. Well, I didn't know about all that, but I knew that whenever she was around and I was on the basketball court, maybe showing the girls how to do something, I got downright light on my legs in her presence. So I told her more words to that effect, you know.

It was a short courtship. We only went together for nine months.

It doesn't take long for a man to know for sure if he knows for sure. With Dorothy, I knew. She was eighteen then and a senior, and I was twenty-six. One day we were out on a date and I said, "Let's get married." She said okay, so it was as simple as that. Dorothy was still in high school, but waiting didn't make much sense. We didn't talk about having a fancy church wedding. My brother Jimmy and his wife had a plan. My parents didn't know. Her parents didn't know. I guess you could say we eloped, because that's what we did. Jimmy and his wife drove us over to this little town. We said the words and signed the papers, then came back. That night, our first night of being married, Dorothy slept back at her home, and I slept back at mine.

That was October 8, 1949, when Dorothy and I got married. We didn't plan to tell anybody until she graduated from high school. We were really in love, and it was hard to keep our getting hitched a secret for very long. People were real happy for us when they found out. Daddy shook my hand and said I had made a real wise choice. Mama made us a special supper. Everybody's folks seemed okay with the arrangement, too, because we got our own place soon—right after Dorothy got out of school in the spring.

That was such a happy time, but Daddy hadn't been his usual self. He was walking slower, coughing more. Things like that. Well, I put Daddy's health out of my mind for the time being and kept working at the mill. Things were slowing down there, too. Coal business can be like that. I was wondering how I was going to be the provider I needed to be when one day Dorothy looked at me with a twinkle in her eye and said she was in the family way.

I was real happy then, and after she was sick a few times, the pregnancy seemed to go smooth. It was a good thing, too, because Daddy got real sick early that spring, and they took him over to the hospital for some kind of surgery on his gallbladder. Things went downhill real quick after that. It was March 1951, and Mom had been at the hospital all night. She went home for some rest, and I was at work, and that's when the hospital called me. I rushed right over to the hospital, then I went home. To my parents' home, I mean. Frankie and Gaynell were sitting in the living room playing double solitaire. I walked through the front door and Gaynell said, "I thought you were working."

"No," I said. "Where's Mother?" That was all I could say. I leaned my head against the wall and started sobbing.

Daddy was real young, much too young to pass like that. He was only fifty-six.

We held a nice funeral for him. We sang hymns and the preacher talked about the hope of a far better place, but I didn't know what to do with myself. Daddy had always been there. Even during the war when I was so far away. Daddy had always been there for our family. Now he was gone.

Less than two months later, on May 3, 1951, Dorothy started having pains real bad, and I sped her to the hospital. They whisked her right inside. I paced around in the waiting room, my hat in my hand, smoking Lucky Strikes by the fistful. That was the first time in a long while I remember asking God for something for myself. If I ever prayed, I don't ever remember praying for myself. It might be more like saying grace at the supper table, or having a moment of silence when somebody died. But as I paced I was saying *"Lord Jesus Christ in heaven, please don't take Dorothy from me,"* over and over again. I couldn't bear the thought of something happening to my wife. I just couldn't bear it.

Well, all those prayers and pains must have been for something good in the end, because that day our son popped out to say hello and decided to stay. He was red like a potato and scrunchy and fat when I held him, and Dorothy said it was okay if I named him Wayne after my good friend from Easy Company, Wayne Sisk. Skinny Sisk was a fine fella and had written me a letter to say that he'd gone and become a minister after the war like he promised God he would. I figured any son of mine would be doing well to follow his example. My son didn't need to become a preacher, I wasn't thinking that. Only that he become a man of character. And I knew Wayne could aspire to that.

Dorothy and me and little Wayne went home and started adjusting to our new life together. The baby was doing well, and I was real proud of all the things he could do. I'd teach him how to throw a baseball soon. Take him out in the woods, you know, and tell him about listening in the forest. Life was real happy, but my work at the mine was getting slow, and I admit it put a lump in my throat, as men are prone to get, a short time after that when Dorothy looked at me again with that same twinkle in her eye. It was a happy lump, but I sure didn't know how we were going to pay for things with her sitting on the nest again. That next July 8, 1952, Dorothy gave birth to our daughter, Margo. Our baby's skin was perfect, as creamy as a peach, and, well, our little girl was about the most beautiful thing I'd ever seen.

About a year went by, and work still wasn't picking up the way I needed it to. A friend from out in California wrote and said times were better out there. I got to studying that letter and knew that I couldn't rightly take Dorothy and the babies out there with no job to go to, no place of our own. So maybe I could head out west and get things set up for my family. I'd call for them later, and they could join me then.

Well, I started praying again, reminding God that I had fairly simple dreams. I didn't know why they weren't coming to pass like I wanted them to. When it came to life, I never dreamed of being someone who folks considered special, you know, someone who folks considered famous or rich or powerful. I was satisfied with who I was and with the direction I was going with my life, and I wanted to keep on being a machinist in the town of Clinchco with my family, the ones I loved the most. But that wasn't meant to be.

In early 1953, I kissed my wife and children good-bye and climbed aboard a train. I was leaving home again, you know. I hated that thought with all my being, but that's what a man needed to do.

15

HOW A MAN WRESTLES WITH WAR

Palm trees swayed in the breeze. The weather was more balmy than I'd felt in a long time. I pulled off the side of the road in the old Chevy I'd recently bought, turned off the ignition, strolled across a little bank into a grove, and helped myself to an orange from right off a tree. Pulling out my pocketknife, I cut the orange into sections and settled back onto the grass, chewing on a wedge. That orange was sun-warmed and sweet. Best-tasting orange I'd ever eaten. So this was California, I thought. Maybe not too bad.

Along with the orange and the sun, I had a job. I hadn't been out West for more than a week, and already I'd been picked up by a machinist company. They had a government contract, and it came with enough work to last quite a spell, they said. I slapped my knee at that thought and grinned. From out of my back pocket I pulled my billfold. Wasn't any money in it except three old wrinkled one-dollar bills. It would need to do until I got my first paycheck. I ignored the money and pulled out a picture I'd been studying a lot lately. It showed me and Dorothy dressed up in our Sunday best clothes. We were lounging beside my car by the side of the road in Clinchco. I had my arms around her and we were kissing. Boy, how I loved that picture. I pulled out two more snapshots, of little Wayne and Margo. I wanted to be with my family. I wanted to forget what I'd been through, and get on with living the rest of my life.

Two weeks passed and I got paid. I sped back to Virginia, loaded up some suitcases and a chair, then Dorothy and me and the kids headed to our new home in Van Nuys. Dorothy settled in and made the best of it, but she remarked more than once how strange it felt living in this faraway place. I knew what she meant. Cars whizzed past, anywhere you went in California. Folks were friendly, but they came in crowds. It took an hour to drive anywhere, and when you did, you needed to study a map. Dorothy found work part-time in an auto parts store to help ends meet, but she confessed to me she didn't like California much. I agreed with my wife. I surely did.

We figured we'd make the best of it. A year passed, and then another, and then another, and then another. We moved to North Hollywood and bought a little house. Sure, we had some good times. One morning, little Wayne and Margo hid in the backseat of my Chevrolet. When I arrived at work for my shift, they popped out from under a blanket with a cheer. Well, I was sure tickled to see them, even though it meant I needed to drive back home. Still, we all chuckled about that for a long while. Most days when I got home from work, I'd throw a baseball around with little Wayne. He was getting real good, young as he was. And Margo would come running to greet me, toddling and squealing. I called her "Marjo" and sometimes "Sissybug." Every once in a while for fun I'd hide a fake fuzzy spider in her bed. She always laughed with a sweet roar. We wanted our kids to remember where they came from, so each year we drove our old Chevy back to Clinchco for a visit. We stopped at motels at night, ate picnic lunches by the side of the road.

One night in North Hollywood Dorothy and me sat looking at each other from across the kitchen table. The kids were long tucked in bed, and I wondered if Dorothy was happy, you know, truly at ease with the life we were leading. It's hard to put that question into words, but I think she was thinking what I was thinking because she looked at me, real straight across the table, and said, "It's all too fast here, isn't it."

I nodded. We went to bed that night, and that's about all we said about the matter. But the next morning when I got to work, the company foreman told us they'd lost the government contract and we were all laid off. I finished the shift, motored home on the new interstate highway, and told Dorothy the news. Getting laid off aggravated us at first, and we fussed about how we were going to pay our mortgage. But then we got to grinning. We stuck up a "For Sale" sign, sold that house in a jiffy, and hightailed it back to where we belonged.

My, it was good, driving back into Clinchco. It was 1957, and oak trees greeted us, their leaves all out in fiery glory. Hickory. Beech. Sycamores. The air felt crisp and clean. A squirrel darted in front of our car and I swerved and screeched on the brakes. He got away fine, and I noticed he was chasing another squirrel all playful up the side of a holler. We were back home, and I slapped my knee for sheer joy. This is where I wanted to spend the rest of our days.

Folks around Clinchco were right friendly welcoming us back. "Where you been?" they asked, and joked, "Hey—stay awhile this time." Jobs were picking up again, and other folks were moving back, too. A machinist job opened up for me at the coal company, and I thought it looked to be an outstanding job. I already knew plenty of the fellas over there. Everybody had nicknames—Shotgun and Red and Pee Wee and Bowtie. Plenty of guys, you didn't even know their real names. I was more or less my own boss in the shop and able to do whatever I wanted, within reason. The coal company gave us good insurance. I didn't want to be any other place for the next long stretch of time.

My job was at a place called the Moss Number 3 Mine. It was actually in the town of Duty, about twenty-five miles away from where we lived, so I had a bit of a commute each morning and evening. I'd go to work about 6 A.M. Get home about 5 P.M. I worked a lot of overtime, too, to keep extra money coming in for the family. I liked the job just fine. About the only thing strange about my job was that every day as I was driving to work, this funny little kid who lived down the road from the Duty coal mine ran out and threw rocks at my car. Her name was Sandy. She was about six years old. I never did know why she chucked rocks at me. I reckoned she was the sassy type who threw rocks at all the passing cars. So that was that. I didn't know then that we'd get to know her a lot better one day.

Dorothy got a job as secretary at the school we'd gone to, and she was happy there. A little while passed, and the kids got to be in school, so Dorothy was able to be around them during the days. Dorothy's mother moved in with us, and that was fine. Truly, I didn't mind having more family in the house. My brother Frankie came to live with us for a spell, then went back into the Navy. We were all real happy, and we settled in to the life we'd always wanted to lead.

I guessed Dorothy and me made a fine young couple around town. We became active in school programs and community events. In my off hours I fished. Trout fishing in a stream was my favorite.

I had two fishing buddies, Pete, and another guy named Claude King. Everybody called him Pee Wee, but I don't know why. Each year, I'd take my family on a big fishing trip. The state held opening days around the end of March, and we'd go out to Whitetop to camp for the weekend and trout fish. I still hunted. Mostly I liked target practice. Oh sure, I'd hunt squirrels, rabbits, birds, but never deer or big game. I got to enjoy fixing things around the house and yard. Lawnmowers. Washing machines. Shoot—sometimes I'd fix a washing machine with a lawnmower part. That set Dorothy to chuckling. Every spring I planted a big garden and tended it all summer. We'd eat real well off that. Tomatoes, corn, beans, peas. Whatever would grow. A couple years I even planted some tobacco. I figured out how to can vegetables, too, because I figured that might come in handy. So I'd can beans by the quartful. Late each summer, my sister-in-law and me would compete to see who could get the most quarts of beans canned. My record was twenty-four quarts. It was real fun.

That was how I coped, you know, as the years passed, although I'm not sure if coping was ever something I gave any conscious thought to or not. I wanted a small life in a safe town, a life where I felt secure and could love my wife and raise my kids. I'd seen plenty of this world's evils and I knew there were plenty of dangers ready to grab at folks. My good friend Pete started having more problems because of his drinking. I saw less and less of him. Some folks called him a drunk, but I never did. After a time, he and his wife divorced, which was sad all around. Sure, I blamed the war for that. Pete could have done things differently, I guessed, but I knew it wasn't easy for a man to put his past aside. Gradually, Pete and I lost contact.

When I thought about Pete, I vowed those things wouldn't

happen to me, but I couldn't say for sure, you know, I really couldn't. Sometimes in the dark of night when I was lying next to Dorothy and she'd be asleep, I'd be peering up at the ceiling, listening closely for any strange sounds. Maybe somebody was trying to bust into the house. Maybe it was the wind pushing on the sides of our home, making the floor creaky, the walls crackling. Maybe it was a ghost. When I slept, these dreams kept haunting me. Memories raced back to me in the night. So much shooting. So much killing. I never talked about these things to anyone. Nobody wanted to hear about the war, I figured. We'd won. America had triumphed over the Nazis and Imperialist Japan. Now we were all aiming to get on with our lives. Rebuild, celebrate, buy that new washing machine—that was the mood in the newspapers. What the world had gone through seemed too hard for anyone to ever talk about again. Once, when Wayne was in ninth grade, his history teacher was talking about the Battle of the Bulge, and Wayne said, "You know, I think my dad was in that." The teacher just laughed at him.

I didn't want to end up like one of those sad-story veterans, you know. You'd hear whispers of other fellas having a rough go of it. It was always, *so-and-sos been drinking too much,* or *that fella tore up the bar real good.* I always carried a .25 pistol strapped to my ankle. I'd carried it ever since I got back from overseas. I always told people it was for the snakes we sometimes get around Clinchco, but the truth was that after the things I'd seen during the war, I plumb felt safer with that pistol there. It dawned on me early on that civilian folks don't work out their differences the same way as men do in the military. In the Army, if I was aggravated with somebody, I either needed to obey him, fight him, or shoot him. When you weren't in the Army anymore, things didn't work that way. Still, on those nights I couldn't sleep, I feared that would be me one day.

It wasn't that I didn't love Dorothy. I loved her with all my being. Same with the kids. I'd never do anything to hurt the life we had together. That's what made me afraid, way back in my mind. Me getting crazy. Me running away and living somewhere on the street without a job. Me getting thrown into jail for a fight I didn't walk away from.

Sports helped. I found that my mind rested whenever I was coaching, so I coached basketball at the high school and Little League baseball in the community. When I was coaching, I wasn't thinking about anything bad, see. My mind was only on the game, and my mind stayed focused on something good. I had the power to do that, you know. I could consciously tell my mind to go to a good place by where I decided that my feet would take me. The kids called me Coach Powers, or just Coach D, and I found it satisfying to help a kid find his way in life.

One spring afternoon, oh, maybe about 1960, I was coaching the Clinchco Cardinals twelve-year-old boys' team. We'd had winning seasons before, but this year we were struggling. It was only the third inning, and the Nora Braves, a team from down the road, were already skunking us—21 to 6. I was never one of these uncompetitive coaches who doesn't care if his team wins or not. But I wasn't a yeller like some other coaches, either. I wanted to win, same as any man, but I never screamed and hollered at the kids. That was never my style.

Well, I did a double take when the other team's coach smirked at the score, hollered for his star pitcher to hit the pine, then called over Rufus Edward Nickles from right field. It was an insult to our team, and I understood what the other coach was getting at. Rufus was about nine years old, as scrawny as a wet squirrel. Everybody called him Shanghai, and his ears stuck out like a late model Ford with the doors open. He'd broken his arm after tripping a few years back while carrying a coal bucket, and his elbow stayed twisted like a sore thumb. His daddy had died a few years back, and I think the only reason anybody let him play was because his big brother was on the team. So now the coach was ordering little Shanghai to pitch. That decision set me to wincing. It didn't matter how badly we were losing. Putting Shanghai on the mound was gonna break that kid wide open.

Shanghai trotted over. He must've decided to give it his best shot, for he wound up and chucked the ball. His first pitch hit the dirt early and rolled over the plate. He dug in his toes and threw his second. It was wide by a country mile. Shanghai's third pitch looked so low and inside it nearly scuffed the shins of my batter. Kids were laughing now. Shanghai was red-faced and sweating. But he spit in the dirt and threw his fourth—a wild outside attempt at a curveball, which walked our batter.

Things went from bad to worse for their team. Shanghai threw eight more balls in a row and walked our next two batters. Now he had loaded bases on his hands. Kids from both teams were hollering. Well, I'll never forget the look of dismay in Shanghai's eyes when he saw that the next player up was Johnny Fleming, one of my best hitters. Poor old Shanghai tossed the meat right over the dish. I mean, that pitch was right over the plate, just begging to be walloped. Johnny hit a grand slam, and all our four players jogged around the bases and came home to score.

I'll give that boy credit. Shanghai was plumb determined. The game continued, and he kept tossing them in. My players kept whacking them out. The coach left him in the game just to get our team's goat, and the game ended with the score 21 to 19 for the Braves.

The kids scattered as soon as the game was over. I've seen some long faces in my life, but Shanghai's was about the longest. I didn't know whether the boy was about to cry or if he was the type who'd take off running, but I walked over to him anyway, put my arm around his shoulders, and said, "Well, cheer up, son. Your team won."

"Yeah," he said, "but I stunk."

"You know, if you're ever gonna make it as a pitcher, you gotta learn how to pull the trigger on the curveball," I said, with all honesty. "I'm not fussing at you, I'm just telling you—you can't over-squeeze the ball."

He looked at me. For the first time in six innings, I saw a grin. I guessed he'd caught the key part of what I said, which was what I wanted him to catch, for he asked, "You actually think I'm going to be a pitcher someday?" Shanghai's face grew real intense. I reckoned if he'd had a notebook right then, he'd be scribbling down everything I said.

I liked to see that in a kid, and a bright idea came to me. After a game, there's always plenty of work to be done, see. Cleaning up the field, sweeping the dugout. So I said, "I'll tell you what, you help me put all the stuff up, and I'll go ahead and buy you a milk shake. We'll talk some more about pitching."

He grinned big at that idea. So that's what we did.

That was the start of a good little friendship between Shanghai and me. Shanghai started practicing his pitches. He didn't even have a baseball of his own, but he threw rocks up behind the supply store until his arm was sore. He'd come hang around my practices, and after a while he got his shot and started pitching for his own team. Wouldn't you know it, the boy showed real improvement.

The year Shanghai Nickles turned twelve, his team had a

champion season. They went 17 and 1, and Shanghai was responsible for pitching fourteen of those games. After the regular season, he played on the all-star team. I was coaching that team, and it was made up of the best kids from all over the league. I picked him first.

When Shanghai turned fourteen, he started pitching for men's leagues. I let out a low whistle at that news. Men's leagues in coal mining towns are made up of some pretty rough customers. Some mine owners even brought in guys and handed them easy jobs, just so they could pitch on their league teams. Well, Shanghai held his own just fine in those men's leagues. I noticed no one else came to watch him play, and as often as not I'd be the first to shake his hand when he came off the field.

Years went by, and Shanghai grew up. He moved out to California and pitched as a semi-pro player for the Glendale Leagues. It was a real job, getting money to play baseball. He never made it to the majors, but it didn't matter none. He was playing at a real high level, and then he retired from baseball, moved back to Clinchco, and became active around the community. He got married. Had kids. Landed and held a good job in radio. Announcing the community games became one of his regular tasks. I told myself that boy turned out real well, and I grinned to think that of the kids I coached, Shanghai's story was just one of many successes. One kid went on to become a doctor. Others I coached became bankers and businessmen, teachers and firemen. It wasn't the jobs they held that made me proud so much as the character instilled in them. They loved their families and communities and were proud to be doing something worthwhile with their lives. I reckoned that was time well spent, out on the mound all those years with those kids, and I knew at the core of me that these kids and their futures were what we'd been fighting for over in Europe.

Most days, most weeks, most years were real fine for me. I settled into a routine, and that's what made life smooth for me. Our own kids grew and kept growing. We went to movies and ball games as a family. Every Saturday we'd go to a little joint called the Pink Room to meet our friends, eat steak, and dance. It was the only real place to go out to for miles around, and sometimes we'd hang around until three in the morning, just laughing and having a good time together.

I'd still have those sleepless nights once in a while. Sometimes two, three hours would go by and I'd get up and pace around in my workshop, trying to shake the darkness out of my head. On those nights I'd think about deeper things, you know, about how my life was going. Mine was a basic life except for that one dark area of the war. I tried praying. I was pretty sure God held some answers to those unsettling questions. But whenever I prayed, I was never quite sure what to say.

I'd always considered myself a Christian, you know. Not that I ever talked about religion with anybody. That business, I figured, is best kept between a man and God. But Mama and Daddy were always churchgoers, so I was, too, at least when it wasn't fishing season. At first, Clinchco only had one church building. Half the Sundays it was used for the Freewill Baptists, and the other half was the Methodists' turn. Dorothy and me got active in the church like most people do in the South, and we were never folks for sitting around with nothing to do, so we taught Sunday School for a lot of years. I liked the thought of a church helping kids make good decisions, so for a while I became the Sunday School superintendent and helped organize all the kids in their departments.

Now, I never fussed about this out loud, but I confess I never much liked the pictures of Jesus that they showed around to the kids at Sunday school. Those pictures often showed him all long-haired and hollow-cheeked, looking as sad and miserable as if he'd swallowed a lemon, you know. So whenever it was my turn to talk to the kids, I'd tell them about the Jesus I read about in the Bible. He was always on the run, turning over tables in the temple, doctoring up sick folks, arguing against the hypocrites, calming stormy seas. I pictured Jesus as a man you wanted to follow into battle. A man you could trust with your life. Sort of like Major Dick Winters, you know. Folks from the Missionary Baptist Association came around in the 1960s, and we liked what they had to say, so Dorothy and me became charter members of a new church they were starting. The church started meeting in houses at first, then we built a building some ways down the road. The congregation grew in size a bit, but we always stayed a small church. Folks were friendly there, and the church had a calm, laid-back atmosphere.

One Sunday a few years later—I was in my mid-forties then—our preacher was talking to us in the pews about getting baptized. The act of baptism showed other folks that you had accepted the hospitality of God, he said. It showed you'd left your old life behind and had decided to start living in the new. Well, how he described baptism like that made me think real hard. I was still carrying around a heavy load of things I wanted to leave behind. Those nightmares, you know, those memories of things I'd done, things I'd seen. So I thought I might do that. One Sunday morning I got down in those waters and the preacher dunked me and I came up again, wet and smiling and fresh, with people singing hymns afterward. That was how I wanted to keep on living—new, like how the preacher described—and I reckon getting baptized after the war helped me go that direction. I never talked about religion with anybody, even after that. But I found it more peaceful when I prayed. And I started sleeping better. I did.

So that's how it went. Years flew by, and all that time I was a working man at the mine caring for my family and enjoying our hometown and coaching sports and going fishing whenever I had the odd free moment, and not doing much else. Our kids grew up. Wayne became a schoolteacher, and a real good one. He ended up marrying that sassy girl, Sandy, the one who used to throw rocks at my car on my way to work. Sandy became a schoolteacher also, and she didn't throw rocks anymore. We were pleased with how things turned out in the end. Margo grew up and married a fine man named Seldon Johnson who worked high up with coal mining products. They did real well for themselves and moved about an hour away. In time, four grandchildren came along—three boys, Jake and Luke and Clay, and a little girl named Dove. They were about the best thing that could ever happen to a fella. The oldest one, Jake, started calling me Pub even before he could hardly talk, and sure enough I had a new nickname that stuck. The grandkids called Dorothy "Guy," so that nickname stuck as well, and for years to come we were known all over simply as Pub and Guy. I gave nicknames to all the grandkids right back. I called Jake, Jakefellar. Luke was Pookus. Clay was Clayfellar. And Dove was Woo.

The grandkids came around our house a lot, and Dorothy and me liked that fine. We were always helping them out with school-work, science projects, taking them fishing, whatnot. Once, Jake and I built a model hurricane with a wooden frame around a hot plate and a tub of water. It cooked up a fine storm. Another time one of the grandsons busted his G.I. Joe. He was sniffling and cry-ing, convinced it would never be fixed. But Dorothy said, "Well, let Pub fix it." It was his bedtime then, and my grandson went to sleep a sad little man. But I went to tinkering with that G.I. Joe down in my workshop, and sure enough by morning, that toy was sitting on the kitchen table, good as new. We all got along fine as friends even, and when Jake was about five, he got bunk beds in his room. He said I was his best friend and asked me to have the first sleepover with him. So I did, me in the upper bunk, him in the lower, and we ate popcorn and told funny stories and had ourselves a real swell time. Luke always enjoyed drawing as a little fella, so one day I commissioned a painting from him. I wanted an owl perched on a tree branch, and after he drew it up and brought it to me, I paid him what was agreed, then raved to everyone about how good it looked. It did look good, you know. That painting hung in my workshop for years. And Dove, well, a fella knows exactly how lucky he is when he's got a granddaughter as cute as her. She was always toddling around and getting into mischief, and we had ourselves a grand ole time, we did.

Those were the seasons of life a fella likes a lot. I was real satisfied with how things turned out, you know. I'd come back from a day's work and sit on my porch and have a cigarette and a drink. On a nice evening, that porch was the happiest place on earth. A train would be running through the mountains, and I'd look out on the world and ponder things. Nothing much in particular. Mostly, just how happy I was.

Now, I did enjoy a regular cocktail most every evening, it's true. When it came to drinking, I did do that a bit, but fortunately it never bit me like it did some men. I liked Early Times whiskey, and once in a long while I drank bourbon. I always enjoyed a vodka tonic. That and a screwdriver were my favorite drinks. We went to several Easy Company reunions over the years, and the son of

George Luz, after he got older, would always bring me a screw-driver first thing after I got in the door. I kept in contact with the guys okay. Fellas get busy when they're raising families, but we'd write letters back and forth. Occasionally we'd go visit them, or them, us. Gordon and Lipton came by, Popeye and Skinny Sisk. McClung. It was real good to see them. Real good.

The fellas from Easy Company used to joke with me that I was basically just a mountain man at heart, and that I was into drink-ing moonshine. I'd never admit or deny it. But one time Sergeant Taylor was giving me a hard time before a reunion. We'd call each other up once in a while, you know. So I said to him, "Well, why don't you bring me some moonshine sometime." So that year at the reunion they brought me a pickle jar with some White Lightning in it. That was a pretty big joke, and I took a sip and said to the fellas, "You know, you have to cook it twice to make it this good." I couldn't tell if it was good moonshine or not, but I figured that I'd let on like I did.

After I'd worked maybe twenty-three years at the mine, I decided to retire. I piddled around in my garden for a while, then helped build my house. It wasn't a big house. Just comfortable, with a good wide porch out in front for sitting. We built our house in 1986. The McClure River ran right next to that house, and a rail-way ran right next to the road. We got an opportunity to name the little road in the neighborhood, too, and Dorothy told me to call it Shifty Lane, so that's what the sign says. The coal trains came regular out of Kentucky and went to Kingsport and beyond, but the noise didn't bother us none. Trains had been around these parts as long as I could remember, and I liked the way they sounded. One of the best things about our new house was that hummingbirds came around. I put up a feeder on our front porch, and I bet there were twenty of them before long. Sometimes the ants crawled up and messed with the feeder, and that was an aggravation to me, but I found if I put a little cooking oil where the feeder was hanging up there, then the ants couldn't cause a fuss. That's what occupied my mind much of the time. Things like that, you know.

Well, I ran for the county supervisor seat somewhere in there, because I figured there were lots of things that a man could do to get things done right, but I lost the nomination. Somebody joked that it was a good thing, too, because I was too honest for politics. So, losing that seat was okay by me. Let somebody else run things. Fine.

I'd always done the grocery shopping for Dorothy and me, for as long back as I could remember. Each week I'd read the newspaper ads and get the best prices. I'd always go to the same place—Food City, it was called, and I got to be good friends with the managers. Oh, sometimes they'd aggravate me, sure. One day they advertised a special sale on chicken. I went and they were all out. I told the manager, "If you're gonna advertise it, make sure you got enough to sell." But they were fine folks there, they really were.

Now, I never told anybody this, maybe only my son Wayne when he grew older, but the real reason I liked grocery shopping was that I'd meet my brothers there each week and we'd slip some brandy drinking into our shopping. We'd each take a nip or two, walk around the store a bit, then go stand outside Food City and talk and have another drink or two, you know. That was our secret, and that's how it went for a long while.

Sad to say, my brothers all died a while back, one by one. None of them were as old as they needed to be before they passed, and it was real sad for me for some time. My mother died, too, around that time, but she'd lived long and healthy and was full of years and joy. Somehow it wasn't as sad when she passed, though I missed her dearly. My sister Gaynelle's still living and going strong. She married young and lives over in Roanoke, about four hours away. I love her richly, I surely do.

Well, most other things went well for me in this latter season of life, but one day I was out trout fishing, see, and my eyes starting blurring to bait the hook. I'd been noticing things go wrong like that for some time, but hadn't said anything. Fortunately, my grandson Clay was with me and he helped bait my hook, but I was worried just the same.

I went to the doctor, and he said my eyesight was about to get real bad. I couldn't say I liked the sound of that one bit. Sure enough, what the doctor said started coming true. The doctor called it macular degeneration, MD for short. It meant I was losing all my eyesight except for my peripheral vision. I kept driving, mind you. I guess I knew the roads around here as good as anyone. But I'd go to Food City, and they'd move things around on me, I guessed, because I couldn't find things like I used to. Or I'd go to watch basketball games, same as always, but things would get real blurry out on the court. I'd talk to Shanghai Nickles, he was usually announcing the game, and say, "Now, Shanghai, you call the game real clear, you hear. You got to be my eyes for me, you know." And he would. But it wasn't the same, you know. It wasn't the same.

Well. Shit. I started having some powerful chest pains one day, and they took me in and said my heart was choked up. They opened my heart right up, they did, and I had bypass surgery. Then I got over that, but then along came prostate cancer, and that sure causes a fella a heap of aggravation. But I took radiation treatments and beat the cancer. So that took care of that.

After my treatments, my eyes started getting real bad. I always loved to read, you know, but it got so I couldn't even see the words on a page anymore, not even out of the corners of my eyes. I loved Westerns—anything by Louis L'Amour. My favorite book of his was called *Last of the Breed*. I used to read it over and over again. I also liked anything by Ian Fleming, the guy who wrote James Bond. And *Last of the Mohicans* was one of the best books ever written, as far as I was concerned. But then I couldn't read anymore, so I got the idea of getting books on tape through the visually handicapped organization. I'd sit in my chair and listen to tapes, but it wasn't the same.

A fella starts feeling real down about himself when his health turns. I'd have good days and bad days, but I started having more bad days than not. The life I was living wasn't the life I wanted to live anymore. I couldn't do the things I wanted to do. I didn't look forward to anything anymore. The devil starts whispering powerful lies in a fella's ear when he's not feeling healthy, and if a fella's not careful, he starts to believe those lies. A man like me had lived his life as well as could be lived, I figured, and there's something to be said for climbing off a horse while it's still kicking, you know. So I wondered, you know. I'd be sitting in my chair day after day feeling bad about things, smoking my cigarettes, wondering if my time was up. I felt so low. Most days. So low. That's how I felt. My kids were worried I was depressed, but I never liked that word much. Still, I wondered if anything could ever make me feel better. And I doubted anything could.

Well, then, wouldn't you know it, one day I got a phone call. And everything got set to change.

16

THE BAND OF BROTHERS

B ack in 1992, a book had been written about Easy Company by this historian named Stephen Ambrose. He'd called me on the phone a few times and we'd talked. That was the input I had in the book. Seemed like a friendly enough fella, and after that book came out he mailed me a copy. Well, I read it, scowled, and mailed it right back. I never fussed to anybody in particular about it, but Mister Ambrose had gotten things dead wrong. Not everything in the book, mind you, just one important section. Important to me, anyway. I don't know exactly who had given him wrong information, but in his book it said that when it was real cold and miserable out there in Bastogne, Lieutenant Shames had given me an order to go out on a patrol, and I'd plumb refused to go.

To an old military man like me, that was a slap in the face. I'd never disobeyed an order. Not even in the worst conditions. I might have grumbled a bit, but I always did my duty. Well, I called up Lieutenant Shames and asked him if he'd seen the book, and he told me he didn't like it either and he'd never said anything like that fool story about me to Mister Ambrose. So somewhere lines had gotten crossed, and I understand how that can happen in a book when an author is talking with a lot of fellas. But still, I wasn't happy.

Time passed, and I pretty much forgot about things. The book wasn't a best seller—not at first. I think one guy from work read it. He said, "Really? You were in all that stuff over in the war? How come you never talked to me about it?"

"I never talked to anyone about it," I said.

My daughter, Margo, wrote to Mister Ambrose and asked him to change things. I think Herb Suerth, the president of the Men of Easy Company Association, did that, too. I heard he told Ambrose I was the best noncom in Easy Company. Well, I don't know about all that, but I guess Mister Ambrose checked things out more and agreed to take that wrong section out of the book. He called me up and explained things, and we had a good talk. He said the section would be removed in a later edition. And it was.

Well, some years passed, and that phone call came, the one that made me much more happy. It came one day out of the blue and was from Playtone Studios, a movie company out in Hollywood. Seemed that two famous fellas by the names of Tom Hanks and Steven Spielberg had read Mister Ambrose's book, and they'd liked it a lot. They figured that enough time had passed since World War II that a lot of folks who maybe hadn't been around then might want to know what had gone on during those years, and they liked the idea that the book traced the story of only one company of soldiers. Plenty of other books about the war had been written, see, but those other books were more about the generals, the higher-ups, the strategy at the upper-brass level. Mister Ambrose's book talked about war from the common man's point of view. That was us.

The fella from the studios wanted to know if they could fly out to Clinchco and interview me. They wanted to hear my words and record some of them for a documentary part of the movie. The idea tickled me. Imagine, someone making a movie with me in it. So I said yes, and they flew out with a camera crew and an interviewer, and we had ourselves a good time. They were real nice folks from Playtone, and I showed them my garden and my rifles, and I let them shoot my M1 off my front porch, like I often did. They asked me all sorts of questions about the war. I knew they wouldn't use all the material, and that didn't matter. I just tried to answer the questions as best as I knew.

I wasn't a complete stranger to moviemaking ways, mind you. A few years earlier a movie had been made, which they called *Saving Private Ryan*. It was a fictional story, but based on true events that happened around Normandy. Mister Ambrose had also written a few paragraphs about the true events in his book *Band of Brothers*. The real "Private Ryan" was a fella named Fritz Niland. He grew up in Tonawanda, New York, about five doors down from Skip Muck. Fritz was in the 101st, but in a different outfit, so he came around every so often to visit Skip when we were in Europe. Don Malarkey and Joe Toye became friends of his, and they met up for beers a few times. Anyway, the interesting thing about that movie was that they'd based one of the characters in it on me—the sniper in the group who looks for Private Ryan. At least that's what was said, but I don't know how close the connection was. I saw the movie and liked it fine, although it showed the sniper fella using a scope on his rifle. I never used a scope. None of us did. I wouldn't say we even had a real sniper in our outfit. McClung, Sergeant Taylor, and me were about the three best shots in the company, but we always just aimed our rifles at whatever we needed to, then hit whatever we needed to hit. Still, I wouldn't fault the movie none for showing a scope on a rifle. It was a really well made picture show. It was.

Well, a while after the folks from Playtone visited, a nice young actor named Peter Youngblood Hills phoned me up and asked if he could also come by for a spell. He was going to play me in the *Band of Brothers* miniseries. From him, I learned this wasn't going to be just one movie, but a lot of different episodes they were going to show on a cable channel called HBO. I said sure, I'd like to meet Peter. It also tickled me to think that some fine-looking young fella was going to play my character on TV.

Peter flew over from London, where they were working on the series. He spent a day and a night with us in our home, and asked me all sorts of questions about my life, about how I did things, how I said things. I showed him how I carried my rifle and what kind it was. Lot of guys used the carbine, you know, and some guys used Thompsons, but I always liked the M1 Garand best. Even though I couldn't see very well, I still knew my way around Dickenson County, so I drove Peter up to Cumberland Gap where you can see several states from this one point. All the while he asked about little mannerisms I had. How I said certain words. He was practicing the way I talked, you know. I told him I talked like everybody else, you know, but he was studying hard to get my accent down, I reckoned that's what they call it. I didn't believe I have an accent, and I told Peter exactly that. He just grinned. Well, Peter was a fine boy, and we were all getting along real swell. I joked to Peter that Dorothy and me might want to adopt him as one of our own. But then we went to town one night and took him to eat. My, that boy could attack a plate of food, and afterward I said, "You know, Peter, you better forget about that adopting business—I can't afford to feed you."

In 2001, the *Band of Brothers* miniseries was all set to come out. HBO flew all of us in Easy Company who were able over to Normandy for the premiere. That was real nice of them, and I hadn't been back to Europe since the war. We were driving to the premiere at Utah Beach, and one of the producers turned around in the van and said, "You know, in about ten minutes your life is going to change forever." None of us old-timers had any idea what he meant. Some of the men were rattled when they saw the showing, but that wasn't what the producer was getting at. We'd still need to find that out for ourselves. Now, I liked the show real fine. It was only a movie after all, close to the real thing, but only close. You could never truly show how scared a man was, how hungry and cold he truly was. You could never explain it. You just had to live through it to understand.

After the miniseries, we all went back home, and life did indeed start to get different. Folks would stop you on the street and say, "Hey, Shifty, I saw you on TV last night." That was the beginning of what the producer was talking about. Those comments felt okay to me, you know, I was the same as I'd always been. In fact, I was happy at what the series was doing. After the war, I just came back to the States and lived my life without talking to anybody, you know. But *Band of Brothers* was serving a greater purpose. It was the first time that things about World War II had been publicized in a big way. For years and years, the war and all the veterans who'd fought in it had gone unrecognized. After the miniseries came out, there was a new sense of gratefulness—for veterans everywhere, not just those who served in World War II.

Now, some folks wondered why all this fuss was being made

over Easy Company, and I thought they had a point. We knew our outfit had been well trained. We were one of the best companies the American Army had at the time, and we were proud of that. Sure. But we also knew that we weren't the only company to do good things or suffer losses. Easy Company became sort of a symbol for all other elite outfits, I guessed. But I wished somehow that all the outfits could have had all the recognition that Easy Company started to get.

About a year went by, and I guess that *Band of Brothers* miniseries did real well on HBO, for soon we got news that it had been nominated for a bunch of Emmy Awards. In 2002, HBO flew us out to Hollywood to take part in the awards show. I had to slap my knee when I saw a bunch of old soldiers all decked out in tuxedos, riding in limousines. There was One Lung McClung, Moe Alley, Hayseed Rogers—all the guys who'd once shared foxholes together were now strolling down the red carpet.

I shook hands with David Schwimmer, the fella who played Captain Sobel in the series. He was a real nice fella and we talked for a while. I thought he did an excellent job of portraying Captain Sobel and I told him so, although the first thing I said to him was, "I think I want to knock the shit out of you." He got the joke and laughed. I wasn't really aggravated. Not after all those years. Captain Sobel wasn't all that bad. I knew all his hard training helped get us through the war.

For the actual awards show, Major Winters stayed in the auditorium for the telecast, but they took the rest of us over to the St. Regis Hotel nearby, so they'd have enough seats for us all. That was fine. The plan was that when the nominations and winners were announced, they were going to combine shots of us with Major Winters and what was happening on stage, split-screen style. I started studying that and thought, You know, I'd like all my hillbilly friends back in Clinchco to see that I'm really here in Hollywood on TV. So I asked the boy in charge if I could move my chair up a few rows. He said okay. But then I got seated up in the front row, and that boy behind the camera was swinging the camera over only so far, and it didn't look to me like he was gonna get me on camera after all. So I pulled him aside, and he recognized my name and that I was known as the sharpshooter in the series, so I said, "I'm noticing that you're not bringing the camera down to where I'm sitting. If you don't move that camera, I'll shoot you right between the eyes." He had a good chuckle, and then, during the ceremony, the cameraman looked over at me. The camera still wasn't on me, so I gave him a stone-faced glare and tapped my finger right between my eyes. I guess that boy got the message, for he brought the camera on over and it showed me on screen.

After the Emmys were over and *Band of Brothers* won five or six awards, we all went to this fancy restaurant in Hollywood called Spago to celebrate. Tom Hanks was milling about over there, and Mister Hanks and I had a real fine talk. We were passing around the Emmy statue he'd won, and he asked me what I might do with it. I said I might take it home and fix it to the hood of my jeep. He had a good laugh.

Well, we all went home from Hollywood after that, but what that producer said to us in the back of the van about our lives never being the same started coming true rapid-fire. I started getting mail. Lots of mail. Fan mail. Folks wanting books signed, pictures, hats. I tried to answer all the mail, sign whatever I could, but it was hard because I wasn't able to see so well. Fortunately, I got to be good friends with a fella named Johnny Sykes, the postmaster at the Clinchco post office. I developed a routine where I'd come to the post office every day at the same time and say, "Hello post office," and Johnny Sykes would take a break and talk with me. He'd read all my mail out loud to me, and help me sign where things needed to be signed. We talked all the while, about politics, taxes, fishing, whatever. Johnny Sykes became a real good friend over time. My fishing days were pretty much over by then, but he'd often catch a mess of fish and bring me some.

I'd get phone calls, too. And I didn't mind speaking to people on the phone. Sometimes folks wanted to come meet me. A fella came with a camera one day and walked up on the porch where I was sitting having a cigarette. I stood to shake his hand and the first thing he said was, "Well, holy cow. You're really real."

We had a couple from Rome, Italy, call us and ask if they could come meet us. We said sure, so they came over and we invited them to spend a day and night at our home. Never knew them before or anything, they just called and wanted to know if they could come on over. So we had a good time.

I started getting asked to come speak to schools and different functions. I went to a couple colleges, some high schools, a couple elementary schools. I found that the kids in the fifth, sixth, and seventh grades were the most interested of anyone. You could hear a pin drop when you went in, and they could ask you some tough questions, too. I'd often fly to different events, different states, different countries overseas to speak. Sometimes other men from Easy Company would come on those trips, and we always had a good time meeting up again. Once I went on a USO tour; my son, Wayne, went with me. It was real good. We did other trips where we visited soldiers stationed in South Korea and Japan. Sometimes it came close to startling to see the reception the men of Easy Company had when it came to visiting soldiers. I guessed *Band of Brothers* had made a real impression on a lot of them. They'd stand in long lines to shake our hands and have us sign books and hats and pictures. Someone said we'd become the rock stars of the military world.

On the Korean trip, we were walking into a place to eat, four Easy Company men and four of the actors who played us in the series, and they had up one of those movie poster cutouts like they have for race car drivers at the grocery store. Well, we went and looked at that poster, and it was me. Peter Youngblood Hills, anyway, the actor who played me. That was strange, you know, seeing that. But it made me grin.

About the only problem I ever had was that sometimes when I was up on stage during all those tours, I needed to use the bathroom on account of my prostate problems. They'd have us all sitting there in a row for a long time, asking us questions, and it was hard for me to get up. So I developed this signal with Wayne. If I put one hand over my nose and pumped my other in the air like I was blowing a train's whistle, well, that meant it was time, you know, because I needed help getting to where I was going. That signal worked out fine.

It was real good meeting all those folks when we were on tour. One fall, it was just me speaking over at Mountain Empire Community College, and a woman stood up during a question and answer time and introduced herself as Jacqueline Havaux Bowers. She explained that when she as a little girl, she lived in Bastogne, Belgium, when it was under Nazi occupation. She was one of those kids we'd see every so often, coming round and asking GIs for cigarettes and chocolate. From where she stood, out on the floor of the auditorium, she said something that really put a lump in my throat. "I want to thank you from the bottom of my heart for what you did for us," she said. "I wouldn't be here at all, my family wouldn't be here at all, if it wasn't for soldiers like you." Then she came up to the podium and gave me a great big hug. That put things into perspective for me, you know. All those years ago. To think here was someone who'd been helped by what we did.

Well, I found I wasn't feeling low at all anymore. After the series came out and after all those speaking events came our way, I had a new reason to get up every morning, sick as I was some days. But most days I was feeling real good. Anytime the phone rang, I'd answer it. Often it was a request to do something, and most often than not, I'd say yes.

In 2004 we went over to Normandy again, for the sixtieth anniversary of the D-day invasion. That was a real good time, seeing all the guys again. Plenty of other veterans came to that event, too, and it was great to see so many veterans get to talk about what they had done and where they had been. The weather got mighty hot over at the dedication, but they passed out water and cookies and things like that. So it was okay.

Major Winters started not feeling well. We used to phone each other now and again, but it got to where he'd have a hard time on the phone. So we'd write now and again. I'd call McClung and Rogers, Jim Alley and Popeye. They'd call, too.

My oldest grandson, Jake, along with his wife, Dawnyale, took me back to visit Toccoa. Jake wanted to run the mountain, and that sounded good to me. Toccoa looked different than I remembered. They'd smoothed the road out. Trees were a lot bigger than when we'd been there. Jake and Dawnyale ran up Currahee, and I ran a bit of it with them. Oh, maybe a couple hundred yards or so. We drove through the town, and it didn't take more than ten minutes until word got out and newspapers showed up. They ran a story with a headline that said, "Grandson Follows Grandfather's Footsteps."

Staff Sergeant Robert Rader was a good friend of ours. He died back in the late 1990s, then some years later they named a bridge in his honor out there in Paso Robles, California, where his family stayed. Eight or nine of the Easy Company guys went down for the bridge dedication, including me and McClung. It was a good time, and I was glad we could honor Bob Rader that way. On the way back to wherever we needed to be, all the fellas were in this van together and got thirsty. So we stopped in at a bar in this little town we were driving through. McClung went in to see if it was a suitable establishment. He came out after a minute and said, "This is our kind of place, boys. The bartender's got two black eyes." So we all piled out and went in, laughing.

In late 2006, McClung and me and several of the guys from Easy Company went back to Bastogne for the first time since the war. We hiked through the woods in the snow, saw the old foxholes that were still there, and met some former German soldiers who, way back when, had been shooting at us from the other side of the road. It sent a shiver up my spine being back in Bastogne. I can't say that I liked being there again, even for a tour. But the trip brought to me a sense of closure, you know. The war was truly over. Finally I could shut the book. We shook those old German soldiers' hands, and they shook ours. And through an interpreter we shared some stories. We were even able to swap some jokes. None of us were fighting anymore.

Well, we went home and I started studying the last few years since the series had come out, and I felt so thankful for the good reception we'd all received. I never could have imagined things would have turned out as good as they did, but I felt like I could do things again, you know. A remembered confidence was coursing through my veins, though this time I felt at peace, like all along I had done what I was supposed to do. I didn't need to explain the things I'd seen in the war. The things I'd done. I was Shifty Powers again, standing side by side with the best friends I'd ever known. I was ten feet tall and bulletproof.

That confidence worked itself out in some peculiar ways. Once, right around then, Dorothy and me were back at our house in Clinchco all alone, when all these motorcycles rumbled up and parked next to the river, a little distance away. It was growing dark and I started thinking they were going to have a wild party down near our house. Well, I didn't want them raising Cain on my property, so I went and talked to a neighbor down the lane and said, "You keep your gun on me. I'm going down there to tell those guys to shove off."

The neighbor agreed, so I hiked to the corner of my property, and, sure enough, all these young fellas had started drinking and carrying on. I walked into the center of those bikers, took a stick, and knocked out their fire. We had a few words along the lines of what I reckoned they'd understand. Then I started walking back to my house. About five minutes later, sure enough, they started up their motorcycles and roared out of there.

It felt good. To be back, you know.

It felt real good.

17

THE LAST GARDEN

I'm sorry to say that my good friend Popeye Wynn wasn't with us when we had all that fun with the Band of Brothers tours. Popeye died in March 2000, right before the series came out. He was a kind, easygoing man and a great soldier. In his last years, he'd bought an old log cabin in Kitty Hawk, North Carolina, where he spent his last days with his family, fishing in the outer banks. I missed him greatly.

A few more years passed, like they're prone to do, and it was a short while into 2008 when I started having chest pains. At first I thought it was congestion, so I brushed it off. I had plenty of other things to worry about. In addition to the chest pains, my eyesight was getting worse all the time. My kids took me to Duke University for that, oh, three or four times. The doctors did laser surgery on me there, but it got to be so there wasn't anything more they could do. I still had a bit of my peripheral vision left, but even that wasn't very good. I hung on to my driver's license, though. I still drove in daytime, only around the roads I knew.

I turned eighty-five that March, and when the weather got warm enough I planted a wonderful garden. It was going to be a real good garden that summer of 2008. Corn. Peas. Tomatoes. Beans. Cucumbers. Beets. Sunflowers—real big sunflowers, as tall as your head. I planted my garden on the north side of the property. We called that section the North Forty, and I also planted another garden on the south side. We called that the South Forty. I got my tomatoes staked up good and high. Deer tended to wander by and eat the tops of my tomato plants. I'd see their tracks in the morning. They'd walk down the mountain and across the river and into my yard.

It was a mild spring, I noticed, when I'd be out cultivating and planting. My daughter, Margo, came over and helped as often as she could. Most days I didn't feel well, but I thought I didn't let on. One day we were both out working in the garden, and I was digging a hole for a tomato plant. I said something—and I regret this so much—I said something to Margo that was short. By the look on her face, I could tell I'd hurt her. I sat down on the bench and said, "Sissy, if I say something that hurts your feelings, I really don't mean it, I just get so tired sometimes." And she knew what I meant, I think, for she came over and gave me a long hug. All was forgiven, you know, but in my bones I felt this tiredness I couldn't put my finger on. A storm seemed brewing on the horizon. The air felt heavy. The sky looked gray.

That summer I made plans to go to Iraq in September with some of the Band of Brothers. We wanted to go encourage the coalition troops. Boy, I really wanted to go on that trip. My chest was still hurting me, though, so I went to the doctor to get an

X-ray and antibiotics for that congestion, but the pills didn't seem to help much.

All this time I kept having some squabbles with a gas company, and that occupied a piece of my mind. I'd always thought that when a body gets up in years, this kind of aggravation would let up, but it didn't seem to. My grandparents had owned about two hundred and fifty acres up on Frying Pan where I used to hunt as a kid. When my grandparents passed, their property got divided among their kids. A few family members sold their chunks, but my family kept ours. Well, a couple of the pieces that got sold had the access road running through them. One gas company bought that property, and they were real nice about letting us use their road to get up to our land. Then the rights got transferred to another company, and the other company leaned more toward the ornery side. They said we couldn't use the road anymore and put a gate on the road and a lock on the gate. I went and talked to them about getting a key to that gate. I talked till I was blue in the face. But that didn't do no good. So I went and shot the lock off the gate.

Now, it was in our legal rights for us to use that road, because there's a cemetery on our property at the top of that road, and nobody can legally block access to a cemetery. So I went over to the Clintwood Courthouse and talked to a boy there about getting a key. The boy at the courthouse said fine and mailed me three keys, but not one of them worked. Sometimes when you cut a key, the way they machine it, things don't line up right at first. So I took a little file and smoothed the edges of the key to get the burrs off. But still it didn't work. So I decided to let things rest for a spell. I reckoned a man needs to let some things go unresolved.

Well, my chest was still hurting, so I went in for more tests. The doctors did every test you could think of and found another cancer outside my lungs. It wasn't lung cancer. It was bone cancer, and none of us were happy about that. They scheduled me for radiation treatments, every day, five days a week, for eighteen days, and I started taking those. Those treatments absolutely wiped me out. I'd get up in the morning, drink my coffee, and go to the cancer center. It's a sixty-mile trip, and Wayne would need to drive me that far. I'd come home, sit around and rest, then go to bed and get ready to do it again the next day.

Those treatments made me real weak. I liked to get out on the deck and shoot my rifle, you know. Nobody lived very close around our house, so it was okay. I couldn't see to hit a target very well anymore, but I knew where they were. I didn't hit them all the time, but I'd hear the gun and smell the smoke, so I'd enjoy that. My M1 was my favorite rifle, but it got hard to lift, you know, and I told Dorothy, "You know, that doggone rifle has gotten fatter since the war." Ammunition for M1s was hard to come by, but my friends would bring me clips. I had a .22 with a scope, which helped me see the targets, so I'd shoot that every so often. Then I had a Lugar that I'd shoot, and a .22 pistol that I'd like to shoot. As a last resort I had a BB gun, and I'd take that out on the deck.

But those days after the treatments, I mostly sat.

Our dear granddaughter-in-law Amanda, who's married to Luke, contracted cancer as well during this time, and she and I had similar treatments. It seemed strange—she, in her twenties, and me, such an old-timer, fighting the same disease. I gave her a nickname, like I did with all my grandkids. I called her Mandy Pandy, and we'd compare notes on how things were going, you know. After we'd both had treatments, her hair started to grow back, and she bleached it blond. I joked with her that I hoped my hair would grow back the same color.

Well, the months went on, and Mandy Pandy started beating her cancer and feeling better, and I was real happy for her and the family, I was. What aggravated me was knowing I wasn't getting the best of mine. Most days I was feeling so weak. After a while about all I could do is sit on the front porch and watch the hummingbirds come around. Then I was staying inside more, sitting in my chair, listening to books on tape. That's what I did on good days.

I got to thinking about all my friends in Easy Company, and how there were only a few men left. At our age, a man couldn't help but look to the other side, you know. Some of the men didn't want to talk about it at all. They were putting off thinking about death, as best as they could, I guessed. Some of the men acted like it was no big deal, you know. But I knew death worried some of the men, too. At our age, it was right around the corner, and we all needed to face it as best we knew how.

My good friend Sergeant Jim "Moe" Alley died that March 2008, and I was sorry to hear the news. Lieutenant Buck Compton and his kids, Tracy and Syndee, went to the funeral, and said it was real nice. I guess old Moe had always been a tough nut to crack when it came to thinking about death and the spiritual side of life. At the funeral, the preacher told a story of how he'd visited Moe plenty of times, even when he was real sick at the end. The preacher always asked Moe if he was ready to go, and Moe always let on that he was fighting his Maker, not willing to give an inch. Then one day, I guess, Moe decided his battling ways were through. That day when the preacher visited and asked Moe if he was ready to do business with God, Moe said yes. So Moe and God did business. Then, just a day or so later, Moe waded through the river and passed to the other side. There wasn't any doubt in my mind that Moe was now walking those streets of gold.

That summer and fall 2008, another author decided to write another book about Easy Company. Seemed like all the folks who'd read *Band of Brothers* wanted to know more about the men's lives. Well, there weren't more than maybe thirty men in the company left by then, and twenty of them agreed to talk. So the author interviewed the last few surviving men from Company E, and asked about our stories. The book was going to be called *We Who Are Alive and Remain*, and it was set to come out in the spring of 2009. I was one of the men he talked to several times for that book. One day we talked, and it was a real nice fall day. Over the phone, I described to him all that was happening around me. The sun was shining, and I could feel its warmth on my face. I was able to sit outside on the deck and drink my coffee and listen to the birds. The leaves were turning color and coming off the trees. We had golden and red ones and brown ones. It was a real good day, and I told him so. A while later, he sent a preview copy of that book to the house, and even though I couldn't read it myself, the rest of the family read it and told me about it, and I liked how things were put. I said to Dorothy that I reckoned that book would be a dandy.

One morning I was thinking about what life might be like for me next spring when that book came out. I hoped I'd be there at the next reunion to see my friends again. But as I walked down the steps from the kitchen to the garage, I took a tumble. My legs were so shaky; my grip on the railing so weak. Dorothy and I talked, and from that point on I knew I had to be careful, so cautious about falling, you know. It was a mess, that cancer. It was really a mess. I still hoped I'd be able to get to the next reunion. The men would call every so often, and I'd call them back, too. Hayseed Rogers, he was ninety and still strong. His voice was always clear over the phone. And McClung, always good to talk with him. So good.

That September, I was all packed to go to Iraq on a Band of Brothers tour of the troops there. I wanted so badly to go, you know. But the night before I was to leave, I toppled over again and broke a rib. I was pretty certain then that my traveling days were over. I wasn't going anywhere with that broken rib inside me. I hated to let those troops down, you know, after I'd already said I'd go. I really did.

Well, things started going downhill more quickly after the broken rib. Nothing was healing right. I vowed I'd fight that cancer with everything I had. More chemo and radiation treatments were scheduled, and I took those. The doctor told me about a new treatment called CyberKnife, real high levels of radiation there, and I took that. He hoped the cancer would go into remission, and that's what I was hoping for, too. But that winter I felt so cold, you know, and my chest hurt all the time, and I wondered if I'd ever see the spring. My hearing stayed strong, and I was able to use the phone. I was glad about that. It's a wonder all the fellas weren't deaf. Those M1s were mighty loud, and we never wore ear protectors during the war, although I'd wear them after whenever I was shooting off my deck.

We were all real tickled near Christmas when Dawnyale, my other granddaughter-in-law, who's married to Jake, announced she was pregnant. I called Dawnyale, "Dawnypoo," as a nickname, and she's a swell girl. A brand-new baby was going to be born in the summer of 2009, and I wanted to see that baby, you know, maybe hold him if I felt well enough. They found out the baby was a boy and named him Gavin, even when he was still in the womb. I thought that was a fine name for my great-grandson. I did.

That March 2009, I turned eighty six. It was a real quiet birthday at home. The weather warmed a bit, and I always liked to do anything outdoors, but it was harder to get out the door to sit on the front porch, and I needed to grasp a walker on the way out. I hated that walker, but if I sat outside, I could hear the train horn blow, then the *chug-chug* and steel-on-steel roar as it came by the yard. Dorothy would come out and hand me a cookie. That was about all I felt like eating. I didn't exactly know why. All my life I'd had a good appetite. My favorite food was beef steak that I'd grill up myself. We always grilled everything—chicken, hamburgers. I loved to barbecue. Sometimes for dessert I'd fix up banana pudding, I liked it so much. I'd cut up the bananas, whip up the custard, and layer it all with vanilla wafers. But that spring, it was just Dorothy's peanut butter cookies. She'd fix up a fresh batch nearly every day. Then, it was every other day, because I wasn't eating as much. Then, maybe once or twice a week, you know. As the weeks wore on, I found I didn't have any appetite at all, you know. Sometimes I'd wake up at four in the morning. I couldn't tell you why, but on the days I felt sickest, I'd feel my best real early in the morning. Somebody would be up then, Dorothy, or maybe Margo if she was helping out, and I'd ask for a cup of coffee and one of Dorothy's peanut butter cookies.

One morning I was up real early, and Dorothy was taking a fresh tray of cookies out of the oven, and I got to studying the way she looked in the kitchen. That coming October 8 would be our sixtieth wedding anniversary, and I thought about how long that is to spend with a person. She walked over to where I sat in my chair, adjusted my pillow, and gave me a plate with two cookies on it. I thought she was so beautiful, you know, with the lamplight on her hair like that. She was as beautiful that day as when I first married her. Shoot—she was more beautiful still. I wondered how

I'd gotten so lucky, you know. To get a woman as good as my wife Dorothy.

The spring of 2009 came around. It got to be about May, and I thought I might go to the garage and grab me a rake, maybe start getting my garden ready for planting. I thought about it for several afternoons while sitting in my chair, rolling the thought of that garden around in my mind. I knew I wanted tomatoes and peas. Some onions this year. Beans. Cucumbers. All the things the family liked best. I was going to plant sunflowers, too, just like last year. They'd grow up big and high and be joyful and bright.

Wayne was over one morning, and I mentioned the garden to him. He put his shoulder under my shoulder and helped me out to the porch. I sat in a chair, breathing heavily.

Margo came around later that morning. She put on gardening gloves and adjusted the sunbonnet on her head. "You just sit, Daddy," she said with a smile. "We're going to plant that garden for you this year."

The warm sunshine felt good on my face. A hummingbird purred on up to the feeder. A few others joined it, darting around, enjoying their meal. I nodded at Margo, then closed my eyes. I could hear Wayne getting the tiller out of the garage.

"You asleep, Daddy?" Margo asked. Her hand was on my shoulder, lightly. Margo had dirt on her gloves. She'd been out to the garden and back again. Some time had passed, but I didn't know how long I'd been sitting there like that.

"No, Sissybug," I said. Real slowly. "I'm not sleeping. I'm just resting my eyes."

Maybe I got to dreaming. I don't know, for I closed my eyes again, and only good memories came to me. One of my grandsons,

Clay Powers, and me, always used to go fishing together. I bought him a boat when he was older, but when he was a little kid we'd go fishing in streams. Once, when Clay was just a tiny boy, we were fishing for carp and the fish were really pulling hard that day. So I tied a rope around Clay's waist and tied the other end to a tree to keep him safe. I wished everybody I loved could always be safe, you know. That was what I wanted most now.

I think it was the day after Wayne and Margo planted my garden that Wayne stopped by the house to take me in for my doctor's appointment. He put his shoulder under mine, but when I tried to stand I found I couldn't.

Wayne carried me to the car. He got me a wheelchair at the doctor's office, sat me in the chair, and wheeled me inside. We waited awhile, then were taken back by the nurse to the room. She took my blood pressure, checked a few things, then Wayne and I sat. After a while the doctor came in. "How you feeling today, Mister Powers?" the doctor asked.

"I feel like shit," I said.

He chuckled, not unkindly. "Well, you're eighty-six years old," he said. "You're supposed to feel like shit."

"No, not like this," I said. I didn't smile back this time. This one was a real good doctor. His name was Dr. Pierce, and I called him Hawkeye, like the doctor's name on M*A*S*H. But today it hurt to even shake my head. I sat there for some time while the doctor checked my heart rate, a few other things. Then he sat looking at my chart. He wasn't smiling anymore. Wayne stood nearby, then took a seat on the extra chair in the corner. For a while, all was quiet in the room. Finally I said, "Hawkeye, I need to know if there's anything more we can do for me. Level with me now."

Even before he answered, I knew what the answer was going to be. Hawkeye looked me in the eye, then shook his head. He shook it slowly as if to be gentle with me. He shook his head no.

After that, I found I couldn't walk anymore. Wayne needed to carry me wherever I went. To my chair. To bed. To the bathroom. Back to the chair. When I wanted a peanut butter cookie or a cup of coffee, I found my hands didn't work so well. Wayne fed me.

McClung wanted to fly out and see me. He called me on the phone, and I said thanks, but no. I didn't want McClung to remember me like this. I didn't say it to him quite in those words, but I think he knew what I was getting at, for he didn't press the question.

Lieutenant Shames drove out to see me anyway. The visit was short, and I wasn't feeling well at all. But I smiled to see him come by the house. He didn't need to do that last bit of kindness, you know—that was several hundred miles for him to drive. But he did anyway. So that was good of him. It very much was.

Even when you're sleeping, you can tell when people are talking in the room, you know. Sometimes, anyway. My daughter-in-law Sandy, well, her mother passed right around then. To make things worse, the night her mother passed, Sandy and her sister were in a car accident coming back from taking care of things. They flew right over the bank, and the car crumpled over on its side. It's a wonder they weren't all killed. In complete darkness, Sandy pulled herself up through the car's window. She climbed on the side of the car, jumped up onto the hillside, and hollered down a passing car for help. Later, she came to see me and told me the story. She bent low so I could talk to her, and I said, "You did good, Sandy, you did good." I meant that. She was that little girl who used to throw rocks at me, you know. I'd always known she was spunky.

A few days passed, and Margo told me it was early June. Frank Perconte was on the phone. Margo handed me the receiver.

"How you doing, Shifty?" Frank said.

"Not too good, buddy. Not too good." My voice was barely a whisper.

Frank said something else, I didn't hear what. Maybe it was *Hang tough*, you know, that's what most of the Band of Brothers tell each other when they're saying good-bye. Margo took the phone back from me. I closed my eyes.

I saw some light and then some darkness and then it was light again. Margo said another phone call was for me. A close friend of the family, Richard Copenhaven, was calling from out in Utah where he lives. He asked how Dorothy was holding up. That was a good question, for when a man's health is ailing, it can be a difficult time for his wife as well. I tried to say something, but I don't know if my words were coming out clear.

Then he said, "Darrell, you got a beautiful bride."

"You got that right, buddy," I whispered. I knew that phrase came out clear.

It was light again, and then dark, and then light. My grandson Jake came into my bedroom. He brought an electric razor with him, and asked if I wanted a shave. He must have been remembering I always liked to have a clean-shaven face.

"Just leave my mustache," I said.

He grinned.

I heard the shaver. I felt Jake's hand holding my face. I closed my eyes.

"What day is it?" I asked.

"It's June 12," Margo said. She was sitting on the corner of my bed. Figures were passing by, dark. It was daylight outside. But the daylight was sad. Margo was holding my hand, and she pressed it to her cheek.

"What's wrong?" I said. I closed my eyes.

"Oh, Daddy," she said. Her voice was a whisper. The tears weren't for me.

"What's wrong?" I asked again. I fought to keep my eyes open.

"Daddy, we lost our baby today," she said. "We lost Gavin."

She was talking about Jake and Dawnyale's baby. My great-grandson. Something had gone wrong with the pregnancy, and the baby didn't make it. Dawnyale delivered him stillborn. Gavin was eight months along in the womb. They didn't have any other children.

Margo was still there. There was darkness in the room. She was holding my hand, and I knew there are powerful times when a daughter just needs her father, you know, even when she's all grown up, and even when he's frail as a fall leaf. I gripped Margo's hand. I gripped it with all my might. "It's okay," I said. My breath came raspy. It took all my air to say those words. I closed my eyes.

Margo bent down and hugged me close. She hugged me for a long time. Then she straightened up and held my hand again. My eyes opened, and she ran the back of her two fingers down the side of my face. Margo sat looking at me. I don't know how long we were like that. Margo holding my hand. Me holding hers. I was so proud of Margo. I knew she'd be there to help her family. I knew Wayne would always be there to help his, too. I was so proud of my grandchildren, of Jake and Dawnyale, as tough a time as they were going through. I was so proud of all my family.

"Your garden's going to be really good this year, Daddy," Margo said at last.

The room was cool and soft, and I got to studying her words.

I knew Margo was right. The tomatoes would be getting higher soon. The cornstalks would be getting leafy, with real good ears on them, you know. The sunflowers would soon be bright and joyful. Soon enough, they'd be as high as our heads.

My last garden had been planted well. I closed my eyes. The darkness was turning to light.

EPILOGUE

S hifty Powers died on June 17, 2009, at age eighty-six, five days
after his great-grandson Gavin Johnson passed. In his last few
days of life, Shifty Powers remained at home in his own bed until
right before the end, when his family moved him to a room at the
Wellmont Regional Hospital in Bristol, Tennessee, which is just
over the state line from Clinchco, Virginia. He died in the hospital.

Shifty's funeral was held on June 19. It was a small ceremony
attended by family and friends. Shanghai Nickles gave the main
eulogy. Now in his late fifties, he was the young boy whom Shifty
had taken under his wing in Little League so many years earlier
and taught how to pitch.

Johnny Sykes was a pallbearer. He was the postmaster at the
Clinchco post office who'd helped Shifty in his last years with sort-
ing through the fan mail he received.

Other pallbearers were Shifty's grandsons, Jake Johnson, Clay Powers, and Luke Johnson, and three longtime family friends, David Robinette, Mike Strouth, and John Wesley Hawkins, a military man whom Shifty had once pinned stripes on in an advancement ceremony.

Following the funeral, a graveside service with military honors was conducted at the Temple Hill Cemetery. Shifty's body was buried in a plot in Castlewood, a town about forty-five minutes from Clinchco. His brother, Jimmy, was buried there, along with some of Dorothy's family. Dorothy plans to be buried there also when she passes.

At the funeral, Luke Johnson spoke the following words in tribute to his grandfather:

> I am the youngest grandson of Darrell and Dorothy Powers, and let me first say how honored I am that the family has allowed me to come up here and read this to you today. For to have the opportunity to eulogize a true American hero would be a privilege to anyone, it is especially so if that hero is your own grandfather.
>
> Darrell Powers was a gentle, soft-spoken man who chose his words carefully and intelligently. He had a wonderful sense of humor. Growing up I can't recall him ever raising his voice to the grandchildren, he didn't have to. Because you didn't want to disappoint him. He was a man who carried himself with such dignity and poise that it made you want to rise to meet that same standard. And to know that you had made him proud was a fantastic feeling. Because even before the books, before the miniseries, the world tours and Emmys, before all of those tremendous accolades, you knew you were in the presence of a

truly exceptional person. In my opinion, one of the greatest men to come out of a generation filled with great men, and though I am honored to have, in the last decade, gotten to know the hero the world called "Shifty," I am especially blessed to be one of the few who were fortunate enough to call him Pub.

I'd like to read to you a portion of a book that Shifty contributed to where he describes his life and what true success means. It is in these simple yet eloquent words where I feel Shifty Powers' voice is truly heard.

My wife Dorothy and I have been married for a good many years. We have two kids, a boy and a girl, four grandchildren, and two great-grandkids. Throughout my lifetime, I've never given a thought to having piles of money or being rich or doing anything like that. Now, I worked hard, and if I wanted something, I liked being able to afford it. But to me, success is those happy times with my family, being able to go fishing and hunting, and just getting out in the woods and enjoying yourself, looking at trees, or watching water go across rocks in a trout stream, things like that. That's always what really mattered to me. My life has been good. All the way back, I've always enjoyed it. *

News of Shifty's passing circulated quickly within the Easy Company circle of family and friends, then to fans of Shifty's who had met him through speaking engagements or who knew him through the series. Within a week, multiple tribute sites had

---

* From *We Who Are Alive and Remain*, page 223. Luke told me that this was Dorothy's favorite passage that Shifty had contributed to the book.

sprung up around the Internet. Literally thousands of messages of condolence for the family and gratitude for Shifty were posted on forum boards, Facebook pages, and tribute blogs. At least a dozen video tributes were made and posted on YouTube. E-mails flooded into the family. A random sampling of messages include these words:

"I want the family to know that America is now grieving with them. Mr. Powers was a very brave and unique individual. Let us emulate his honor and integrity in our actions."

"Thank God for men like Sgt. Powers. They are becoming harder and harder to find. He is truly a hero."

"I and all Americans living are in debt to you and your comrades. I am deeply grateful for all of your sacrifices—but that is not enough. This country owes all who served a debt that can never be repaid."

"His actions throughout his life made this world a better place."

"My condolences to all the Powers family at the loss of your husband, father, grandfather, and friend. I do not know any of you, but was saddened none the less. I am grateful for the sacrifices he made for our country."

"It was because of people like Shifty that I was allowed to live a free and productive life. My respect and sadness cannot be expressed to the fullest."

"I never knew Darrell Powers except from the movie *Band of Brothers*. I do know that I owe him and his comrades an eternal debt of gratitude for their sacrifice for my freedom and my family's. It is with great sorrow that we lay this hero to rest."

On July 7, 2009, a businessman named Mark Pfeifer living in Charlotte, North Carolina, was watching the widespread news coverage that surrounded the passing of pop singer Michael Jackson, who had died just after Shifty, on June 25, 2009. Pfeifer said in later interviews that he was never against Jackson, he simply thought it was time that Shifty got a bit of recognition and "that people started paying attention to things that mattered." Pfeifer had met Shifty once in an airport, but other than that, he had no connection to Shifty or the Powers family. Pfeifer drafted a short e-mail with the subject line "Memorial Service: You're invited" and sent it out to about twenty of his friends.

The e-mail read:

We're hearing a lot today about big splashy memorial services.

I want a nationwide memorial service for Darrell "Shifty" Powers.

Shifty volunteered for the airborne in WWII and served with Easy Company of the 506th Parachute Infantry Regiment, part of the 101st Airborne Infantry. If you've seen Band of Brothers on HBO or the History Channel, you know Shifty. His character appears in all 10 episodes, and Shifty himself is interviewed in several of them.

I met Shifty in the Philadelphia airport several years ago. I didn't know who he was at the time. I just saw an elderly gentleman having trouble reading his ticket. I offered to help, assured him that he was at the right gate, and noticed the "Screaming Eagle," the symbol of the 101st Airborne, on his hat.

Making conversation, I asked him if he'd been in the 101st Airborne or if his son was serving. He said quietly that he had been in the 101st. I thanked him for his service, then asked him when he served, and how many jumps he made.

Quietly and humbly, he said, "Well, I guess I signed up in 1941 or so, and was in until sometime in 1945 . . ." at which point my heart skipped.

At that point, again, very humbly, he said, "I made the 5 training jumps at Toccoa, and then jumped into Normandy. . . . Do you know where Normandy is?" At this point my heart stopped.

I told him yes, I knew exactly where Normandy was, and I knew what D-Day was. At that point he said, "I also made a second jump into Holland, into Arnhem." I was standing with a genuine war hero. . . . and then I realized that it was June, just after the anniversary of D-Day.

I asked Shifty if he was on his way back from France, and he said, "Yes. And it's real sad because these days so few of the guys are left, and those that are, lots of them can't make the trip." My heart was in my throat and I didn't know what to say.

I helped Shifty get onto the plane and then realized he was back in Coach, while I was in First Class. I sent the flight attendant back to get him and said that I wanted to switch seats. When Shifty came forward, I got up out of the seat and told him I wanted him to have it, that I'd take his in Coach.

He said, "No, son, you enjoy that seat. Just knowing that there are still some who remember what we did and still care is enough to make an old man very happy." His eyes were filling up as he said it. And mine are brimming up now as I write this.

Shifty died on June 17 after fighting cancer.

There was no parade.

No big event in Staples Center.

No wall to wall back to back 24x7 news coverage.

No weeping fans on television.

And that's not right.

Let's give Shifty his own Memorial Service, online, in our own quiet way. Please forward this email to everyone you know. Especially to the veterans.

Rest in peace, Shifty.

"A nation without heroes is nothing."

Roberto Clemente *

Pfeifer never could have guessed what a splash his e-mail would make. About four or five days later, he started seeing his own e-mail again. The e-mail was being forwarded. And forwarded. And forwarded. The e-mail had taken on a life of its own. It went viral, being forwarded again and again all over the world. No one knew exactly how many times it got forwarded, but estimates range from the hundreds of thousands to the millions.

For a while, a guessing game ensued. People wanted to know who had written the e-mail. Pfeifer hadn't signed his name. Apparently, someone forwarded it to retired Major General Chuck Yeager, who forwarded it on. For a while, people attributed the e-mail to him.

Reporters from Fox News were first to call Pfeifer. They noted

---

* Original e-mail, courtesy Mark Pfeifer.

that his name was encrypted far back in the e-mail, and they wanted to know if Pfeifer knew anything about who had written it or how Pfeifer fit into the whole thing. At the time, the reporters suspected the author of the e-mail was astronaut John Glenn, Pfeifer said.

The *Army Times* and the *Navy Times* picked up the story, and the e-mail started to show up in military circles. Various redactions and corrections of it appeared—some versions of it contained a lot more anger toward Michael Jackson, which was never what Pfeifer intended, he said.

The e-mail began to show up as the subject matter on local television shows around the country. It was the subject of multiple talk radio shows. News began to trickle out that an obscure, former Dow Jones employee was the author, and Pfeifer began to get e-mails from all over the world. The farthest away was from someone in the Kamchatka Peninsula, in the Russian Far East. The English was not very good and the name was Russian, so Pfeifer assumed it wasn't a U.S. serviceman stationed over there. The e-mail said simply, "Hey, good for you for recognizing Mr. Powers."

NBC News picked up the story, and national anchorman Brian Williams eulogized Shifty Powers on the evening news, although they initially attributed the e-mail's authorship to Chuck Yeager. NBC News is the most-watched major network news in America, averaging as many as ten million viewers each night.* The soft-spoken machinist from Clinchco was now a household name.

The watchdog website Snopes.com picked up the story and initially classified the idea of meeting Shifty in the airport and the Yeager authorship as "probable but undocumented." Pfeifer

---

* http://www.nytimes.com/2010/04/02/business/media/02tele.html, accessed May 2010.

e-mailed them to say that the story of meeting Shifty was true, and that he was the author. Snopes representatives didn't do anything to change their classification for some time, Pfeifer said. But then a variety of other sites started posting that Pfeifer was the author. Finally Chuck Yeager's people came out with an official statement, something along the lines of "While we agree with the content of the e-mail, he didn't write it," Pfeifer said. Snopes confirmed the authorship,* and representatives for NBC News wrote an article clarifying it also.†

The constant forwarding of the e-mail, as well as the national news coverage, created a larger grassroots effort to honor Shifty. More sites and messages promoting a day of honor started appearing all over the Internet. Word was spread on a variety of cities' Craigslist message boards. On July 20, 2009, an unofficial day of memory and honor in Shifty Powers's name was held. No fewer than nine memorial pages on Facebook carried the tribute. The largest garnered more than five thousand fans.‡ Messages flooded the boards.

Pfeifer was happy when he saw this. The point, Pfeifer said, was never that the e-mail itself would gain a lot of attention. It was always that Shifty would receive the honor due him.

At the sixty-third annual Easy Company reunion, held October

* http://www.snopes.com/politics/military/shiftypowers.asp, accessed May 2010.

† Tom Gusto, "War Hero E-mail Goes Worldwide—But Who Really Wrote It?" July 16, 2009,
http://abcnews.go.com/Politics/story?id=8100838.

‡ http://www.facebook.com/profile.php?ref=name&id=1277460425#!/group.php?gid=102678943567&ref=ts, accessed May 2010.

29 to 31, 2009, in Columbus, Ohio, Herb Suerth, Jr., president of the Men of Easy Company Association, held a moment of silence for Shifty Powers, as well as for Easy Company members Forrest Guth and Jack Foley, who had also died that year. About one hundred and fifty people attended the reunion, including extended family and friends of Easy Company members, and eight remaining veterans, including Shifty's good friend Earl McClung. An open mic time was held, and a variety of stories, both humorous and poignant, about Shifty were told.

Margo Johnson, Shifty's daughter, sent a letter to the reunion. Margo wanted to attend in person, but the thought of going to the reunion without her daddy felt too overwhelming; her grief was still too raw, she said. Margo's letter was read from the podium at the evening banquet by Carrie Smith, Shifty's great-niece. The letter said in part:

> *On behalf of my family and myself we wish to thank you for your generous expressions of sympathy. It is a comfort and honor beyond measure for me to count myself a member of the Easy Company family. Before the book, before the miniseries, before all the accolades, you were a breed apart, a close-knit family that has only grown closer through these many years.*
>
> *. . . We strive to be brave as Daddy was brave, we strive to be strong as he was strong, and we strive to live our lives as he lived his—with quiet dignity and the determination that no matter what trouble may come, we will be strong enough to endure. "Shifty" would expect nothing less.*

And the legacy of Shifty Powers continues.

UNDERSTANDING SHIFTY POWERS'S POSITION IN EASY COMPANY, 506TH PIR, 101ST AIRBORNE

Shifty started the war as a private and eventually became a sergeant. As a sergeant, Shifty led a squad in the Third Platoon of Easy Company. This was a low position on the front lines of the battle, nothing glamorous or glorious here. But NCOs like Shifty are considered the backbone of the military. They are men who get the job done.

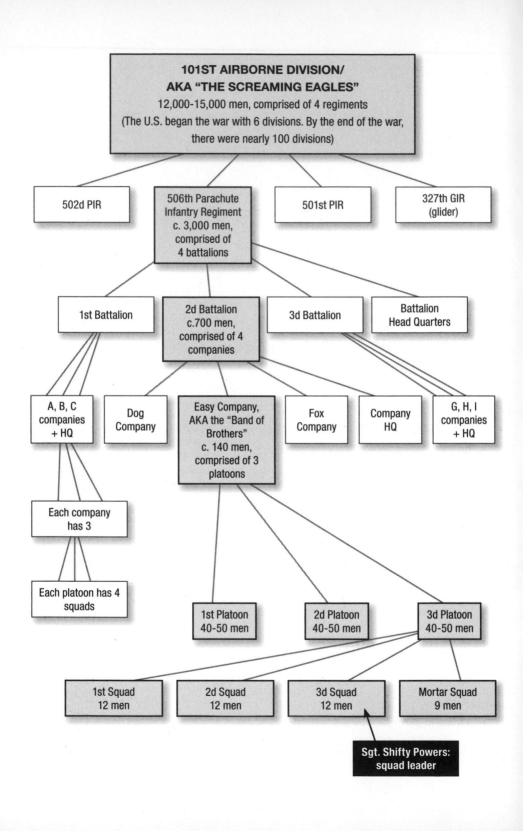

ACKNOWLEDGMENTS
AND SOURCES

In the fall of 2009, the last few remaining veterans from Easy Company, 506th Parachute Infantry Regiment, 101st Airborne Division, held a reunion in Columbus, Ohio. I attended the reunion, and we held a book signing at a nearby bookstore with the veterans who wanted to participate. It was a good time, many of them told me later. Some of their wives told me that their husbands had been looking forward to this event for months. Shifty Powers had died a few months earlier and he was fondly talked about and remembered often during the weekend.

Coming home from the reunion, I remember thinking that my time with the Band of Brothers was nearly finished. I had authored two books and coauthored another on the subject, and was not seeking to do another book about the men. But a few weeks after the reunion, I received a short e-mail that said simply: "Hi Marcus, I'm Sandy, Shifty's daughter-in-law. My husband, Wayne, is very interested in speaking to you regarding a project involving his father. Could you please give him a call?"

I phoned Wayne Powers the next day and we spoke for some time. He described how there were still stories to tell about the Band of Brothers. His father had been so loved by so many, and the outpouring of expressions of gratitude since his death had been overwhelming. The family wanted to talk from their hearts about the man they knew and loved so well. Would I be interested in writing a book about Shifty Powers?

Yes, I was very interested, but I was also wary. The book business had suffered a sharp downturn in 2008 and 2009, and publishers weren't offering contracts for anything except "the surest things." My agent, Greg Johnson of the WordServe Literary Group, and I had recently pitched two other veterans' memoirs, and they had both been rejected. I e-mailed Greg and described the project about Shifty Powers. He was also initially wary, as it usually takes quite a bit of work even to prepare a full proposal package to publishers, but he said he'd mull the idea around a few days.

Now, Greg is a fairly cut-and-dried type of businessman. He's not one given to hearing voices or seeing visions. But early the very next morning, Greg e-mailed me back. "Okay, I kept having dreams about Shifty Powers last night," Greg wrote. "I can't get him out of my mind. The more I think about this, the more I think this is something that we ought to pursue."

We prepared a proposal document and sent it to acquiring editor Natalee Rosenstein at the Berkley Publishing Group, and she offered us a contract immediately. The folks at Berkley are pure professionals, straight-shooting and courteous, and they've always given us honest feedback if they believe a book project will find success or not. We've worked with them on several projects now, and many thanks are given to Ms. Rosenstein, Michelle Vega, Caitlin Mulrooney-Lyski, and the rest of the publisher's team. Within a few weeks, I flew to Clinchco, Virginia, to visit the family of Shifty Powers. I wanted to see firsthand the lay of the land and understand more what made this small mining community so special. Shifty's daughter, Margo, and her husband, Seldon Johnson, picked me up at the closest airport, in Bristol, Tennessee, which is just across the line from Virginia. It was nearly midnight their time when they picked me up, yet they took me to a hotel and we sat in their car in the dark with the snow falling outside, and we talked for more than an hour, reminiscing about their dad. I'd say we enjoyed an immediate connection.

The next day we drove out to Clinchco. The town is so small there is no hotel, so I stayed in a spare room at the Ralph Stanley Museum and Traditional Mountain Music Center in Clintwood. The next few days were filled with interviews with the Powers family and trips to see various parts of the land. Wayne drove me in Shifty's jeep up to Frying Pan, where, once you near the top, you can look out and see ridge after ridge, and they're all actually blue.

The Powers family was truly gracious. They went out of their way to make me feel welcome and provide all the information, documents, and photographs needed. Many thanks to Shifty's widow, Dorothy Powers; Wayne and Sandra Powers; Margo and Seldon Johnson; Clay and Kayla Powers; Dove Powers; Jake and Dawnyale Johnson; Luke and Amanda Johnson; Caden Powers; and Cooper Powers. I also spoke on the phone with Shifty's last remaining sibling, Gaynell Sykes, who lives several hours away in Roanoke.

While in Clinchco, I spoke with friends and acquaintances of Shifty's, including Shanghai Nickles, Teresa Mullins from the *Dickenson Star* newspaper, Cody Mullins, Carol Robinette, and Johnny

Sykes. Thanks for all the stories they shared, and thanks go to long-time family friend Richard Copenhaven, whom I spoke with later.

When I got back home, I conducted more interviews while researching the book. Many thanks go to the many members of Easy Company who contributed stories for this book, including Earl McClung, Buck Taylor, Paul Rogers, Don Malarkey, Buck Compton, Ed Tipper, Joe Lesniewski, Herb Suerth, Jr., Bill Guarnere, Babe Heffron, and Ed Shames. Some men I talked to directly, some men spoke about Shifty on various recordings I listened to. Thanks are due to Carlton and Sandra Lowry, the family of Popeye Wynn, who sent me pictures as well as correspondences that took place between Popeye and Shifty.

Peter Youngblood Hills was a wonder to talk to and had much to contribute regarding the mannerisms and gestures of Shifty. Thanks also go to Mark Pfeifer for telling me in detail the story of his amazing e-mail.

Thanks go to the many people and companies who faithfully preserved Shifty's words and thoughts over the years, including the Makos family and Valor Studios; the Men of Easy Company Association; the Army & Navy Club; Scott Vaughn and Richard Clark from *The Groove 1320* radio show, WMSR Manchester; Nick Roylance and Alex Hedley with Genesis Productions; Cowen/Richter Productions (the original HBO tapes); the Dickenson County Historical Society; and the students and faculty at Southwest Virginia Community College, the University of Virginia's College at Wise, and Mountain Empire Community College at Big Stone Gap, Virginia. Gratitude is expressed to the Powers family for allowing me access to their archives.

Thanks are extended to the authors and publishers of the many books surrounding Easy Company, which I used as source material,

ACKNOWLEDGMENTS AND SOURCES

including *Band of Brothers* by Stephen Ambrose, *Parachute Infantry* by David Kenyon Webster, *Beyond Band of Brothers* by Major Richard Winters and Colonel Cole Kingseed, *Biggest Brother* by Larry Alexander, *Brothers in Battle, Best of Friends* by S/Sgt. Bill Guarnere and P.F.C. Babe Heffron with Robyn Post, *Call of Duty* by Lt. Buck Compton with Marcus Brotherton, *Easy Company Soldier* by Sgt. Don Malarkey with Bob Welch, *From Toccoa to the Eagle's Nest* by Dalton Einhorn, and *In the Footsteps of the Band of Brothers* by Larry Alexander. (Note: for people looking to complete a library about the Band of Brothers, there are two other coffee table–style photo books, quite rare, which I didn't consult for this project—*The Way We Were* by Forrest Guth and Michael de Trez and *Easy Company* by Genesis Publications.) Many thanks also go to the veterans who contributed to *We Who Are Alive and Remain*, and the families and friends of the veterans who contributed to *A Company of Heroes*.

Currahee!, the scrapbook compiled by Hank DiCarlo and Alan Westphal and published by the 506th PIR in 1945, was also invaluable. Gary and Marci Carson loaned me their copy, most generous of them, as it is an extremely rare book.

I am indebted to the families of Burton "Pat" Christenson, Mike Ranney, Gordon Carson, Carwood Lipton, and Robert Van Klinken for allowing me to view their unpublished journals and notes while researching *A Company of Heroes*. These journals and notes were consulted for this book as well.

Thanks go to the greater community that surrounds Easy Company, people who work to preserve and maintain documents, photographs, files, memorabilia, and stories, and those who champion veterans' tributes and remembrances, including Jake Powers, Rich Riley, Steph Leenhowers, Chris Langlois and everybody from the Easy Company family forum, Steve Toye, Joe "Mooch" Muccia,

Peter van de Wal in Holland, Paul Woodage from www.battlebus
.fr, Vance Day, George Luz, Jr., and Colonel Susan Luz, Robyn
Post, Ian Gardner, Larry Alexander, Tony Coulter, Linda Cautaert
from www.majordickwinters.com, Don Burgett, Captain Dale
Dye, Tracy Compton, Syndee Compton, Rob Stark, Tim Gray
Media Productions, Curt and Shonda Schilling, Conan O'Brien,
James Madio, Donnie Wahlberg, Flint Whitlock and *World War
II Quarterly*, Barbara Embree Webster, Renay Fredette from Art-
4Causes, and the incomparable C. Susan Finn.

Continual thanks go to Tom Hanks, Steven Spielberg, the
Playtone Company, and Merav Brooks and everyone at HBO.

Newspaper journalists Dorothy Brotherton and H. C. Jones
carefully read each chapter and offered valuable suggestions along
the way.

I am ever grateful to my wife, Mary Margaret Brotherton, for
her strong support in this project and her love always.

Final thanks go to the international community of fans who
continue to preserve the legacy of the Band of Brothers and hold
closely what it means to live in freedom.

Regarding sources used, and where certain stories came from, I
thought it might be interesting to provide a short section at the
back of this book, sort of like a DVD's commentary. Forgive me for
not providing footnotes, but I thought they'd only slow down the
reading experience through the actual book.

Of course, most of the stories in this book came from Shifty
directly. Yet here are some chapter-by-chapter explanations of
where a few of the other stories came from.

Chapter 1

Shifty told his son-in-law, Seldon Johnson, that he had killed the specific number of eight men during the war. The specific line Seldon remembers was, "I know I killed eight men. It could have been more, but I don't know for sure. People think they know what killing's like, but they don't." Other than that occasion, Shifty seldom answered that question straight out if asked. If he was talking to adults, he'd brush it off, if to children, he'd get very elusive in his answer, almost white lie-style.

Shifty's well-known statements about the German soldiers perhaps being just like him were spoken directly by Shifty and shown in the vignettes feature of episode 10 of the miniseries. Interestingly, in transcripts of the full interview with HBO, Shifty added the line "He might have been a basketball player, you never know," which was edited out of the series.

The big red Nazi banner that Shifty got as a souvenir from Berchtesgaden is still around, stored in a box in the Powers family's garage. Wayne Powers hung it in his dorm room as a college student.

The scene of Shifty talking with Major Winters was shown in the HBO miniseries but probably fictionalized. Shifty was asked in a newspaper article if the incident happened like that. "If it did, I was so excited I don't remember," Shifty said. "If I didn't, I should have, because he was an outstanding officer." [Douglas Durden, "Bringing the Toll of War Home," *Richmond Times-Dispatch*, September 5, 2001].

The story about the men of Easy Company in Bastogne drinking creek water with human remains was recounted by Bill Guarnere and Babe Heffron in an interview with *Valor Magazine*, Adam Makos, editor (issue 15, volume 4, number 3, pp 13–14). Whether

or not Shifty was in proximity to hear their conversation is imagined, though it's probable and likely that he would have drunk the
same water.

It's verified that one man out of the four in the back of the truck
died from wounds received during the head-on collision in Austria,
although it's not known if he was the man from D Company. I
made that up, along with the description of what he looked like, to
help put flesh on the man for the story.

Chapter 2

Most of the background information about Shifty in this chapter
came from his sister, Gaynell Sykes, and other family members.

Shifty told me the story about shooting a dime. He said a good
friend of his observed this, but he never mentioned specifically if it
was Pete. I think it likely was.

A joke in Easy Company circles is that Shifty got his nickname
from bootlegging moonshine whiskey in the mountains around
Clinchco, meaning, as "an old hillbilly from the holler," that he was
always on the "shifty" side of the law. Shifty perpetuated the rumor
to a certain extent as a participant in the joke, but clarified to several people that his nickname really originated from his basketball
days and his ability to be "shifty" on his feet.

Shifty never was one to swear much, but his family noted that
the one coarse word he frequently used was "shit." That's authentic.

Chapter 3

The information about the legends of Low Gap and Dave's Ridge
came from Cody Mullins, a lifelong Clinchco resident who had
interviewed Shifty for a school project when Cody was in fifth
grade, then kept in touch with him over the years. I wasn't able to

verify if these legends also existed when Shifty was a boy, but I liked the idea of a small town having these spooky stories that are passed down from generation to generation. Undoubtedly similar stories, if not these, were in place when Shifty was young. I used these legends to start this chapter because I wanted to show the difference between the imagined fears of boyhood that Shifty was just emerging from, and the real fears of war that he was about to head into.

Wayne Powers told me the story of the gang stopping Shifty in their car. According to Wayne, this line is spot on: *I got no problem with taking you on. All I ask is that you come at me one at a time.* I really like the grit it shows in Shifty. He wasn't afraid of a fight, but he preferred to walk away from one if he could.

Chapter 4

Information about each man mentioned in Toccoa comes from either *We Who Are Alive and Remain* or *A Company of Heroes*. I don't know if Shifty actually talked to all the men mentioned in this chapter on the first day in camp, but I wanted to give a brief snapshot of some of the real men and what they were like. We do know that he became friends very quickly with Skinny Sisk.

The information about the obstacle course came from pictures and text inside the 506th scrapbook.

Unfortunately, not much is known anymore about Shifty's good friend Bill Kiehn. Whenever Shifty talked about him, it was only that he was a good friend and that he died in Haguenau. I was unable to locate any of his family members, but Buck Taylor recounted orally the story of Bill Kiehn coming into the company with a chip on his shoulder, and taking him out one morning for some one-on-one close order drill, which soon brought him around.

Shifty mentions orally that Bill Kiehn came home with him to Clinchco once after they both received their jump wings.

Much of the detail and description about the hike from Toccoa to Benning I read in Mike Ranney's unpublished journal, courtesy the Ranney family.

Chapter 5

Stephen Ambrose (*Band of Brothers*, p. 41) tells how an enlisted man located a cache of whiskey and passed it around just prior to the *Samaria*'s voyage, and that many of the men, while familiar with beer, were unfamiliar with the effects of harder alcohol. It's unknown whether Shifty participated or not, but it's likely that he did because he hung out with all the guys, and he wasn't much of a drinker before enlisting. Ambrose notes that "the next morning, the air filled with the moans and groans of the hung-over men, the company marched down to the docks. A ferry carried the men to a pier, where hot coffee and doughnuts from the Red Cross girls helped revive the near dead."

Shifty recounted orally on several occasions his memory of seeing the people in Aldbourne practice defending themselves with only garden implements. During some of his public talks after the war, he made a strong case for maintaining the legality of privatized gun ownership in the United States. This issue was about the only time he ever made a public political statement. Shifty believed that citizens had a right to own guns to defend themselves, while acknowledging that problems came if guns fell into the wrong people's hands. Nevertheless, he stayed a strong proponent of personal gun ownership rights his whole life.

The story about Joe Lesniewski coming in as a replacement and being befriended by Skip Muck and Alex Penkala was told orally by Joe and mentioned in *We Who Are Alive and Remain*. When he told me this story over the phone, Joe "sang" a few bars of one of the old Western songs he and the boys sang. It was a very good moment. When Joe got to telling about Skip and Alex's deaths, he found it very difficult to talk anymore. He was still very choked up about it, more than sixty years later.

Earl McClung told me the story about Shifty and him shooting at other men's targets to help them pass their marksman tests. He still chuckled when he told it.

I mention the story of McClung receiving his nickname here, but it's positioned slightly ahead of sequence. He rejoined the company during Carentan, some days later.

Chapter 7

Stephen Ambrose reported that Shifty and an unnamed friend found the wine shop and sampled the contents in Come-du-Mont, and that it happened before Carentan (*Band of Brothers*, p. 90), but Shifty swore it happened in Carentan after the bulk of the fighting was all over.

Don Malarkey and Alton More scrounged a U.S. army motorcycle and sidecar in their last few days in Normandy and received permission from Lt. Buck Compton to take it back to England. Malarkey told me it was probably More, not himself, who drove Shifty up to Worcester on the back. Shifty recounted the story of hearing somebody from a different outfit call his name. Although he never knew who it was, it cheered him greatly, Shifty said.

When I first heard the incident of Earl McClung shooting up the whorehouse while Shifty was upstairs, the location was stated as London, which undoubtedly made sense sequentially in the storyteller's mind because London followed Normandy in the company's experiences. But after reading this manuscript, McClung told me that the incident (while it most certainly happened!) could not have happened in London because they weren't carrying their rifles when they went into the city on passes. Most likely, McClung said, the incident happened in Cherbourg right after the company's fighting in Normandy was finished and just prior to the men boarding the ship to head back to England.

Chapter 8

Pat Christenson wrote in his unpublished journals that "many" of the Germans in the truck were hit by the men's rifle fire, and doesn't mention taking any of them prisoner. But when Shifty told the story, he said not a one was hit and that they were all taken prisoner. Earl McClung said that two Germans were shot. So there is some discrepancy in the numbers. Winters and Ambrose don't mention the incident in their books.

Chapter 9

Don Malarkey wrote in his book that it was a fourteen-hour truck ride from The Island to Mourmelon-le-Grande (p. 149), but the 506th Scrapbook describes it as taking thirty-six hours. When the men first arrived, "their first look around was anything but reassuring . . . but there were beds everywhere so everybody crawled in and slept." The Scrapbook mentions the Germans had used it previously as a tank depot.

I asked Buck Compton if he remembered any of the names of the players on the Champagne Bowl football team, but he didn't. He said it was an extremely tough group of guys, though, as he was able to pick players from all three thousand men in the regiment, not just from the company. I mentioned Joe Toye watching the game in this section because, as the toughest man in Easy Company, on a good day, he probably would have been one of the players. I checked with Joe Toye's sons. They had also wondered if their dad was involved with the game because he loved football so much, but they'd never heard him talk about it, and had always assumed the wounds their dad received in Holland precluded him from taking part in the game.

Chapter 10

Band of Brothers purists will notice a slight overlap between chapters 10 and 11 in the sequencing of some of the stories presented. For instance, the night of hard shelling that claimed the lives of Muck and Penkala happened just after Buck Taylor was wounded.

I included the story of Popeye telling a joke in this chapter because Shifty said that in spite of all the horror in Bastogne they occasionally found time to tease each other to lighten the mood and break the tension. Shifty said they'd sometimes shake snow from a tree branch down on a man just to mess with him, or tell stories or jokes. The incident of men urinating on their hands or rifles to warm them up is confirmed, although I don't know if Popeye actually did this or not.

The story of Shifty being in the same vicinity when Don Hoobler fatally shoots himself in the leg with the Luger is shown in the miniseries, but I never found one instance of Shifty talking about it after the war. In *A Company of Heroes*, several men reported that it was a very significant incident to them, and the memory haunted them for years, so the absence of Shifty's recollection makes me wonder if he was out on patrol when the actual incident took place. As such, I didn't mention it in the book.

Chapter 11

Earl McClung tells the stories of being on a train, heading back to Haguenau, and getting a stove full of coal and shooting the locks off train cars to get food inside (see *We Who Are Alive and Remain*, pp. 163–164). Other still-living men from the Third Platoon don't dispute the stories. Elsewhere, it's said the men rode on trucks, so it may have been some combination of both forms of transportation.

Shifty told the account of shooting a sniper in Foy differently from how it was portrayed in the miniseries. This account reflects how he told it. C. Carwood Lipton wrote unpublished notes about a variety of the men from the company. He described the incident this way:

> One of the men in the 3rd platoon of E Company, 506th had excellent eyesight, and he was also an outstanding marksman with a rifle. He was Darrell C. "Shifty" Powers, a tall, part-Indian, from Clinchco, Virginia.
>
> Shifty's marksmanship paid off for us on January 13 when E company received orders to attack and clear the town of Foy. We moved around to the south of the town and attacked to the north into it. The Germans defended it strongly, and we had a number of men hit. At one point, several of us, including, Shifty, Popeye Wynn (Shifty's closest buddy), Bob Mann, R. B. Smith, and I were pinned down by a sniper that we just couldn't locate. R. B. Smith caught a bullet in the leg. Then Shifty yelled, "I see 'im." And there was a rifle shot. We weren't pinned down any more so we continued the attack.
>
> When things had cleared up later that day I went back to see where that sniper had been. When I found him, Popeye had already found him. We stood there looking down at the dead

German and at the bullet hole centered in the middle of his forehead. Popeye looked over at me and said, "You know, it just doesn't pay to be shootin' at Shifty when he's got a rifle."

How right he was.*

Chapter 12

The story of Skinny Sisk, one of the most incorrigible men in Easy Company, having a foxhole conversion during the shelling in Bastogne is one of those you hear every once in a while in Easy Company circles, but I wasn't able to verify if the initial conversion actually happened in the foxhole or later on. For the first few years after the war, Wayne Sisk suffered extensively from flashbacks and PTSD, evidently choosing to cope by drinking. It's verified that in 1949 he underwent a significant spiritual conversion experience, which he reported in a letter to Dick Winters. Evidently it did change his life fully and help him cope (*Band of Brothers*, p. 299). That same year, 1949, Skinny Sisk was ordained as a Baptist minister. His obituary, which you can easily find online, notes that he died July 13, 1999, in Charleston, at age seventy-seven.

In the miniseries, Shifty is shown going on the patrol across the river, but McClung confirmed that Shifty wasn't on the patrol.

The miniseries shows Bill Kiehn walking along with a sack of potatoes when he gets hit with a shell, but that was a fabrication for story's sake, said Paul Rogers, who was in Haguenau and saw Kiehn's death when it occurred. Rogers's experiences are recorded

---

* Unpublished notes of C. Carwood Lipton. Courtesy the family of Carwood Lipton via the family of Popeye Wynn.

in the chapter. Still, I liked the story of the potatoes that HBO added and kept the reference to potatoes in the story only because it showed that men were dying over very small things by that stage in the war. Margo Johnson told me that Shifty had told her once (as an adult) that Bill Kiehn was an only child.

Chapter 13
Ambrose records the story of Shifty getting a new rifle that he hated (*Band of Brothers*, p. 236).

Chapter 15
For information on Fritz Niland, the real "Private Ryan," see *Band of Brothers*, p. 59. For information about Skip Muck's longtime friendship with Fritz Niland, see *A Company of Heroes*, pp. 272–273.

Chapter 16
The Powers family noted that the release of the miniseries and subsequent speaking engagements for many of the men featured brought Shifty out of the depression he was feeling on account of his declining health. They speculate that the series bought Shifty an extra few years of life.

Chapter 17
Shifty's final words to various family and friends are all related as they remembered.

INDEX

Page numbers in **bold** indicate 101st Airborne Division's organization chart.

ABOUT THE AUTHOR

Marcus Brotherton is a journalist and professional writer, known internationally for his literary collaborations with high-profile public figures, humanitarians, inspirational leaders, and military personnel. He is the author of the national bestsellers *We Who Are Alive and Remain* and *A Company of Heroes*, and the coauthor of *Call of Duty* with Lt. Buck Compton.